THIS IS THE CANON

DECOLONIZE YOUR BOOKSHELF IN 50 BOOKS

JOAN ANIM-ADDO

DEIRDRE OSBORNE

KADIJA GEORGE SESAY

greenfinch

First published in Great Britain in 2021 by Greenfinch
An imprint of Quercus Editions Ltd
Carmelite House
50 Victoria Embankment
London
EC4Y 0DZ

An Hachette UK company

A CIP catalogue record for this book is available from the British Library.

HB ISBN 978-1-52941-459-2
eBook ISBN 978-1-52941-460-8
TPB ISBN 978-1-52941-884-2

10 9 8 7 6 5 4 3 2 1

Designed and set by seagulls.net
Cover design by Sumuyya Khader
Printed and bound in Great Britain by Clays Ltd, Elcograf S.p.A

Papers used by Greenfinch are from well-managed forests
and other responsible sources.

CONTENTS

AFTERWORD

Decolonizing the Literary World 333

INTRODUCTION

DECOLONIZING YOUR BOOKSHELF: INTRODUCING *THIS IS THE CANON*

Welcome to *This is the Canon: Decolonize Your Bookshelf in 50 Books*. Before you lies a reading journey like no other. Within these pages you will encounter a wide-ranging collection of fiction from around the world. Each title has been carefully chosen as a result of our commitment to diversify the traditional literary canon of novels and short stories available in the English language.

We read books for all sorts of reasons: as a leisure activity, for comfort or escape, for information, for educational study. Fiction, however, holds a unique power to displace us – in the most positive and universal ways – into imaginatively rendered worlds, which may and may not resonate with our daily lives. Crucially, it can transport its readers beyond their prior experiences. Stories can excite and unsettle, provoke and inspire, and offer opportunities to explore different ways of reading and interpreting the world through the characters' lives

– which can be alike and unlike their reader's. Andrea Levy (see entry 40 in this book) told an interviewer that there was no essay 'so powerful an agent for change as a James Baldwin short story' (see James Baldwin, entry 13). In encouraging you to view reading – in relation to the decolonization of the literary canon – as an enriching and worthwhile endeavour, we are confident that the books sampled within *This is the Canon* will help you on your way.

The impetus for co-authoring this book has been to centralize fiction produced by writers of African descent, Asian descent, and Indigenous Peoples, to offer a corrective to reverse the dominance of white-dominant literary canons. As three women used to working collaboratively, with commitment to the collective politics of racial and social justice, we share longstanding track records in reading, teaching, researching and writing against the grain of canonical entrenchment. Our work is grounded in community contexts through the wide demographic of the people with whom we have worked. Joan Anim-Addo's eminent career as an academic, poet and publisher has paved the way for recognizing Black people's diasporic histories in the UK. She is the Director of the Centre for Caribbean and Diaspora Studies at Goldsmiths, University of London. Deirdre Osborne has taught literature in prisons, schools and universities, and has made a pioneering contribution to the critical writing and publishing of Black British drama. Her current work centralizes the legacies of imperial–colonial rule and its aftershocks in contemporary writing. Joan and Deirdre co-founded the MA Black British Literature in 2014 at Goldsmiths, which remains the only degree in the world in this field. Kadija George Sesay has been a lifelong literary activist and is Publisher of *SABLE LitMag* and Series Editor of the Inscribe imprint for Peepal Tree Press. She co-founded the Mboka Festival of Arts, Culture and Sport in The Gambia. In her roles as editor, poet and publisher, she has influenced the lives and careers of many Black British writers and writers of African descent and Asian descent in the UK.

Anthologies of writing or edited collections of short stories, or series by a range of authors, can often introduce readers to work that falls outside traditional canonical spaces. While *This is the Canon* points readers in many directions on the literary map, the books we profile are fiction – novels or short stories – by individual authors. Poetry, plays and life writing may lie beyond the parameters of this book, but definitely *not* beyond our reading horizons.

This book is unquestioningly transnational in its outlook. It is responsive to the multiple heritages that any one of the 50 writers might embrace, and also to the plurality of cultures and geographical locations to which they might be affiliated. Three oceanic regions perhaps best indicate the conceptual and geographical reach of the literature covered in *This is the Canon*: the Atlantic, the Indian and the Pacific Oceans. What difference does it make to literary canons when these three regions are brought together? While these oceans are geographical realities, they are also intellectual and cultural constructs. Unlike continents, all three oceans are interconnected and create continuity. The recognition between global regions, as read through the literature, is what makes this book distinctive.

Readers may notice that over a third of the authors profiled in this book were born or live in the United States. This highlights the challenges we faced in not wishing to generate new hierarchies of decolonizing, where the restoration of one cultural history that is absent or minoritized in white dominant canons, then discounts another. Instead, this book foregrounds its limitations by acknowledging its omissions, its uneven representativeness. You will also find writers whose decolonial works have created sensibilities that have dismantled the power of imperial languages, even as they are of that heritage, in this book. Not only have such authors transformed the European novel through their alchemy of magic realism with historical accountability, but also their sensitivity to foregrounding and learning from pre-existing cultures is intrinsic to their creative process. We hope this book will act as both a guide and a catalyst for you to seek out literature beyond the traditional canon's borders. This is a first step in 'firing the canon'.

FIRING THE CANON

'What does it mean to engage in canon formation at this historical moment?' asked the philosopher, scholar and activist Cornel West in 1987. His question remains pertinent today and fits perfectly with the ethos of this book. Protest, pandemic and climate catastrophe have produced conditions and changes in living on this planet that were unimaginable in 2019. Together, they have created the 'historical moment' for *This is the Canon*. However, these consequences emerge from the deep roots of history. As cannons and other artillery enabled European empire-building, 'canons' served as their cultural strong arm, both within the imperial nations, and as exported to and imposed upon the vast areas of the globe that were colonized across centuries.

As will be explored in more detail later on, canonicity involves the elevation of certain texts as judged by critical literary consensus to represent exemplary quality. To decolonize the canon, we must begin by asking: who are the people making the judgements, what equips them to do so, and by what criteria? The existence of a largely unchallenged canon has ensured the cultural legitimation and hence, continuity of certain literary works. The literary canon is shaped by the various national, social, political, educational and economic factors that position people's identities according to intersecting categories of sex, gender, race, class and so on. The work of white males has dominated canon formation. In Britain and the US, for example, its legitimacy has been reinforced at various points by influential figures such as F R Leavis's inclusions in *The Great Tradition* (1948) or Harold Bloom's defence in *The Western Canon: The Books and School of the Ages* (1994).

A canon, therefore, becomes a benchmark. It also shapes who is published and what is read. Writers who can be most closely aligned with European literary traditions and aesthetics still achieve the most sustained recognition. *This is the Canon* is an intervention that offers opportunities for readers to explore a broader reach of works than those that are perennially taught and examined, or promoted. In engaging with this book, you will also be engaging in contemporary canon reformation. We can refer to this as democratizing the canon – or, at least, starting the process.

Although our title states: *This is* the *Canon*, it should be understood as much to mean this is *a* canon, neither replacing nor adding to what has existed previously, but one of many possible selections. We are aware that certain novels still remain centre-stage, attracting attention, leaving minoritized authors in the 'shadows' of the dominant culture. *This is the Canon* is no shadowland, but instead builds a robust structure that houses fiction from across the world. It opens its doors to all readers who wish to explore new literary horizons, that is, to decolonize their bookshelves.

DECOLONIZING YOUR BOOKSHELF

Decolonizing can be defined literally in relation to the imperial–colonial legacy derived from empires. As will be further examined, it is a dismantling of the oppressive hierarchical power relations that, in the example of nearly four centuries of the British Empire, left hardly any region of the world untouched by its reach. A crucial limit to our work here is the availability of texts. There is a whole body of wonderful work yet to be translated into English. The issue of translation is a pressing one. This frequently connects back to the colonial legacies of contemporary writers' contexts. The imperial scrambles for territory set the linguistic primacy of English, French, Spanish, German, Portuguese, Danish, Norwegian and Finnish in many regions from which the authors in *This is the Canon* hail or reside. For example, Lebanese author Leila Baalbaki's *I Live* (1956) is a milestone in Arab women's literature and was on the Arab Writers Union's 'Top 105' novels of the 20th century. Published in French as *Je vis!* (1958) and in German as *Ich lebe* (1994), lamentably no work of Baalbaki's has yet appeared in English.

Turning to Northern European regions and indigenous Sámi people, you will not find any Sámi-language fiction authors published in English. Although Kirsti Paltto's debut short story collection *Soagnu* (*The Proposal Journey*) was published in 1971 and the 1986 Finnish translation of the novel *Guhtoset dearvan min bohccot* (*Run Safely My Flock*) was nominated for the Finlandia Prize, no English translations exist of her eight works of fiction. The first published novel by a Greenlandic woman, Mâliâraq Vebæk's *Búsime nâpíneq* (*Meeting on the Bus*) was translated into Danish by Vebæk herself and into Russian and Sámi, not English.

In the long period of European imperial rule which divided up much of the globe, we should not forget the reach of Britain, France, the Netherlands, Portugal and Spain into regions geographically distant from Europe, such as Vietnam, Indonesia, East Timor and the Philippines, and how many of these areas were subsequently in the orbit of US foreign policy at a later point in history. We should also remember the imperialism of other empires, such as Russia and Japan. For people in Korea and China, occupation by Japan is a period of history often overlooked in European contexts. Concerns with Westernization present a distinct theme in fiction from Japan and China that adds further nuance to what decolonizing literature might entail. Countries in Scandinavia were effectively complicit in colonialism and its suppressing of indigenous languages, without having actual colonies.

We are mindful that we produce this book in Britain, that the books we champion in order to support the vast project of decolonizing and diversifying reading practices are chosen because they are all available in the English language.

The Black Lives Matter (BLM) protests around the world provided a pivotal movement in the international solidarity against racism in 2020. But just how far did the overdue changes demanded of social, cultural and political institutions truly become adopted? Or were the responses merely wallpapering, performative acts in words only? In many nations, Indigenous Peoples still endure colonial conditions in the 21st century. Meanwhile, 'caste' and 'class' continue to oppress and define lives. Nor can we overlook the fact that, in decolonizing reading, we include literature written from the perspectives of those people who identify as LGBTQIA+ and of disabled people, and of the possible interfaces in self-terming. Literature can open a window on representing the fullest ranges of lives.

Therefore, to decolonize our bookshelves and democratize the canon, we should finally consider the routes to these widening horizons in which publishing, both print and digital, plays a crucial role.

DEMOCRATIZING THE CANON:
NEW READING HORIZONS

To what degree do publishers support or constrain decolonizing literature in their commissioning and selling – in what gets offered to the reading public? Markets drive publishing just as publishing can create new markets. But are mainstream publishers ever able to truly engage with minoritized cultures?

For commercial publishing houses, providing a decolonized fiction list involves tuning into cultural sensitivities that were not previously considered. Trying to be respectful of the content of books – and not wishing to replay adversities or grim subject matter that has become negatively associated with one particular cultural or ethnic group in white-dominant representation – presents certain dilemmas. Should a publisher not reprint books that foreground disturbing or taboo topics, especially as these are such an important part of a great deal of fiction? Could this constitute a form of censorship? What if these difficult topics are written from the perspectives of that group as a key step in developing literary agency? Might the publisher's approach be misguided? There are many complexities at play. Bad memories and disturbing experiences are the subjects of much fiction. As you will read, many of the 50 titles in this book might be characterized in this way if viewed by topic alone. We ask readers to remember that it is *who* tells the tale that is important – and that it is not the *only* tale that can be told.

The precarities of publishing not only determine who gets into print, but whose work stays in print. The determination of feminist and queer and critical race scholars since the late-20th century to retrieve 'lost' works and authors, teach them, and create new markets in order to return books to centrality, has long been the means of recognizing the fuller literary landscape. The 2019 Booker Prize winner Bernardine Evaristo's (see entry 36) project with Penguin to reprint Black British novels that have fallen out of print is one such achievement of cultural correction. The dedicated independent publishers and literary activists who have nurtured and published work across decades are discussed in the Afterword.

The 50 writers represented in *This is the Canon* are but the tip of the iceberg of possibilities. To extend the reading list further, each of the individual entries is supplemented by recommendations in the 'If you like this, try…' sections at the end of each entry.

Diversifying who and what we read can only broaden our imaginative horizons and enlarge our awareness of different cultures and traditions. But *how* we read what we choose to read, the act of reading itself, is also illuminated as a vital benefit when we set our compass in a decolonial direction. Psychologist and writer Charles Fernyhough (2017) observes that as 'we internalize dialogue, we internalize other people.' Reading can be simultaneously defamiliarizing and revelatory. It can unlock one's experiences of particular socio-cultural contexts, such as school, family, community, friendship group, and highlight awareness of gaps in understanding the world.

The list of 50 titles provides a snapshot of the last 70 years, but not a blueprint for a linear reading experience. The sheer variety represented by nationalities, literary genres and styles, alongside the period in which authors are writing, being published or translated, unsettles such an approach. We urge readers to venture across chronological time zones, national identities and cultural affiliations. The anarchic, absurdist whirlwind of G V Desani's *All About H. Hatterr* (1948) pairs well with Paul Beatty's subversively satiric *The Sellout* (2015); the hierarchical family politics of Eileen Chang's *Love in a*

Fallen City (1943) resonates with Daniyal Mueenuddin's feudal landowning order depicted in *In Other Rooms, Other Wonders* (2009), just as the edgy delicacy of Yūko Tsushima's episodes composing *Territory of Light* (1979) melds beautifully with the introspection of Zadie Smith's *NW* (2012).

We must also remember that the shadow of European imperial–colonial legacies still haunts today's access to literature. How many languages were outlawed, erased and lost through empire building and consolidations of acquired territories? Much literature in this volume was written in resistance to the European lingua francas forced upon colonized nations that suppressed indigenous languages and cultures. Three of our authors, Assia Djebar, Patricia Grace and Ngũgĩ wa Thiong'o, were denied speaking their mother tongue – Arabic, Māori and Gĩkũyũ respectively – while growing up.

While we mourn the fact that much writing has not been created in its author's indigenous language, and more often in the language of the oppressor, we can celebrate how these majestic works defy this legacy through fashioning innovative narrative voices. Trinidadian academic and writer Kenneth Ramchand (1988) describes an example of this virtuosity in Sam Selvon's *The Lonely Londoners* (see entry 5). He notes that Selvon is a writer 'trying to invent an orthography for the dialect' while at the same time signalling that 'he knows what the "correct" English would have looked like.'

As Salman Rushdie's often-quoted character from *The Satanic Verses* (1988) Whisky Sisodia parodically stutters, the 'trouble with the Engenglish is that their hiss hiss history happened overseas, so they dodo don't know what it means.'

Only too well, however, did these 'overseas' regions know English history and its cultural export of the literary canon as reinforcing colonial rule. A necessary question must be asked. What kind of knowledge is needed to understand and appreciate indigenous writing from cultural positions or geographical locations that have no contact with – or little awareness of – the lives of the Indigenous Peoples concerned? Colonial rule violently foisted a 'vanishing act' upon colonized peoples' presences and languages. Histories of space and place became reconfigured and overwritten by the imposed language of empire – of treaties, reservations, protectorates, missions, residential school systems, bands and reserves – and by terms such as 'terra nullius'. The application of *terra nullius* – meaning land belonging to no one – justified the British invasion of Australia and the genocidal policies towards the continent's Indigenous people.

A refrain throughout the fiction by First Nations peoples in this book is one of ongoing recovery: to recover kinship ties, and languages and lands; to recover *from* the legacy of genocidal politics and environmental devastation. Despite such odds against survival, the sustenance of rich cultural traditions by many communities is evident even in the wake of irrecoverable loss. Such lifelines are shared by books from Turtle Island, Aotearoa, the generically clustered 'Central and South American' nations, and the continent of Australia (comprising over 600 language groups). The work of Tony Birch, Alexis Wright, Albert Wendt, Patricia Grace, LeAnne Howe and Eden Robinson in this volume all testify to loss, but also to Indigenous sovereignty of unceded lands. They speak to a determination to restore, record and speak the words of previous generations and to foreground kinship between human and non-human as a fundamental understanding for existing in the world.

Reading diverse writing helps us appreciate how interconnected human experiences can be. This is highlighted in Maya Angelou's sparkling reminder in her poem* 'Human Family' – that we are more alike than we are unalike. We hope this book ignites your interest to investigate authors from the regions, nations, traditions and literary histories touched upon in these 50 titles.

---

* From her collection *I Shall Not Be Moved* (1990, Random House).

DECOLONIZING THE CANON: WELCOMING DIVERSITY

The demand for 'decolonizing' has moved from the margins to the centre of former colonial empires. The cry is now loud and unmistakable, and it keeps growing, particularly in the wake of the global Black Lives Matter (BLM) movement. Decolonizing insists on change regarding practices and responses that oppress *others*, notably those burdened by historical injustices dating back to colonialism and slavery. The argument goes that residual and persistent colonial oppression – most evident as racism – not only damages individuals and groups, it corrodes society and ultimately inhibits human progress and potential.

To relate decolonizing to the shaping of a literary canon – of novels and short story collections – we necessarily turn to questions of diversity, or a plurality, of literatures. Those who oppose or criticize the act of decolonization often fear contamination or a lowering of standards. To reassure readers, we are emphatically opposed to exalting books that are mediocre, or outside the possibility of literary success, however conventionally and narrowly defined that might be. Yet, in tracing diversity concerns to their source, we find that elitist thinking, nostalgia and lack of exposure to the widest range of literary art are at play. Alongside this viewpoint is the belief that change comes only at the expense of quality, examples of which are encompassed within a literary canon created in the 20th century by and for a privileged, white minority.

THE LITERARY CANON

We understand the canon in terms of aesthetic excellence, sophistication, exemplariness and so on. Such superlatives indicate the quality by which a work of art – literary or otherwise – is measured and selected in order to be considered canonical. Yet, awareness is required concerning *who* decides on the canon. The traditional canon is in danger of containing only the novels that those who make literary decisions know how to read. Change means asking different questions of the books they read. This matters because the canon becomes the norm across classrooms and in publishing, and against which other writers might measure their own writing.

There already exists a multiplicity of literary canons linked to nation states, and increased awareness of this is gradually shifting the incorrect notion of a single, indisputable canon measured by impeccable Western values. Our aim in this book is to illuminate the canon of the present-day, the contemporary moment and its absences. In this context, a consideration of nations alone – and the story they tell of themselves – is inadequate. We must go beyond this.

To establish a canon in the global 21st century is to recommend books on account of their excellence, to present the best in literature and to celebrate the best of a nation, of the world. This, of course, raises many fundamental questions. As we have seen, at issue is the breadth of the pool from which those selections are made, who decides, and the nature of the aesthetic principles applied. Selecting the titles for this new canon, we have undertaken just such a process, but from a diverse pool of writing. Importantly, the process questions how a body of work identified as prestigious relates to nations and nationalism. In *This is the Canon*, we are acutely aware of how answers to such questions correspond to the world's greater understanding of a common humanity, a situation with which we humans must urgently come to terms. In considering decolonizing, we need to ask how colonialism has come to be linked to the Western literary canon and what might be done about it.

That crucial question remains: who decides on a canon of work? The answer is institutions and the exclusionary structures and frameworks they maintain. For literary writing, key players are publishing houses and universities. The canon is also determined, or greatly influenced, by other institutions, such as literary prizes and the media. Increasingly, social media plays a key role in recommending books and this can be celebrated as a form of democratization. The university more usually *preserves,* through reading lists that are occasionally adjusted, the canon that is already historically justified. In tandem, the publishing houses keep those works in print, with new editions and introductions. There is, however, a growing demand from students for new voices.

Western universities exported their colonial models in the age of empire. Literature, as an academic discipline, is linked to 18th-century canon formation. As maps of colonialism confirm, by the mid-18th century, Britain, France, Portugal, Spain and the Netherlands each had colonies across the globe. Spanish settlers in South America, for example, readily established universities in their colonies, while Britain and France did not. As colonial goods and peoples were crossing the Atlantic, the ideas shaped by European thinking – justifying its colonizing role – were also being transported. Many of those ideas were to be found in books. Some of our 'classics' derive from that period; along with their limited ideas of the human as being primarily the European.

Dr Johnson, the distinguished writer and critic, referred to the 18th century as the 'age of authors'. However, the explosion of literary writing from that celebrated British period was not taking place in a vacuum. The 18th century was Britain's 'heyday' as a nation trafficking in and exploiting Black human bodies. The period ensured the decimation and displacement of Indigenous Peoples from the Americas to Australia, in order to build a colonial empire and to claim land. Writing became a key tool of colonial domination. Besides published fiction, this writing involved the publication of various justifications for the colonizers' trade in bodies, and its attendant racialization.

The influential philosopher, David Hume, noted in his 'Of National Characters' of 1753: 'I am apt to suspect the negroes, and in general all the other species of men (for there are four or five different kinds) to be naturally inferior to the whites.' One might imagine how students from different parts of the globe still negotiate such thinking as Hume's, perhaps especially when the majority of their teachers are often white. Fortunately, we now understand from our historical vantage point that central to a perception such as Hume's is a compulsion to think hierarchically, placing the white male at the top of the pyramid. This outdated perception does not recognize or appreciate diversity, whether human or cultural. Over two hundred years later, the Latin American scholar Walter D. Mignolo writes about such ideas as 'the darker side of Western modernity', which refers to the colonial idea that history begins with the European man. Mignolo's writing has been important in making the contemporary argument for decolonial action accessible to the English-speaking world.

This is the Canon embraces the challenge of thinking through concerns about decolonizing, especially in terms of the writers we have included in the selection. We aim to unsettle generally accepted and unquestioned ideas concerning the literary canon. We suggest that it is the refusal of institutions to acknowledge the diversity of the body of literary writing available that has led to demands for an active decolonization of the literary canon.

DECOLONIZING LITERATURE AND ITS CONCERNS

Decolonizing is best understood in two ways. Firstly, as a date-specific event that has taken place in a former colony, and secondly, as a political practice against colonial ideas and perspectives. Decolonization takes the view that colonialism did not end when political independence was granted to previous colonies in the 20th century. It continues through the generations, having been deeply ingrained within the institutions, the infrastructure and the colonizers' language – itself disseminated by the written word, for example, in the reading prescribed for schools and universities in former colonies.

Literary historian Stephen Greenblatt, in his book *Marvelous Possessions* (1991), delves into the power of written language in considerable detail. He makes the point that 'a distinction between peoples who have writing and those who do not' becomes 'crucial' following Europe's colonial encounter with non-European peoples. That is because writing – in its everyday sense, such as in establishing regulations to remove native peoples from their land, and in its specific, literary-artistic sense of the novel – readily functions as a tool of domination.

Thinking about decolonizing and the history of literature as art, the links between the written word and structures of power are self-evident, so we come back to the question: is literature political? The larger question is similar: is art, in its broadest sense, political? Though purists might argue otherwise, observation of the art world as well as that of books suggests that *both* are political. The evidence, across fiction and nonfiction writing alike, points to the act of writing, its dissemination – or not – and its reception, as being one of political enfranchisement. Not that long ago, the voices of half the population – women can hardly be considered a minority – were largely absent from literature. Women writers were obliged to point to the many ways in which literature *is* political, despite the persistent rhetoric invoking a kind of aesthetic purity around the published canon, while ignoring the selective conditions of publication. The published writers were men, and so were the decision-makers.

In the UK, currently, debate centres on the absence of Black and Asian British writing, as recent research, including 'Writing the Future: Black and Asian Writers and Publishers in the UK Marketplace' (Spread the Word, 2015) and 'Rethinking "Diversity" in Publishing' (Goldsmiths Press, 2020), confirms. Yet, these reports only tell us what was already known and voiced among those excluded from the industry and their allies. Why this absence persists is certainly rooted in coloniality. Knowingly or not, gatekeepers are guarding against *impurity* creeping into the body of literature, preventing the disruption of the status quo.

To decolonize the canon, both event and practice require *delinking* from the dominant views and practices of colonialism. As Walter D. Mignolo warns, colonialism took charge of 'the modes of knowing, of producing knowledge, of producing perspectives.' To perpetuate this is damaging, especially in our increasingly globalized societies, and must be addressed. Hence, our focus in this book is on literary art from those whose experiences carry the complex residue of colonial rule, or who live in a country with a long history of the complexities experienced through centuries of empire. The process of steering the world into a more equitably shared future for the benefit of all is clear, if not urgent.

The use of literature – with the European novel offered as the pinnacle of literary art – remains, perhaps, an underestimated part of the colonial process. Again, borrowing from

Greenblatt, to consider colonialism as three stages helps. In the first stage, written proclamations and treaties are created that signal acquisition of property: humans, lands and territories. Secondly, new rules and codes of behaviour are published. The third stage involves a re-fashioning of those who are colonized, in the image of the colonizer. Britain, in its third stage of colonial rule in the late 19th and early 20th centuries, engaged a paternalistic colonialism in which literature was taught – or utilized – in privileged classrooms. The emphasis on *civilizing* involved canonical writing like Shakespeare, Scott and Kipling. Native languages were ruthlessly suppressed, while in classrooms empire-wide, the pinnacle position of the white colonizer was being glorified, not least since colonialism had already designated Black and Brown people as either *not* human or in hierarchical gradations of the human.

Unsurprisingly, there are many concerns about the ways in which the contemporary practices of publication replicate colonial exclusion of those of African descent, Asian descent and Indigenous Peoples, as does the teaching of literature itself. Specifically concerning the teaching of indigenous traditions, primarily in the US, Australia and the Americas, the history of colonization, as well as the highly racialized policies of assimilation after decades of neglect and lost generations, make the relatively recent claiming of a literary voice not only necessary, but pressing.

In teaching literature – primarily Caribbean, but also Black British – for decades within the UK university system, one listens attentively to students. It is clear that a younger generation insists on being able to read with confidence the world in which they live. That world, globalized and diverse, is one with which they are already familiar. They puzzle over ways in which the Black and Brown people drawn from their own lives resemble, and yet do not resemble, *others* represented in the writing that they read. They experience this with discomfort in the university classroom. Also important is the absence of that world from their prescribed reading, despite their knowledge of the UK as a nation with a centuries-long multicultural, multiracial presence. Where are the characters, the narratives, they ask? This is felt keenly, as the world they experience outside the university is one of interculturality and cultural entanglements, multilingualism and multiracialism. For students of literature, their sense is that the traditional, little-questioned canon consists of many texts that they would never read unless required to do so.

All members of a society should expect to be able to be imaginative, creative and to make art in which they are reflected. That is, unless one subscribes, consciously or not, to the colonial view that some groups, specifically those designated 'other' in some way, are less capable of artistic endeavour. Such racialized bias has been problematic, especially for Black British – and emerging Black European – writing, and for postcolonial countries around the world. The problem raises concerns about who is permitted to produce knowledge and culture, and who is designated mere consumers of knowledge or culture. This is further compounded by the absence of Black scholars in the classroom. Notably, in 21st-century Britain, Joan Anim-Addo was the first Black British Professor of Literature. In the US, with its tradition of Black universities influencing the mainstream, the first US Black professor dates back to the mid-19th century.

In Europe, the situation, even compared with England, seems more bleak. Primarily through courses on Postcolonial Studies in countries such as Italy, Spain, Greece and Finland do students gain the opportunity to study 'other' literatures; all helped by the academic movement that the EU has established.

In the 21st century, for minoritized Black women's writing, the concern with belonging in university classrooms is a reality. Though not in the minority in literature classrooms, women often continue to feel marginalized. This is even more the case for Black and Brown women who are in a 'minority'. The situation for the teaching of a more inclusive body of literature continues to cause concern for many students, who continue to bear the load of raising issues about exclusion. The UK's action is late and little, with some minimal shifting since the BLM movement's call for decoloniality began ringing through the universities. At the same time, in too many Humanities contexts, Black students find themselves co-opted into the study of artistic representation from which they understand themselves to be effectively excluded. The situation is alienating and holds repercussions for the classroom and for writing as well.

SELECTING A NEW CANON

Although there is noise in many universities about decolonizing the curriculum, this usually amounts to little more than an updating of reading lists and the continued instruction by predominantly white lecturers. The majority of English departments in

Western countries are adamant that 'English' is what those interested in literature want, despite a constant cry that students are not engaging with the traditional canon. Could the answer lie in a more diverse range of novels for study?

Opportunities to study the kind of literature selected for this book are rare in the UK and in many parts of the world, and it cannot be a surprise that there are so few long-standing champions of decolonizing or diversifying the canon. A structural issue remains internationally. In order to be studied or enjoyed, books must be in print. As we have indicated, publishers have an important role to play in considering the responsibilities of their literary custodianship and the wider cultural context of their work – over and above market forces.

Perhaps an immediate question concerns whether diversity is ever enough when considering literature or any other art form. The answer is no. Nor is diversity alone the basis of our choice for this volume, which has held true to our concern with quality that interlinks with diversity. Drawing on years of studying, teaching and writing, we have evaluated the individual works of fiction. We have rediscovered the range of forms that are available as literary fiction. We have maintained sight of the pleasure that great fiction gives.

We have brought to the selection process multiple viewpoints, including that of seasoned scholar, writer and activist. Though in the past, such decisions have involved the test of time, we bring to bear additional tools. These include the recognition of excellence through a range of prestigious prizes. Many of the selected novels have tested ideas about the universality of standard English and have brought regional writing to the fore, so that a sense of place is heightened. The variety of the selection indicates the extent to which the novel has evolved in form and substance since the height of the Western tradition. Voice, language, writerly preoccupations, characters are differently emphasized. Settings are infinitely more varied. Women authors are much more prevalent.

This book's decolonized canon references a present in which nation states – if only because of unprecedented international or diasporic movement – play a diminished part in the consensus about literary merit as always reflecting the story of that nation or the West. As a result, whether or not 'the canon' might have been perceived in the past as 'closed', its openness today is visible and necessary. Evidence of openness lies in award-winning authors, many of whom were not born in the West and whose writing displays a style drawing on multiple traditions. We have unpicked the complex literary expressions of an increasingly transnational body of writing in relation to its readers. This book is about artistic excellence in a context mindful of a common humanity, and the urgent need for us to read each other. Our hope is that you, the reader, reaching for change, will grow in confidence about the potential that the act of reading holds as a vehicle for decolonizing. Above all, we want you to be nourished by the rich and diverse selection offered here. Thereafter, it remains for you to champion the writers, their regions and beyond – all of which you are set to discover.

THE
CANON

LOVE IN A FALLEN CITY AND OTHER STORIES

EILEEN CHANG

1943

The novella *Love in a Fallen City* centres on a divorced Shanghai woman, Bai Liusu in the period leading up to the Japanese bombing of Pearl Harbour and the occupation of Hong Kong during the Second World War. It is a psychologically ambiguous and bewitching account of how marriage and concubinage are maintained by the same sexual politics, but produce vastly different consequences for women.

Liusu's family politics resembles a sea of circling sharks and Chang names each of them numerically – Fourth Master, Sixth Young Lady, Third Mistress, and so on – each identifiable in the hierarchy of significance and order of birth. We learn that it has been seven years since Liusu fled a brutal husband. With his death, she refuses to be wrecked upon the rocks of her divorce. Nor will she let her future be capsized by her greedy, self-seeking relatives who have spent all of her money. Liusu is an intriguing character and Chang makes sure readers' allegiances lie with her. Her cool appraisal of her physical appearance at 28 years old, is of not being 'too old yet', with an attractive small face and a slender figure. However, as she notes, a woman close to 30 can grow haggard in a moment; she is on borrowed time. Liusu is clever, more so than her family, much to the particular displeasure of her brothers. Her incisive remarks always expose their ignorance and yet, as a woman, she has no security without them.

The 32-year-old playboy Fan Liuyuan is designated for Seventh Sister, the 24-year-old Baolu, but instead prefers Liusu. He contrives a trip to Hong Kong with Liusu, benefiting from the complicity of marriage arranger Mrs Xu. Although Liusu deduces this is all part of a plan to woo her, she is shocked at his disregard for the protocols of respectability. She must observe these at all costs to avoid becoming an outcast and a disgrace to her scornful family. Liusu's thoughts in evaluating her situation are at odds with the facade she displays in order to achieve her goal of matrimony. Readers can appreciate her struggle and the compromise she has to make, one that involves acknowledging her powerlessness over determining her destiny merely because she is a woman.

Liusu's instinctive understanding of Liuyuan's sexual strategizing is confirmed when she discovers he has booked them adjacent rooms in the ostentatious, but unnervingly named, Repulse Bay Hotel. Like Liusu, the reader is drawn into his web. We are privy to Liusu's inner assessments and reassessments of him. Is she his prey or is he the romantic outsider displaying increasing devotion to her? Liuyuan's manipulativeness is revealed when Liusu realizes some people call her Mrs

Fan. His snare has captured her reputation in a double-bind. If people assume she is his mistress, she will be forced to acquiesce and forgo any chance of marriage. If they mistakenly think she is his wife, it means that she has been 'trapped by appearances'. All Liusu's skills of diplomacy and clear-sightedness are needed to ensure her security. She requires marriage, while he offers love. When Liusu decides to return to Shanghai, her family are alert to the reputational consequences of her failure to secure Liuyuan. They visit friends and relatives to urge their silence, driven by their collective view that 'a woman who was tricked by a man deserved to die, while a woman who tricked a man was a whore.' Such are the stakes for Liusu.

It is a slow-burn narrative, reminiscent of a measured dance in which each performer knows the formations and steps, but edges around the other, maintaining a distance. Courtship in this context also evokes skirmishes between two sides, reinforced by militaristic language. Plans are made, competitors or enemies are to be outwitted. Mrs Xu attempts 'a two-pronged attack' in 'scouting' to find husbands for both Liusu and Baolu. Liusu remains afraid that Liuyuan will 'suddenly drop the pretence and launch a surprise attack.' She might appear calculating in displacing Baolu, but Liusu's knowledge of how men operate saves her, as it is clear to her that he is 'used to lying to women.' Liusu unsentimentally and carefully pursues her goals in a game to be played with two different outcomes: hers practical and tactical, his heedless and hedonistic.

When she ultimately capitulates to sharing a house with Liuyuan, despite being unmarried, his immediate intention to depart to England without her raises suspicions as to her fate. However, there is an abrupt change of fortune, as plans are suddenly taken out of their hands. In early December 1941 the bombing starts. Wartime conditions disrupt national borders, as well as boundaries around expected and accepted social roles and codes of behaviour. When his boat cannot sail from Hong Kong harbour as a result of the invasion, Liuyuan returns to take Liusu to what they hope is a safer place, the Repulse Bay Hotel. Suddenly freed from social conventions, more natural responses bloom into new understandings of the world and each other.

Chang creates an enchanting portrait of morals and manners that absorbs lyrical aspects from Chinese classical literature while conveying a contemporary sensibility. The apparent lightness of touch is misleading, however, for the issues are weighty. The story also charts the division between traditional etiquette and customs, and capitalist-impelled modernity. The shadow of the Japanese occupation atrocities and the sexual enslavement of women as weapons of conquest are unspoken factors for any woman in the context of 1940s Hong Kong and China. Chang disingenuously truncates the tale with the fiddle-like *huqin* playing its desolate sound, with which she also opens her novella in the ultimate tantalizing withholding '—oh! why go into it?'

Chang's work is legendary throughout China and Taiwan. The award-winning Taiwanese film director Ang Lee directed the adaptation of her novella *Lust, Caution* (2007), and high-lighted her importance internationally, noting that with 'these excellent new translations, English readers can discover why she is so revered by Chinese readers everywhere.'

THE COLLECTION

First published in China as 傾城之戀 in 1943, *Love in a Fallen City* is available in an English-language edition (2007) in the Penguin Modern Classics series. It comprises four novellas, one of which provides the title for the collection, and two short stories, written when the author was in her twenties and variously translated by Karen S Kingsbury and Chang herself.

THE AUTHOR

Eileen Chang (張愛玲) was born Zhang Ying (张瑛) in 1920 into the elite Qing Dynasty. Her aristocratic father was a brutal opium addict, while her mother, who renamed her daughter Zhang Aìlíng was independent, educated and travelled abroad. Chang studied English Literature at the University of Hong Kong. When the Japanese invaded in 1941, she returned to Shanghai. In the 1940s she wrote for newspapers in both English and Chinese languages, and published short stories, essays and a novel – *Half a Lifelong Romance* (1948). She fled to Hong Kong in 1952, as her elite background and the perceptions of her as a lightweight writer were problematic; her books were banned by the People's Republic of China until 1978. Chang emigrated to the US in 1955. Her fame grew from the 1970s, but she became a recluse and was found dead in her Los Angeles apartment in 1995. *Love in a Fallen City* was successfully adapted as a film, directed by Ann Hui (1984).

IF YOU LIKE THIS, TRY...

Snow Flower and the Secret Fan (2005), a subtly feminist novel set in the Qing Dynasty during the 19th century by Chinese-descent US author Lisa See. It reconfigures stereotypes of women in regards to foot-binding practices and arranged marriages through the lifetime sisterly relationship between Lily and Snow Flower. Yáng Jiàng's Baptism (1988) represents the era of 1950s Beijing where, after the 1949 Communist Revolution, the intellectual classes had to find ways to 'perform' an acceptable identity as the purges began. To Live (1993) by Yú Huá is a novel that follows the fortunes of Xu Fugui, a dissolute young man who finds himself at the centre of key moments in Chinese modern history. In Notes of a Desolate Man (1994) by Chu T'ien-wen, a middle-aged man flies from Taipei to Tokyo to care for his friend dying of AIDS in a unique portrait of Taiwan manners and mores, love and ageing, set against a tragic backdrop of personal loss.

ALL ABOUT
H. HATTERR:
A GESTURE

G V DESANI

1948

Described as the 'Indian *Ulysses*', Desani's novel is an inventive, biting satire that pillories and parodies storytelling itself. It invigorates, disorientates and enthrals all at once. The prose goes beyond grammatical limits to stimulate readers to consider just how far we understand and apply these rules – and what fun is to be had. Examples range from pompous archaic usage, 'Thereon, an eternal unto-death struggle is being waged', and Edward Lear-esque nonsensical coinages, 'young Always-Happy' or 'Bishop Walrus', to colloquialisms, clichés and mimicry, '*Me-dams! and Ma-sewers!*'. With italics used for emphasis throughout the book, and short sentences of vernacularized and standard English, every sentence exists potentially as a stand-alone statement. A more energetic and mischievous form of novel writing would be hard to locate. The reader seems to be allowed in on the joke, but just who is the narrator making fun of? Is anything to be taken seriously? This tale, pitched truly beyond words, led T S Eliot to declare, 'In all my experience, I have not met with anything quite like it.'

In Desani's dextrous narrator Hatterr – recalling Lewis Carroll's 'Mad Hatter' – we experience not just his voyage of self-discovery, but also the liberation of constantly changing perspectives on everything. The novel's labyrinth of allusions and red herrings defy conventional ideas about character, plot or narrative. After a beguiling opening chapter, we are led to believe that the author is tracing the book's chaotic prov-enance. We meet 'Betty Bloomsbohemia', a 'Specialist' whom Desani the author consults, followed by 'Pius Prigg Pilliwinks'. They advise 'Desani' to change, that is 'correct', his manuscript. The narrator 'Desani' leads the reader to believe he does *not* do this, although Desani the author in real life did rework and refine further versions.

After his white Scottish father's death (his Malay mother's whereabouts are unknown), Desani's narrator, the eponymous Mr H. Hatterr flees from the English Missionary Society, which has adopted him. He takes with him the mission funds and three books: an English dictionary, and Latin and French primers. He then embarks on a personal odyssey, starting in colonial India and ending with Independence. A 'sage' from 'Calcutta, Rangoon, Madras, Bombay, Delhi, Mogalsarai-Varanasi' and finally of 'All-India' introduces each of the seven chapters with an anecdote to Hatterr. These place names remind readers of the history of the British Empire period when its colonized territories were renamed, reflecting its ethos of divide and rule.

Hatterr proves to be a delightful shape-shifter, deftly bringing together all forms and registers of English, Indianisms,
French, German, Latin and Hindi, veering from formality to
informality, effortlessly relayed in an often whirlwind sentence.
The chapter titles are presented as rhetorical questions, under
nonsensical headings on the 'Contents' page. Each adds a twist
of the narrative thread: can anything be relied upon? How
accurately do these indicate what is to come?

As an adventuring imperial subject, Hatterr seeks his
fortune in colonial India. He joins the exclusive Sahib Club
after giving another club member access to his wife, Kiss-curl,
and passes as an Englishman. When he is dismissed from the
club for unpaid debts, he then embraces his Indian heritage,
but at the same time loses status. A number of jobs follow: a
newspaper reporter, antique furniture renovator and meeting
a fake seer who runs a racket in impersonating holy men. His
wife humiliates him with her new lover as he tries to win her
back through acquiring a title and an honorary music degree.
In rejecting the material world for mysticism and charlatan
holy men, the book reveals the misleading facades of aspira-
tion, nationalism and spiritualism. Hatterr explains that in
India you need only 'cast off clothing' to transform yourself
into 'a semi-Benedictine, a sacred chicken.'

There are laugh-aloud moments in the novel's absurdist
humour and yet, there is an edge that constantly alerts us to
the more disturbing aspects of Hatterr's origins. His mixed
parentage is as much personal – 'Biologically, I am fifty-fifty
of the species' – as the character is symbolic of the consequences of the empire's clash and crush of cultures in colonial

rule. What exactly is Desani drawing our attention to? Perhaps he sums it up in that first chapter, intentionally *mis*appropriating language to unveil the formula of imperial success. He suggests using cunning to accumulate goods and property, 'by legal sanction, by religious warrant...by right imperial motive.' The novel parades the repurposing of the colonizing language, a process just as turbulent as the fight to win Indian Independence proves to be.

Desani positions his protagonist as challenging the white, male Anglophone literary canon (Shakespeare, Kipling, Joyce) and their cultural legacy on behalf of colonial and formerly colonized subjects. There is a teasing undertone, which provokes readers to reflect on their grasp of Desani's word-play and 'In'(dian) jokes. Unlike Joyce's *Ulysses*, or the complete works of Shakespeare, there is no annotated version to help readers in deciphering its mysteries. That is the key to its anarchic appeal. We can all join in with puncturing both pomposity and the canonical cultural balloon. This balloon, for Hatterr, is filled with hot air and as Desani infers, the narrator might very well be too!

Desani's quirky typography demands reading aloud, or even acting out. The cacophony of the narrative is populated by unforgettable presences that weave together myth, anecdote, digression and contradiction into a richly entertaining and thought-provoking experience. This post-war novel's brilliance lights the way for later Indian writers in English like Salman Rushdie, who observes the text as 'the first genuine effort to go beyond the Englishness of the English language.'

THE NOVEL

First published by Francis Aldor, London in 1948 and in the US in 1951 by Farrar, Straus and Young, Desani's book has been kept in print through many editions. A revised edition, with an introduction by Anthony Burgess was published as *All About H. Hatterr: A Novel* in 1970 by Farrar, Straus and Giroux in the US and The Bodley Head in the UK. In 1972 it was reissued as a paperback for the Penguin Modern Classics series. In 2007 it was published as part of the New York Review of Books Classics series.

THE AUTHOR

Born in Nairobi, Kenya Govindas Vishnoodas (G V) Dasani (1909–2000) grew up in pre-partition India. At the age of 17 he travelled to London and by 25 was a foreign correspondent for *Times of India*, changing the spelling of his name to Desani. Living in the UK (1926–8) and (1939–52), Desani lectured at many institutions including the Royal Empire Society, and Oxford and Cambridge universities. During the Second World War, the British Ministry of Information sponsored his talks throughout the UK to thousands of people. *All About H. Hatterr: A Gesture* was published to international acclaim in 1948. It was followed by *Hali*, a poetic work, five years later. Moving to India in 1952 Desani spent 14 years in seclusion, immersed in Hindu and Buddhist mysticism. He was a special contributor to *Illustrated Weekly India* in the 1960s. Desani moved to the US in 1968 to teach Philosophy at the University of Texas, Austin.

IF YOU LIKE THIS, TRY...

Afro-Colombian writer Arnoldo Palacios's 1949 *The Stars are Black* is a trailblazing rendering of the impoverished lives of Black people in the remote Chocó region. Mumbai-born Suniti Namjoshi's *Goja: An Autobiographical Myth* (2000) also unsettles categories and conventions. It employs polarized class-caste perspectives to recreate the life of a family retainer through imagined conversations that undo boundaries between fact, fiction and myth, entwining personal and public histories.

Ambai's short story collection *In a Forest, A Deer* (2000), translated from Tamil into English by Lakshmi Holmström unearths women's hopes from beneath the layers of social expectation. Combining myth and nature, these tales explore the forbidden and silenced experiences of characters seeking worlds beyond repressive contexts. The Zimbabwean author Dambudzo Marechera's *The House of Hunger* (1978) grasps the brutalities of repressive colonial legacies and explodes the depths of their consequences in both language and plotline, combining nightmarish satire with shock to prevent any 'comfort' reading of his mesmeric masterpiece.

THOUSAND CRANES

YASUNARI KAWABATA

1952

Thousand Cranes opens with a dilemma. Kikuji Mitani, a man in his early twenties, has been invited yet again to a tea ceremony, despite his apathy towards the ritual itself. It has been arranged by his late father's former mistress, Kurimoto Chikako, and the reason behind the invitation puzzles him. Kikuji finds himself drawn into an increasingly unsettling psychological game resulting not only from Chikako's attentions, but also those of his late father's final mistress, Mrs Ota, her daughter Fumiko and a young woman, Inamura Yukiko, whom Chikako has earmarked as Kikuji's potential bride.

Through the deceptive simplicity of a Japanese tea ceremony and its four Zen Buddhist principles of harmony, tranquillity, respect and purity, a saga unfolds where the past entanglements between two families, the Mitanis and the Otas, sets the course for a creeping tale of shame, secrets and suicide, told against a backdrop of the encroaching Westernization of post-war Japan.

While the tale is told through Kikuji's perceptions, the presence of an omniscient narrator hovers nearby, pointing out a discrepancy, an irony or a more ominous angle to be read into a character's actions. This upends the apparently subdued and enigmatic calm of the tea ceremony ritual. All is not what it seems.

Stirring emotions reside beneath the outwardly mundane interactions between Kawabata's characters. Just as the reader might feel they have understood the motives of Kikuji, Chikako, Mrs Ota and Fumiko, this is undermined by a contradictory self-reflection or an action or reaction resulting in a surprising plot twist.

This lyrical novella is composed of five chapter-like episodes. Despite its brevity and compactness, there is a complex mystery of gradually unravelling lives, holding the reader fast within its grasp. The intimate moments between characters or their private thoughts also creates a sense of intrusive witnessing that is almost unseemly. Kikuji recalls an unpleasant childhood memory of seeing the birthmark on Chikako's breast, which still repels him and by extension, appears to infuse his attitude to women. The misogyny that surrounds descriptions and observations of women's bodies, established on the first page with Kikuji's memory of the birthmark, is set alongside the idealized purity and compliance expected of a young woman destined for marriage. In such a context Yukiko and Fumiko must find husbands.

In a world dominated by the politics of the marriage market and altering family fortunes there is much wryness of tone. Alongside the seemingly mundane, there is an edginess that is both disorienting and gripping. Carefully placed symbols throughout the book cry out for interpretation. What are the 'thousand cranes' of the title meant to evoke? Sadako Sasaki, an irradiated victim of the Hiroshima bomb folded over 1,000 paper cranes before dying in 1955, aged 12. In traditional Japanese culture, folding 1,000 origami cranes grants a special wish. But for Kikuji there are complex layers to the symbolism. The 'thousand cranes' pattern on Yukiko's scarf transfixes him, and yet it is Chikako, who he resents, who has orchestrated the meeting with her.

We discover that the Mitani family shares an odd history with Chikako. After her displacement by the younger Mrs Ota, Chikako then becomes companion to Kikuji's mother and moves in with the family. Our brief glimpse of the late Mrs Mitani shows her to have been insightful and stoic about her husband's infidelities. We gradually realize that there is an absence of moral judgement over this arrangement. Chikako's birthmark is implicitly the reason she has never married. The double standard is clear for, as Kikuji's mother observes, any man with a birthmark would be able to simply 'laugh when he was found out', whereas for a woman, it is not so. The cost of physical imperfection in this society is seen to be great.

Chikako is resourceful, setting up her own business for training young women in the art of the tea ceremony, which also creates matchmaking opportunities. Kikuji is baffled, even unsettled, by Chikako and Mrs Ota's acquaintance; not to mention their ostensible joint purpose. After he sleeps with Mrs Ota, there begins a chain of events punctuated by death, deceit and cross-generational sexual encounters, where 'the mother's body was in a subtle way transferred to the daughter.' This is a world in which women's physical age and appearance are forensically scrutinized. While daily life appears bland, the depths of daydreams operate as a contrasting subtext. The seemingly mild-mannered Kikuji harbours disturbing thoughts, but it is unclear whether he enacts them.

Kawabata admired the haiku poetry form of three lines containing seventeen syllables and adopted this in his prose to resist the Westernization of Japanese culture. Much of his narration in *Thousand Cranes* employs compact sentences of few syllables as he aims to preserve Japanese traditions through language. The intriguing history of the tea-making wares and the artistic styles for the bowls, vases and containers going back to the 16th-century Seto period or the Edo period (1603–1867) and images by 10th-century artists, celebrates how sustained this history is. The treatment of the tea ceremony utensils serves as a compelling metaphor for the decay and disillusionment with post-war social relations and expectations.

Western influences infiltrate the novella's society, represented in the form of Occidental buildings, and in the loss of tradition and heritage. The apparent passivity and compliance of the defeated nation to the victorious forces is reflected in the outward indifference of the characters to each other's emotional pain. Who is the villain of the piece as it reaches its shocking denouement? Is it Kikuji, full of menace, and presenting a diffident demeanour to the world? Are Mrs Ota and Fumiko self-sacrificing victims of male exploitation, or manipulative and strategic? Is Chikako, who weaves a powerful web of vengeance around both families, justifiably vindicated, or the destructive enemy?

THE NOVEL

Published in Japanese as *Senbazuru* or 千羽鶴 by Chikuma Shobō in 1952, after having been serialized (1949–51), the novel was translated into English by Edward G Seidensticker and published by Alfred A. Knopf in 1958.

THE AUTHOR

Yasunari Kawabata (1899–1972) was the first Japanese author to win the Nobel Prize in Literature (1968) for three of his acclaimed novels: *Snow Country* (started in 1934, first published in 1937 in Japanese and then in English in 1956), *Thousand Cranes* and *The Old Capital* (1962). He was born in Osaka and orphaned when he was four, growing up with his paternal grandparents who had both died by the time he was 15. Kawabata first majored in English at the Tokyo Imperial University, changing to study Japanese literature. Beginning as a short story writer and journalist for the *Mainichi* newspaper, he became author of 13 books and rated *The Master of Go* (1951) as his best. Kawabata was honoured by an Ordre des Arts et des Lettres from the French government (1960) and received the Japanese Order of Culture in 1961. It is considered that he ended his own life in 1972, but this remains debated.

IF YOU LIKE THIS, TRY...

An epic, intergenerational tale that is also a lament to loss, *Song of the Crocodile* (2020) by Indigenous writer, Nardi Simpson.

Simpson depicts the Billymil family, who are Yuwaalaraay people living on the edge of the fictional country town of Darnmoor in Australia, a place with secrets – swathed in colonial racism – that are violently revealed. The novel is suffused with grief, but is also a defiant celebration of life in the face of settler ignorance and destruction. In Madeleine Thien's *Certainty* (2007), Gail, a radio producer from Vancouver, returns to Malaysia to find out more about her father's wartime experiences under Japanese occupation and to track down his friend Ani. Instead, she discovers complicated family secrets.

Haruki Murakami's classic *Norwegian Wood* (1987, translated into English by Jay Rubin) is told from the first-person perspective of a young man, Toru Watanabe. It concerns his relationships with Naoko, the ex-girlfriend of his friend (who committed suicide) and Midori, who he meets at university. Naoko gradually retreats from the world and also ends her own life, while, in contrast, Midori's feistiness and earthiness offer a release from the world of death in which Toru is psychologically fixed. Set in 1960s Tokyo, it shimmers with the submerged emotions of a society restrained by internalized protocols and morbidity.

THE LOST STEPS

ALEJO CARPENTIER

1953

The Lost Steps is a story on a grand scale and offers readers a gateway to Latin American writing. Considered a masterpiece of 20th-century writing, the novel holds an important place both in the literatures of the world and of Latin America. Carpentier imagines in this narrative the place of the New World in the artist's quest for meaningful art. The plot, characters and setting open up questions about Western values and artists who are rooted in the New World. What are the frustrations and the possibilities? We follow the narrator's journey, from New York City deep into the Amazonian jungle and witness his self-discovery unfold; the journey's slow pace appears to stop time itself in search of answers. What is important in the context of decolonizing the canon is the world that Carpentier investigates, along with his demonstration in the novel that the West does not always know best and can at least attempt to learn from the South. The world that he represents and what it envisions have been little explored.

Central to the novel is the unnamed narrator-protagonist, a composer who questions his place in a world of art dominated by declining European ideas. He is also disillusioned with his job writing music for advertising. His real desire is to compose a serious work. He is dissatisfied, too, with his marriage. His actress-wife's job consumes much of her time and attention. With a holiday period looming, he receives an invitation from his old university to undertake some funded research in his field of musicology. The research involves finding primitive instruments still being used in South America, where he spent his childhood. Feeling acutely out of touch, he initially rejects the offer until his lover, Mouche, persuades him to accept it and make the trip a holiday for them both. She announces the trip to their friends.

Events are largely driven by the three main women characters. Mouche, unable to write poetry as she had once hoped, is interested in the Amazonian project only as an exotic holiday. She even suggests that they fake his findings. With the narrator's wife, Ruth, absent from the marital home at the beginning of the novel, Mouche catapults the narrator into his journey. Ruth, too, has lost sight of her artistic ideals as her current acting role has become mechanical and meaningless. As time passes, Ruth imagines her husband to be lost and organizes a rescue plan to find him.

Meanwhile, to return to his language and his roots, the narrator lands first in a South American city that is in the grip of political upheaval, with factions fighting in the street. It marks the start of his challenging journey through place and time. As he travels with Mouche further into the interior, he becomes increasingly attracted to an Indigenous woman and fellow traveller, Rosario.

Recognizing Rosario as central to his quest, he engineers Mouche's return to the US by arranging, when she is sick, for someone to accompany her back home. In Mouche's absence, he commits himself to Rosario, who, in turn, gives herself to him. Their 'secret language' allows him to thrive as they travel deeper into the interior. By the time they reach the remote village of Santa Mónica de los Venados, he finds inspiration in all that they share and he decides to live in that community with her.

Rosario plays a crucial role. Her world, outside of and unknown to, Western art remains to be discovered. When the narrator and Mouche first meet her, she is a fellow traveller on the rattling bus taking them into the interior. Rosario, 'mestizo', of Indigenous, African and European blood, represents the interracial synthesis typical of the Caribbean region. Drawn to Rosario, the narrator's understanding of his quest as more important than collecting instruments begins to unfold. Their meeting lends greater meaning to his journey, which he recognizes to be about the place of his art in the world. Through Rosario, he gradually begins to understand more of the forgotten language of his childhood. At the funeral of Rosario's father, 'the language of the dead' triggers deep memories and connections that increase his understanding, and create a bridge between the lovers. The narrator's quest gradually becomes a search for his origins.

In Santa Mónica de los Venados, we are introduced to the village's founder, the Adelantando. His territory becomes the secret place in which the couple find happiness. Like the narrator, the Adelantando is driven to establish something new. Unlike the narrator, he is without artistic pretensions.

His wish is to create a place where people might live together, which he gradually achieves. Unlike the narrator, he has developed an unparalleled familiarity with the landscape and its peoples. His village is one to which he always returns, and to which he selectively invites others. It is the Adelantando who locates the instruments required by the narrator and who guides him into the unspoiled Amazon.

In the village, the narrator as artist comes into his own. He rediscovers his creativity, writing 'real' music, and while tracing the origins of music itself, he loses all track of time. When Ruth's search party finds him, he must choose to return with them immediately or stay. He chooses to return, as he explains, to purchase paper and equipment for his composition, which at last is flowing. For Rosario, though, his art is all but meaningless in the jungle. She does not understand his need for paper, nor does she believe that he will return.

Back in the city, newspaper headlines announce him as the husband rescued from the jungle by his devoted wife. This complicates his plans to return to Rosario, and further complications arise when Mouche goes to the press with the story of their affair. Finally resolving his messy domestic affairs, he attempts to return to the Amazon village, Rosario and his creative life, but is unable to remember how to get back into the village. He has effectively lost the steps to return to that which he believed he had discovered.

Two contrasting settings serve *The Lost Steps*: the city and the primeval jungle. The narrator's disenchantment with the city as a place of superficiality and artistic pretension leads him into the depths of the Amazonian jungle. There, closed off from city life, he gains a sense of himself and the origins of art. Away from the city's influence, his composing is untainted by the world, where everything appears to be inauthentic. Watching the shaman, for example, he is deeply moved by the authenticity of the experience. At the same time, he remains blind to the sharp difference between shaman and artist. There is considerable irony in the narrator's situation in which, whether in city or jungle, he finds himself superfluous as an artist. Carpentier leaves open precisely what the narrator learns from his journey – and especially what he learns by his inability to find his way back.

THE NOVEL

First published as *Los pasos perdidos* in Mexico (1953), then translated from Spanish into English for publication by Victor Gollancz (1956), *The Lost Steps* is considered to be Alejo Carpentier's masterpiece. It was the first novel by Carpentier to be published in the US and was awarded the Prix du Meilleur Livre Étranger in 1956.

THE AUTHOR

Alejo Carpentier (1904–80) was a prolific and influential writer, musicologist, composer and journalist. He grew up and lived predominantly in Cuba, being absorbed in its culture and promoting an alternative view on literature from the South. His work has shaped many writers and fired debate about literature, not only in Cuba and Latin America, but also much further afield. *The Kingdom of the World* (1949) focuses on the Haitian revolution and introduces his far-reaching ideas about 'the marvellous real' and the fantastic in nature, specifically in relation to magic realism. He is also noted for a style that richly references larger questions about the arts. His last novel, *The Rite of Spring* (1978) borrows from Stravinsky, and *Explosion in a Cathedral* (1962) draws on the name of a Goya painting.

IF YOU LIKE THIS, TRY...

Helen Oyeyemi's *The Opposite House* (2007) which explores the thin divide between myth and reality through a focus on two female characters who must recuperate their suppressed memories. Until they are able to reconcile both worlds and languages, the European and the Afro-Cuban, they will not know peace. Conceição Evaristo writes from the perspective of a Black Brazilian woman. Her debut, *Ponciá Vicêncio* (2003), was published in English (2007), translated by Paloma Martinez-Cruz. Ponciá, a young psychically gifted Afro-Brazilian woman, journeys from the land of her enslaved ancestors to urban life. Augusto Roa Bastos's *Hijo de hombre* (1960) published in English in 1965, translated by Rachel Caffyn, interweaves multiple narratives using magic realism to represent his Indigenous Guarani-Paraguayan history.

5

THE LONELY LONDONERS

SAMUEL SELVON

1956

Britain's Empire – in the form of a group of young 'immigrants' travelling from the Caribbean by sea – comes home to the motherland, to London, the heart of the empire. Selvon's lonely 'boys' find themselves in varying states of despair in post-war London and turn towards the novel's central narrator, Moses Aloetta, who appears seasoned to London's discomforts, and to its racism.

Blackness is not the primary lens of the boys' perception of themselves. Neither do they see themselves as 'West Indians', a general term that camouflages a range of ethnicities and attendant mixtures generated through the region's intercultural history. Rather, they are, foremost, specific islanders from the Caribbean: Trinidadian, Grenadian, Jamaican. However, in the post-war metropole they must accommodate a shared initial identity, being referred to as 'West Indians', even as they learn about and resist this demeaning construction through whiteness. As the novel reveals in its opening pages, neither the press nor the British Parliament seem able to fathom the incoming characters' desire to migrate to Britain. The stories of these unwelcome visitors' lives in London are intricately woven into this masterwork with humour and pathos; it soon becomes clear that much more than loneliness is at stake.

Having made the journey from Trinidad ten years earlier, Moses brings to the narration the peculiar experience of being racialized, together with a forbearance tinged with irony. Selvon invites the reader into the world of the newcomers primarily through the flawed figure of Moses, who adds substantially to the irony that is played out in the course of the entire novel. Mindful that 'things bad enough already,' Moses finds himself manoeuvred into functioning 'like a welfare officer' to a steady flow of new arrivals. He wearily predicts that the boys streaming off the boat-train at Waterloo, are destined for serial disappointment, despite their enthusiasm for London. Crucially, they will struggle to comprehend that though schooled as citizens of the British Empire, by virtue of their 'colour' they are considered *other* and will be treated as such. This is gradually revealed through their experience of discrimination in housing, employment and much more.

The novel turns on Moses' grudging generosity and his puzzlement at the manifestation of an othering through 'colour' that converges on his lived experience. In a pathbreaking intervention, Selvon's London contains an array of Black characters. Previously, this had been a stark absence in the English novel, despite the centuries-old presence of a Black population in Britain, particularly in port cities such as

London. This important dimension of *The Lonely Londoners* encourages readers and writers to become increasingly attuned to a transcultural world – their own, and that of Selvon's characters. Beyond the inclusivity of the characterization, Selvon also brings a fresh, melded style of narration infused with Caribbean and Creole Englishes, along with a carnivalesque humour. This is a distinctive portrayal of collectivity or shared experiences, drawing on the cultural emphases within the region of his birth.

Back in 1950s London, Selvon's collective foreshadows a global turn in literary writing represented by the boys who must negotiate – beside 'loneliness and fright' – a bewildering racism. This predominantly Caribbean group includes the newcomer and fellow Trinidadian, Henry Oliver, promptly nicknamed Sir Galahad, and the Jamaican, Tolroy. Arriving at Waterloo Station to meet his mother, Tolroy becomes immediately distraught to find several members of his extended family waiting, unaware of the problems their numbers will bring him. There is also 'Big City', an illiterate who hopes to make his fortune, Bart whose attempt at passing as Latino fails, and 'the wandering Nigerian', known as Cap(tain). In tune with the Caribbean carnivalesque, these 'boys' behave badly, specifically in terms of sexual politics.

Selvon uses narrative strategies drawn from the carnival tradition that is part of the annual cultural practice of his island home, Trinidad. Central to that tradition is calypso music, which by its very nature is inclusive. This genre pays precise attention to both audience and current affairs, and is also often risqué. To function to greatest effect, calypso performs an airing

of an open or shared collective secret. Its intention is to enter-
tain artistically and humorously. Ultimately, and as a measure
of its success, calypso points a finger at major topical issues,
particularly those involving the more powerful taking advantage of the more vulnerable. These aspects, over the plight of
any individual character, merit the reader's particular attention.

Transferring key elements of calypso – including satire, the
risqué and vernacular or Creolized language – to the modern-
ist literary form, the novel reveals its characters' collective
plight. Readers witness the boys' struggle to belong, despite
their paper entitlement (detailed in the 1948 Nationality Act),
and the long-lived distortions and exclusions of empire. True
to the situation of the day – latterly referred to as the Windrush
era – Selvon offers a reading, from the inside, of the boys' challenges. They are unaware that their arrival in London marks a
key moment in contemporary history, namely the making or
acknowledgement of multiracial Britain.

On one level, Selvon offers a social, realist novel of London,
which is acutely observed as a place of 'little worlds' not easily
accessible to migrants, especially those racialized as Black.
Galahad is pulled up short by a growing awareness of racism
to the extent that his sleep is interrupted by the memory of a
'black bastards' accusation, which he attempts to accommodate. On another level, Selvon is to be credited for an inventive
crafting that balances storytelling – replete with laugh-out-loud
moments, as well as bathos – and historiographical veracity.

Importantly, this novel succeeds in opening up questions
about colonial origins at a time when the debate insisted on
focusing upon race. Decades later, this remains a powerful

read that seemingly withholds almost as much as it reveals. Its reputation has rested largely on its representation of a varied 'West Indian' experience and its portrayal of the process of becoming the immigrant 'other' in Britain. This urges a wider re-reading that includes questioning Britain's deeply hierarchical story of empire and its attendant toxic human relations, thinly disguised under the cover of paternal colonialism.

THE NOVEL

First published in 1956 by Longman, Selvon's critically acclaimed novel is recognized not only as telling an important story about West Indian experience in London, but also as an iconic book about a changing post-war London. The novel has been adapted for radio a number of times in recent years. It has paved the way for a wave of published writing by Caribbean authors and for those experimenting with the Caribbean vernacular as literary language.

THE AUTHOR

Samuel Selvon (1923–94) was born in Trinidad. Leaving school at 15, he turned initially to journalism in the *Trinidad Guardian*. He travelled to London in 1950 with the intention of developing his writing career and, like several Caribbean writers in London at the time – such as Edward (Kamau) Brathwaite, George Lamming, V S Naipaul and Andrew Salkey – gained exposure through the BBC World Service's *Caribbean Voices*. Selvon's first novel *A Brighter Sun* (1952) is set in the

Caribbean. Other novels include *Moses Ascending* (1975) and *Moses Migrating* (1983), in which Selvon returns to the character of Moses Aloetta. He has also written many plays, and his screenplays include the collaboration with Horace Ové on the film, *Pressure* (1976).

IF YOU LIKE THIS, TRY...

James Kelman's Booker Prize-winning novel, *You Have to be Careful in the Land of the Free*, Penguin (2004). Written decades after Selvon's trailblazing novels, Kelman acknowledges the impact of Caribbean writing to which Selvon has been central. He singles out the influence of Selvon's insistence on a literary language inflected by varieties of English on his own particular Scottish sensitivity to the politics of language. George Lamming's *The Emigrants* (1954) explores similar themes to those of *The Lonely Londoners* and was published two years earlier. Selvon and Lamming famously travelled on the same ship to Britain and were said to have shared a typewriter on board.

6

THINGS FALL APART

CHINUA ACHEBE

1958

In Achebe's debut, set in the 1890s, we meet Okonkwo, a renowned warrior and wrestler from the village of Umuofia in the eastern region of Nigeria. He is also a man who lives in fear that he will be considered weak and lazy, like his father – a musician, who, having shunned field labour in life, had died (to Okonkwo's shame) in debt to several people. Okonkwo has had to work hard from childhood, with no paternal support, to become a wealthy farmer; he is determined to be the exact opposite of his father. This resolve drives his success, yet his three wives and seven children perceive him as a harsh and intolerant man who hides his emotions.

Early in the story, the village gives Okonkwo the honour of being the caretaker of a boy, Ikemefuna, from another village. The boy was a life given to Umuofia to prevent further bloodshed between the two villages. Three years later, The Oracle of the Hills and the Caves informs the village that the boy must die. Ikemefuna has become like a son to Okonkwo and so the elder, Ezeudu, warned him not to participate in his slaughter.

Not wanting to be perceived as a weak man, however, Okonkwo ignores this warning, yet, Ikemefuna's subsequent death profoundly unsettles Okonkwo, and he does not eat for days afterwards. Okonkwo, recalls the elder's warning when he hears of his death. At the funeral ceremony of Ezeudu, Okonkwo accidentally kills his youngest son. In accordance with custom, Okonkwo and his family must be exiled for seven years, and his compound cleansed of his presence. They are welcomed into his mother's village during this period.

This story is steeped in the way of life of the Igbo people, one of the largest ethnic groups in Nigeria. Conversations are populated with Igbo proverbs and words and phrases that are part of the narrative. The course of people's lives is determined by oracles and *chi*s, similar to personal guardian spirits. Achebe's use of repeating seemingly innocuous dialogue enhances the storytelling form, making it easy to become engrossed in this book and notice the early signs that foretell Okonkwo's downfall.

In the second part of the book, the first white Christian missionaries appear and converge on the villages, followed by British colonial authorities. One day Okonkwo's friend Obierika visits him while he is still living in exile; Obierika has seen Okonkwo's eldest son Nwoye attend the church in Umuofia. Nwoye had never been as warrior-like as his father wanted and had not come to terms with the death of his older 'adopted' brother, Ikemefuna. To the disgust of his father, Nwoye had turned to the church for answers.

Okonkwo and his family return home in the third part of the novel, and although his friend had warned him of the changes, he is shocked at the extent of the white presence there, and at the challenges he faces to regain his status. At a village meeting, the decision is taken to fight against the colonial and ecclesiastical authorities who have installed themselves in the village. Okonkwo swiftly takes the lead when colonial messengers try to break up their meeting and he kills one of them with his machete. However, no one follows his lead and his warrior-like action draws condemnation instead of the admiration he expected. He realizes then that the village will never fight back. For Okonkwo, this is the end of life as he knows it. It is as if the entire village has been emasculated, undermining everything that he believes in.

A dominant theme in *Things Fall Apart* is the idea of community as family within the Igbo culture and tradition, which falls apart when infiltrated by a foreign body. The coming of white people is foretold by the arrival of locusts – later recognized as a Biblical 'warning'. The villagers joyfully capture, cook and eat them as a rare delicacy – without realising the true devastation that awaits them.

A similar, critical scene involves a conversation between the white missionary, Mr Brown and Akunna, one of the village leaders, comparing Christianity with Indigenous faith. Mr Brown prefers a tentative approach to conversion, gaining trust and slowly undermining the community's customs. The villagers believe that their way of life has roots strong enough to withstand this intervention. Newly converted Christians know they are physically safe and will not be banned from the village, as long as they do not upset the internal structures of community life and Igbo traditions. The church presented one

God as an alternative deity to ask for their needs. This God did not require human sacrifice, since He had already sacrificed His Son, whereas the villagers' Indigenous faith demanded that newborn twins must be buried in the Evil Forest. Some villager-converts begin to challenge the way of life that they have been born into. One zealous convert, Enoch, decides to cause deep division in one swift action that alters the power balance in the community. He rips off the devil's mask in a village ceremony and then flees to the church building for protection. This dramatic and tense turning point marks the beginning of the end of Umuofia's stability.

Although *Things Fall Apart* is a story simply told, it is not a simple story. The stages of intervention into Africa are clear, showing how the combination of Christianity and colonialism tore the region apart. The story represents change enforced by tragedy that cannot be healed in one generation.

Things Fall Apart combines the intersection of traditional Igbo life, with the arrival of white Christian life in the 19th century. The impact of colonialism has been woven into many stories from those countries colonized by Britain. Nigeria's situation and circumstance as told in Achebe's story, through his characters, are symbolically replicated in other countries.

THE NOVEL

This was the first novel published in the ground-breaking Heinemann African Writers Series by William Heinemann in the UK; it has been translated into 57 languages. *Things Fall Apart* was voted one of Africa's 100 Best Books of the 20th

Century, and is featured in *Encyclopaedia Britannica*'s list of '12 Novels Considered the "Greatest Book Ever Written"'.

THE AUTHOR

Chinua Achebe (1930–2013) was born in Nigeria. He wrote five novels, two short story collections, six poetry collections, seven books of nonfiction and four books for children. He received several accolades, including honorary degrees, both during his lifetime and posthumously. His first major award was a Rockefeller Fellowship in 1960. *Beware Soul Brother* (1971) was the joint winner of the first Commonwealth Poetry Prize (1972). Achebe was awarded the Nigerian National Order of Merit (1979) and the American Academy of Arts and Letters (1982). He was appointed Goodwill Ambassador to the United Nations Population Fund (1999) and awarded the Peace Prize for Literature from the German Publishers and Booksellers Association (2002). He won the Man Booker International Prize (2007) and the Dorothy and Lillian Gish Prize (2010). Posthumously, he was honoured with the Grand Prix de la Mémoire (2019) and in the same year, a memorial bust was unveiled at the University of Nigeria, Nsukka. He is referred to as the father of modern African literature, although he refuted this title.

IF YOU LIKE THIS, TRY...

A number of Nigerian fiction writers in the same generation as Achebe and beyond have received accolades for their books since *Things Fall Apart*. These include books such as *Jagua Nana* (1961) by Cyprian Ekwensi, *The Famished Road* by Ben Okri (1991) and *GraceLand* by Chris Abani (2004). *Measuring Time* by Helon Habila (2007) is about twin boys in Nigeria who try to escape from their harsh father, with one becoming a soldier, the other, a historian. More recently, both *The Fishermen* (2015) and *An Orchestra of Minorities* (2019) by Chigozie Obioma have been critically acclaimed. *Omenuko* (1933, translated into English by Ernest Emenyonu in 2014) by Pita Nwana, was the first novel written in Igbo. It tells the life story of the politician, Igwegbe Odum. Books by women writers who embed the Igbo tradition in their work include *Ogadinma : Or, Everything Will Be All Right* by Ukamaka Olisakwe (2020), *The Son of the House* by Cheluchi Onyemelukwe-Onuobia (2019) and *Sky-high Flames* (2005) by gay activist, Unoma Azuah.

7

CHILDREN OF THE NEW WORLD: A NOVEL OF THE ALGERIAN WAR

ASSIA DJEBAR

1962

Anguish, loss and the power of anti-colonial resistance are the backbone of Assia Djebar's profoundly moving and multi-layered novel. In the shadow of the Tell Atlas Mountains, where flames and smoke indicate another battle raging between Algerian liberationist fighters and the French army, the women of the city of Blida live in fear of reprisals, but also in solidarity with the insurgents. It was from Blida that the first attacks were launched on French bases in 1954 to ignite a war for independence, which Frantz Fanon described as, 'Terror, counter-terror, violence, counter-violence' and 'the circle of hate, which is so tenacious and so evident in Algeria'.

In *Children of the New World*, no one falls outside the circle of hate's reach, but the circle is also threaded with love

– of family, friends and community – and especially the bonds between women. These bonds reflect the knotty interactions of European and Arab cultures under French colonialism, be this through inter-marriages or through France paradoxically providing refuge for Algerians fleeing persecution by French colonial authorities. The traditional wives include Cherifa, who is married to her second husband Youssef, the local guerrilla leader, and Amna, married to the increasingly ostracized policeman, Hakim. The modern women are Salima, the school teacher; Lila, who is married to the radicalized medical student Ali; Lila's French friend Suzanne, who is the wife of Algerian lawyer Omar; Touma, a Frenchified young Arab woman who rejects tradition and wears European fashions; and Hassiba, a 16-year-old girl who ends up in the mountains as a combatant. The women form a poignant and personal chain, recognizing what each other endures and defies. Lying to Hakim to save Youssef, Amna, decimated by too many pregnancies, articulates her precious bond with Cherifa as so close they might as well have shared the same mother's milk.

The story centres on the events of a single day, 24 May 1956, and loops back on itself, revisiting incidents from a new angle, opening up a different viewpoint in a magical maze that is not chronologically sequenced. But this is by no means a disorienting reading experience. Djebar lists her 22 characters by name, age, relationship, nationality and location. The result is a tantalizing set of co-mingling perspectives, a beguiling matrix of a character's inner thoughts and enthralling cross-hatching plotlines.

In this period an Algerian woman's space is expected to be strictly in the home, hidden from public view, behind curtains and the veil. Lila reflects that she has no photograph of her mother, a custom to ensure that even a woman's image does not leave the home. However, the aerial raids bring the war directly to the home front. The book opens with Lla Aicha, Youssef's mother, being killed by a shell on her terrace. From this moment on, there begins a complex web of alliances and subterfuge as each character makes a radical, life-changing decision. Cherifa needs to warn Youssef that he has been betrayed to the police, but being house-bound in the traditional way, 'how for the first time to *act*?' Middle-class women only go outside for funerals, to women's baths, for parties or ceremonies and 'the escorting spouse walks in front of her'. So as not to draw attention to herself, Cherifa knows she cannot risk asking for directions, and appraising male eyes burn into her as she walks, veiled, across the city. In doing so, she passes Touma in one of the cafés. In an instant Cherifa knows Touma is an informant and both women silently clock this mutual recognition. Touma's blatant Europeanization, a misguided assertion of independence in a context of national liberationist struggle, leads her to being in the pay of Martinez, the European policeman. Although vanity and materialism motivate Touma's quest for a sense of power over her destiny, the reader can understand how her desire to live without traditional constraints motivates her collaboration. Djebar is unrelenting in meting out Touma's eventual fate.

While Hakim is cruelly triumphant over torturing Saidi the former café owner to death, Djebar represents his dehumanization in bringing this violence into the home, beating Amna after a day's work. The heartlessness of the colonial regime towards resistance is starkly portrayed. No one is safe.

People are denounced, collaborators are killed. In her prison cell, Salima laments that the screams from those being tortured will make her 'go mad', before falling back asleep knowing she could be next. Denounced by her concierge, Lila rehearses her resolve, to refuse to confess under torture. Will she withstand it? The anticipation is chillingly juxtaposed with Ali, unaware of his wife's danger, encountering a little girl and her grandmother as the only survivors of a bombed mountain village, exemplifying the suspense and heart-wrenching nature of this book.

Anti-colonialist revolution was interwoven with the agency of writing in Arabic, a driving force for many writers of Djebar's generation. She dedicated a ten-year period to learning Arabic, while memorably describing French as 'the booty of war'. *Children of the New World* portrays how liberation from colonial rule, the 'New World' must extend to women's emancipation from patriarchal control and unequivocally recognizes that independent Algeria owes as much a debt to the traditional woman as to the freedom fighter.

While Gillo Pontecorvo's timeless film *The Battle of Algiers* (1966) captures the war from the perspectives of ordinary Algerian citizens, Djebar foregrounds the roles women played, roles much forgotten in Algerian political life as post-1962 conservative politics reinstated oppressive measures against women's independence. This novel is a tender tribute to their contribution to Algerian history. It is an evocative, transformational novel that remains fresh and relevant to the struggles today across the Maghreb, the area of the coastal plains and the Atlas mountain range in northwest Africa.

THE NOVEL

First published in French as *Les enfants du nouveau monde* (1962) by R Julliard, the novel was translated into English by Marjolijn de Jager and published by Feminist Press at the City University of New York in 2005 – the year of the 50th anniversary of the Algerian war.

THE AUTHOR

Filmmaker, novelist, translator and scholar, Assia Djebar is the pen name of Fatma-Zohra Imalhayène. Born in 1936 to an Arab-Algerian father and Berber mother, she was initially educated at an all-male school where her father taught. Her debut novel *La Soif* (1957), translated into English as *The Mischief* (1958) by Frances Frenaye, was the first novel by an Algerian woman writer published outside Algeria. In feminist solidarity, Djebar oversaw the French edition of Nawal El Saadawi's *Woman at Point Zero* (see entry 15) in 1983.

Djebar was awarded the Neustadt International Prize (1996), the Marguerite Youcenar Prize (1997), the International Prize of Palmi (1998) and was the first Muslim Maghrebian woman elected to the Académie Française in 2005. For a feminist anti-colonialist figure, it attracted controversy, as the institution is dedicated to protecting and monitoring the French language. Djebar wrote over 15 novels in French and her work translated into over 20 languages. The Assia Djebar Prize is considered the foremost prize for novelists in Algeria. Set up in 2015, the year of her death, it promotes literature in Arabic, French and Tamazight.

IF YOU LIKE THIS, TRY...

Algerian writer Abdelouahab Aissaoui's *Sierra de la Muerte* (*Mountain of Death,* 2015*)* won the Assia Djebar Prize. Not yet translated into English, it follows the fate of Spanish communists incarcerated in North African prison camps after the Spanish Civil War. Aissaoui's *The Spartan Court* (2020), as a winner of the Booker-backed International Prize for Arabic Fiction, will be translated, financed by the award. David Diop's 2021 International Booker Prize-winning Francophone novel of 2018, *At Night All Blood is Black* was translated into English by Anna Moschovakis. It follows the tragic fate of Senegalese colonial infantryman Alfa Ndiaye. Fighting in the French army in the First World War brutal trench warfare, his comrade's death triggers his psychological breakdown.

The Bridges of Constantine (1993, English translation by Raphael Cohen in 2013) by Tunisian writer and globally bestselling Arab woman novelist, Ahlam Mosteghanemi, is the first novel in Arabic written by a Maghreb woman. It exemplifies the refusal to write in the occupiers' language and traces 50 years of Algerian history from the 1930s to the 1980s, through independence fighter Khalid. Now a famous artist, he returns from self-exile in Paris and falls in love with novelist Hayat, the daughter of his former revolutionary commander. It combines passion and personal loss with a searing critique of contemporary Algeria.

8

WIDE SARGASSO SEA

JEAN RHYS

1966

Wide Sargasso Sea is a literary *déjà vu* in response to Charlotte Brontë's *Jane Eyre* (1847), published when the British Empire was ascendant and Caribbean plantations had supplied the wealth upon which its power was established through two centuries of enslaved Black people's toil. The setting for Rhys's novel is newly post-abolition Jamaica, 1834, when Britain paid financial compensation to plantation owners, rather than formerly enslaved people – incurring a government debt so shockingly huge it was only settled in 2015. Rhys wrote her revisionary novel in another era, that of the 1960s when 24 nations gained independence from Britain in a decade characterized by decolonizing politics.

Rhys places Rochester's first wife, Bertha, who he has incarcerated in the attic of Thornfield Hall in *Jane Eyre*, at the emotional centre of *Wide Sargasso Sea*. In Bertha, Brontë created one of the most enthralling and haunting figures in English literature. By reimagining her life and foregrounding Bertha's backstory, Rhys represents the consequences of enslavement and colonial violence through Black and Creole society in the crucible of the Caribbean. As a region that the imperial European powers of England, France, Spain and the Netherlands had competed over as they invaded and colonized, the Caribbean is overlayed with these histories and those of the original indigene Taino and Arawak peoples and Amerindian cultures.

The story is told from the first-person perspective by three narrators, suggesting insider access to a character's mind: Antoinette Cosway, the troubled heroine as a child in Part 1; the unnamed character who we understand is Rochester dominates Part 2; and Part 3 is prefaced by Grace Poole, but narrated by adult Antoinette. As both a prequel and a sequel simultaneously, it is a novel of the outsider, the excluded, of those people who do not meet the criteria of social and racial majorities. This is memorably signalled by the opening lines: 'They say when trouble comes, close ranks, and so the white people did.' White cockroach is how the Black servant girl Amelie refers to Antoinette as an impoverished white colonial Creole. Antoinette is marooned from any secure sense of belonging, wondering who she is and which country is her homeland.

The animalization of Brontë's Bertha is replete with the racist ideology that arose from assumptions and paranoia concerning racial purity. The paradoxical situation of Antoinette is that her husband fears she has Black ancestors. Elizabeth Barrett Browning's father was a plantation owner and the poet expressed her father's wish that she not marry and have children, in case miscegenation was revealed. This real-life example reflects Antoinette's husband's worst prejudices regarding her sexuality in relation to her non-European heritage. He wonders whether Amelie and Antoinette are related: 'It's possible, it's even probable in this damn place.' Shame, rage and humiliation course through the novel. The assertion of Anglo-Saxon 'civilizing' superiority by which the empire was maintained is refused by Rhys's portrayal of 'the other side of a story', as she described her inspiration to write it.

In leaving Antoinette's husband unnamed, Rhys's novel underscores undifferentiated white male power and its invisibility – everywhere controlling but nowhere named. By contrast, Rhys's naming of Antoinette replays the colonizing act of renaming, as her husband changes it to Bertha when he displaces her to England.

Brontë's Gothic elements – the uncanny, the supernatural, untamed and remote countryside, storms, the sublime – articulate what is repressed by the genre of realism and within Victorian society. In the colonial context of *Wide Sargasso Sea* these elements are reworked into a vivid tropical climate and a personified environment, which acts as a witness. Trees 'shiver', gather strength and 'wait'. Colours, symbols and imagery evoke the loss of nerve that Antoinette's husband experiences as he is immersed in a sultry arcadia that overwhelms his senses. He, the white male colonizer, keeps losing his bearings while asserting his assumption of unquestioned power. Jamaica is a sensorial cacophony and voices are everywhere in Rhys's text, emulating the spread of gossip and defamation of character. Antoinette's former nanny Christophine – who is a formidable obeah woman and during enslavement was perturbingly given as 'a gift' when a child to Antoinette's Martinician mother

Annette – notes that Antoinette's husband 'hears too many voices.' He is unable to decipher truth in a world in the grip of secrets, hearsay and spectral goings-on. The uncanny sense of foreboding is ever present. For readers who are familiar with *Jane Eyre*, there is the accompanying anticipation of when the two books will come together through the fate of Antoinette and Bertha once the former is brought to England.

This is a novel about the impossibility of finding love that lasts and where ownership of others and their labour distorts and defines relations, be it through enslavement, indenture or marriage. Both Antoinette, and Annette before her, must sell themselves into advantageous marriages to secure their futures. While Christophine is Antoinette's emotional anchor, this relationship is problematized by remembering that Christophine was formerly Annette's property.

At the time of its publication, there were few books written in England that had tackled history and the imperial–colonial legacy in as haunting a reconfiguration as Rhys's landmark novel achieves. It is sometimes heralded as a 'postcolonial' novel, but can it really be classed as this? None of the Black characters speak directly, they are narrated through either Antoinette or her husband. While Christophine's powerful influence frames the novel, she is unable to transcend the racial oppression of her situation and so, just how much power does she actually exert?

The revenant quality of coming back from the dead is the compelling thread by which to follow this tragic tale of passion, revenge, displacement and loss.

THE NOVEL

Wide Sargasso Sea was first published in 1966 by André Deutsch in the UK, and edited by the writer Diana Athill. It won the Royal Society of Literature Award and the W H Smith Award in 1966.

THE AUTHOR

Jean Rhys (1890–1979) was born to a white Creole mother and a Welsh father on the Caribbean island of Dominica. She felt an outsider in Dominica as a white woman descendant of enslavers and she left at 16 for London to continue her schooling, where she was ridiculed for her accent and colonial origins. Her peripatetic life included living in Paris (where Ford Madox Ford encouraged her writing), Bloomsbury and South-West England.

In her 52-year writing career, Rhys published novels and short stories, alongside other forms such as diaries and poetry. Titles include: *The Left Bank and Other Stories* (1927), *Quartet* (1929), *Voyage in the Dark* (1934), *Tigers are Better Looking* (1968) and *Sleep it Off Lady* (1976). Her letters were published in 1984. Her unfinished autobiography, *Smile Please*, was published posthumously in 1984 by André Deutsch and Harper & Row. Despite receiving critical acclaim for her earlier work, it was *Wide Sargasso Sea* that rescued her from obscurity and destitution; she described this as having come 'too late'. She was appointed CBE in the 1978 New Year Honours list.

IF YOU LIKE THIS, TRY...

Witi Ihimaera's *The Whale Rider* (1987) is an uplifting portrayal of one girl Kahu's determination to overturn male-centred traditions and prove her leadership as a descendant of the legendary 'whale rider', Kahutia Te Rangi. Erna Brodber's *Jane and Louisa Will Soon Come Home* (1980) is a work of poetic prose that represents Jamaica's colonial past through the character of Nellie, growing up in the 1940s. Brodber's aim was to prioritize complex feelings in her writing over plotline. She represents recovery from trauma by a self-narrating female subject through Nellie's experiences of the US and Jamaica, and particularly the power of the *kumbla* – a metaphorical space that serves as protection and refuge.

Edward P Jones's Pulitzer Prize-winning *The Known World* (2003) is an epic work of historical fiction, redolent of 19th-century novels. Henry Townsend, a Milton aficionado and a freed man, is now a plantation proprietor himself. The challenging moral universe of this novel is distinctive, echoing the Devil's assertion in 'Paradise Lost' – he prefers to rule in hell than be subservient in heaven. Timeframes and references are on a collision course with a character's past and future, often contained within the same sentence.

A GRAIN OF WHEAT

NGŪGĪ WA THIONG'O

1967

As the day to celebrate independence from Great Britain draws closer, the challenge for Kenyan people is to make it an exciting and memorable moment. The village of Thabai designates Mugo their hero because he sheltered Kihika, the local leader of the Mau Mau resistance movement. Mugo was also praised for trying to stop a policeman beating a pregnant woman; she was then left to die in the trench that surrounded the village. Mugo is sent to a detention centre for this defiant act.

The elders and businessman Gikonyo, who is also the Uhuru (freedom) celebration day organizer, demand that Mugo give a speech, after which the 'highlight' will be to publicly expose Kihika's betrayer. A village traitor had informed the British colonial administration of Kihika's location, where they captured him. Kihika was then hung in a public field for his parents, siblings, friends and passing villagers to see as a 'warning'. Mugo initially agrees to speak but later reneges, preferring to remain in his hut on the outskirts of the village, nursing his secret – that he was Kihika's betrayer.

We meet the full cast of characters early on in this novel, as it moves between the two historical turning points of the 1952–60 Emergency, when the entire country was under a form of house arrest, and the forthcoming 12 December 1963 Independence from the British colonial power which instigated the Emergency. Real political figures such as Jomo Kenyatta are part of the backdrop of the story and we come to know the villagers of Thabai through their memories, their tragic misunderstandings and unrequited loves, which simultaneously reveal the history, culture and myths of Kenya.

Although A Grain of Wheat is a political novel, at its centre are the two universal themes of love and betrayal. Betrayal is committed on all levels, from the most intimate between husband and wife, to community betrayal by the local politician; from a secret Mau Mau oath to betrayal of one's dignity and self-respect for the love of a woman.

Both love and betrayal are at the heart of the changing relationship between Gikonyo (who had also been detained) and his wife, Mumbi. The ever-present symbol of betrayal between them is the child that Mumbi, Kihika's sister, bears for her first love, Kiraji, while married to her husband, Gikonyo. Mumbi's son is a constant reminder to Gikonyo, after he returns home from the detention centre, of his wife's adultery and he cannot touch her or talk to her. The bitter irony is that he himself betrayed his oath in order to earn immediate release from detention because of his overwhelming desire to be with her. But his action backfires, he is betrayed and it is six more years before he is finally released.

On the flip side of Mumbi's betrayal, we encounter her deep loyalty within the love triangle between herself, Gikonyo and Kiraji. She is devoted to family life and love for her husband and his mother during the difficult times of the Emergency, when they were forced to abandon their village to make way for white migrants who wanted to live on their fertile land. While Gikonyo was in detention, Gĩkũyũ people were forced to rebuild their homes elsewhere within two months or be punished by the colonial authorities. Gikonyo is unaware of Mumbi's care and loyalty to his family, but his mother appreciates her and stands by her.

Mumbi is also a beacon for the change to come in post-independent Kenya. Through her we see the younger generation of women in control of new power dynamics partly due to many of their menfolk being detained for several years. They must subvert tradition and, like Mumbi, fend for their families. Rather than accept the end of their marriage after being called a whore by Gikonyo, Mumbi tells him they need to talk through their issues before forging a new future as husband and wife. Her decision parallels the situation of the new Kenya, which cannot return to the time before the country and its people were abused by the outside force of colonialism.

Eventually, Gikonyo learns to look beyond his wife's mistake once he has contemplated and admitted that he had also been treacherous in the past and kept a secret. Throughout the novel betrayals are exposed and lives irrevocably altered – echoing events played out on an international stage during the unfolding of Kenya's independence. The novel ends ambiguously, but a resolution of sorts is found in the understanding and acceptance of human fallibility.

A Grain of Wheat achieves an enormous amount in a relatively short novel. The multiple ways of interpreting the story mean that each version offers a different emphasis. Each version is equally pertinent to the multifaceted storytelling of Kenya's political and social history and one in which the author skilfully incorporates Kenyan traditional culture and relates it to modern ideals. Alongside being a political narrative, it is also a moral tale and a social epic.

In his masterful approach to storytelling, wa Thiong'o experiments with multi-narrative voices told from different angles, rather like a film camera. Through one of these lenses, the author reworks Kenyan folk stories and there are hints of the Gĩkũyũ creation tale in *A Grain of Wheat*. His recent book, *The Perfect Nine*, is the creation tale told as a novel-in-verse. The ghostly but ever-present cloud of colonialism permeates everyone's lives and it is in these everyday lives, and the stories that could emanate from any close community, that the most moving aspects of the novel lie.

This story also shows that British colonial authorities aimed to prove to the world that their presence in Kenya was of paramount importance in order to 'civilise' Africans or to wipe them out. As Thompson, one of the 'civilised' British colonial officials, prepares to leave Kenya on the day before independence, he leaves behind the legacy of his barbaric actions: of torturing and starving men in detention centres, brutally castrating them and burying them alive. Thompson had concluded that African people were not human but merely 'vermin', and this was his justification for annihilating them.

THE NOVEL

First published in English in the Heinemann African Writers Series in 1967, this novel was voted one of Africa's 100 Best Books of the 20th Century. It is available as part of the Penguin Modern Classics series (2002).

THE AUTHOR

Ngũgĩ wa Thiong'o (1938–) was born in Kenya. He is the recipient of 11 honorary doctorates, including one from Yale University (2017) 'for showing us the potential of literature to incite change and promote justice, for helping us decolonize our minds and open them to new ideas.' He has published 19 books of nonfiction including memoir and essays, 4 books of plays, 8 books of fiction and 3 books for children. His *Decolonising the Mind: The Politics of Language in African Literature* (1986) won the 2019 Erich Maria Remarque Peace Prize.

His 2016 short story, 'Ituĩka Rĩa Mũrũngarũ: Kana Kĩrĩa Gĩtũmaga Andũ Mathiĩ Marũngiĩ' ('The Upright Revolution') has been translated into 98 languages. *The Perfect Nine: The Epic of Gĩkũyũ and Mũmbi* (2020) was longlisted for the International Booker Prize (2021). Ngũgĩ wa Thiong'o was a 2010, 2017 and 2019 Nobel Prize in Literature nominee. He is an Honorary Foreign Member of the American Academy of Arts and Letters, and is currently Distinguished Professor of English and Comparative Literature at the University of California, Irvine.

IF YOU LIKE THIS, TRY...

Yvonne Adhiambo Owuor's *Dust* (2014), like wa Thiong'o's works, covers the period of Mau Mau resistance. The book starts with a killing similar to the assassination of the young political activist Tom Mboya. *The Autobiography of President Kwame Nkrumah* (1957) is as important as Nelson Mandela's *Long Walk to Freedom* (1994) in the reading of colonial resistance. At the centre of African and Caribbean resistance is the historical biography of Toussaint L'Ouverture and the Haitian Revolution in the classic, *The Black Jacobins* (1938) by C L R James. *Miramar* (1967) by the Nobel Prize-winning author Naguib Mahfouz also plays with multiple narrative voices, although his most well-known books form *The Cairo Trilogy* (1956–7).

THE BEAUTYFUL ONES ARE NOT YET BORN

AYI KWEI ARMAH

1968

Ayi Kwei Armah's debut novel was published to critical acclaim following the demise of British colonialism in Ghana which was the first country in Africa to gain political independence from Britain. The setting is the residential and coastal areas of 1960s Ghana. The novel follows the last years of Kwame Nkrumah's government, leading to his overthrow in a military *coup d'état* and the arrest of his ministerial cabinet. The action takes place between Passion Week in 1965 and 25 February 1966, the day after Nkrumah's overthrow. The novel does not detail the action of the fall of the regime but remains throughout with the protagonist, telling instead how the events touch his life.

Despite its realistic setting and possible reader expectations of a realist tale, Armah presents a morality tale, or fable for postcolonial times. The novel takes its title from the 'carefully lettered' inscription on the back of a local bus and in light of this local wisdom, Armah undertakes the telling of Ghana's tragic tale of promise and betrayal. On the one hand, there is the immense hope built on socialist promises. On the other, the country is overtaken by decay as corruption spreads nationally following independence. The novel questions the action an individual might take to resist the rot of political corruption and considers the likely impact of resistance.

Armah's characterization is minimalist and centred on 'the Man', an unnamed *everyman*. The Man is a railway clerk whose unrewarding job pays little. By steadfastly refusing bribes, he becomes unpopular with those around him and alienated from his family, causing him acute loneliness. His position is met by incomprehension both at home and at work. We see him in his railroad office when a member of the public, a timber contractor, visits for the purpose of bribing the clerk to ensure that his timber is transported rather than left to deteriorate. Blocking every manoeuvre by the contractor – not responding to being referred to as 'brother', insisting that any discussion should be held with the booking clerk – he leaves the visitor 'struck dumb by incredulity' at his thorough lack of interest in a possible bribe. When the contractor leaves, the Man ponders 'the easy slide' into corruption and how 'unnatural' someone refusing corruption now seemed.

Living in impoverished conditions, his family struggle to minimize the effect of everyday degradations. Shoes are needed for his older son, and meals are a meagre affair. As the 'gleaming' Koomson – the government minister portrayed in the novel – discovers, the Man's family does not own a toilet, but instead shares a communal latrine. Filth and bodily functions feature prominently in the narrative, on both a metaphorical level and in terms of setting, plot and character. Though acutely aware that his family cannot enjoy the imported goods that are increasingly prized, on the rare occasion when his wife insists upon them, he finds himself torn. He savours briefly the approval of shopkeepers and fellow customers alike, despite being aware of the corrupt path to such items.

Corrupt practices are seen in the novel to give a 'gleam' – as promise or reality – to the lives of everyone, especially those involved in politics. The Man's wife, Oyo exhorts him to be like everyone else in order to raise their standard of living. His mother-in-law invokes the gleaming lifestyle of Koomson, the Man's relative and former classmate. A dockworker turned politician, Koomson's lifestyle is signified publicly through his chauffeur-driven car, an imported Mercedes-Benz. When Koomson suggests they could all be included in one of his moneymaking schemes, involving the ownership of a fishing trawler, the pressure from his family threatens to break the Man. He refuses to sign documents fraudulently indicating co-ownership of the boat, so his wife does. The hoped-for wealth does not materialize.

If the Man is an archetypal character representing the everyman who chooses a moral path, Koomson is the opposite, representing Ghana's post-independence. Koomson's 'bold, corrupt leap' has led him from being a railwayman and a docker to being a government minister. As the Man notices, in Koomson's house 'light glinted off every object in the room'. Filled with imported luxuries, his home reflects his rapid success. He has exchanged the 'big rough man' that he was, for a slick version of a privileged citizen accustomed to frequenting the status hotel, the Atlantic-Caprice, liveried servants and the pursuit of wealth. During the military coup, Koomson hides in the Man's house, placing him in another moral dilemma. This time it is one of life or death.

The Man consults his friend and mentor 'Teacher' when he is at his most despairing. In similar ways, both have been rendered outcasts because of their seemingly deviant behaviour in unfailingly refusing to take bribes. The difference between them is that despite their similar moral positions, Teacher has withdrawn from the world. He has cut himself off from friends, family and employment. His has become a 'half-life of loneliness'. In terms of his moral position, however, there is no guise; he is naked – physically and metaphorically – to the world.

Meanwhile, the new elite – the Koomsons of the nation – have superficially reconfigured the most desired spaces for their benefit. The Upper Residential Area, once the residence of white colonials, is now owned by the new 'big men' of the nation. The manicured lawns of the big villas overlook the town. The prestigious Atlantic-Caprice Hotel beckons white in the distance to the Black elite. All the time, the 'climbers' at different levels of society are accruing and displaying their imports such as radios, televisions and cars. Meanwhile, the poorer areas are evident through overflowing dustbins that are as likely to be stained by urine, as by food waste. Filth is everywhere. Armah looks askance at much of this, frequently through darkness or dim light. The country is a wasteland against which the sea offers some respite.

The final pages of the novel, denouncing Ghana's elite in the post-independence era, hold no long-term hope since the new rulers are military dictators. While the constitutional and corrupt government has been overthrown, the incoming group, having seized power, carries no credibility as an elected body. Ordinary wisdom, inattentive to detail, appears to have declared that 'the beautyful ones are not yet born.' Yet, a modicum of hope lies even in that much recognition of the collective situation.

Since Armah was writing about recent and dramatic events, the novel was set to be topical. For supporters of Nkrumah, controversy centred on the novel's apparent anti-Nkrumah stance. For those opposed to Nkrumah, the novel offered evidence justifying the coup. African writers, too, were divided, with Chinua Achebe questioning the novel for its 'existential writing' style in the face of real difficulties.

THE NOVEL

The novel was first published by Houghton Mifflin in the US (1968) and in the Heinemann African Writers Series (1969). This is Ayi Kwei Armah's first novel. It received widespread critical attention for its uncompromising representation of the Ghanaian elite's role in the demoralizing defeat of democracy and the spread of corruption that followed.

THE AUTHOR

Ayi Kwei Armah (1939–) is an acclaimed Ghanaian author, poet, essayist and translator. Since his first novel, Armah's writing has been the subject of much controversy. He has lived mainly outside of Ghana. He has taught at the University of

Massachusetts and in Tanzania, Lesotho and Senegal. His essays are published in journals such as *Black World* and *West Africa*. His novels include *Fragments* (1970), *Why Are We So Blest?* (1972), *Two Thousand Seasons* (1973), *The Healers* (1978) and *Osiris Rising: A Novel of Africa Past, Present, and Future* (1995). Armah's memoir, *The Eloquence of the Scribes* was published in 2006.

IF YOU LIKE THIS, TRY...

Ayi Kwei Armah's *Two Thousand Seasons* (1973), in which his writing style draws greatly on the African griot tradition. Chinua Achebe's *A Man of the People* (1966) was published in the same period as Armah's *The Beautyful Ones* and is also critical of corrupt practices.

Mission to Kala (1957) by Mongo Beti is a coming-of-age novel set in Cameroon just before West African countries were granted independence. A young, educated man returns home to be given a special mission to a remote village called Kala.

THE BRIDGE
OF BEYOND

SIMONE SCHWARZ-BART

1972

Simone Schwarz-Bart takes the reader to a faraway island and
a time that is at once historical and mythical. Long considered a masterpiece of Caribbean writing, this spellbinding
and intricate tale is built on the Creole tradition of oral storytelling. Set on the island of Guadeloupe in a period spanning
four generations, the narrative unfolds around central women
characters such as Telumee Lougandor, who has observed
and experienced much in her long and challenging life. These
generations span the one hundred years between the abolition of slavery and the 20th-century setting of the novel,
underscoring the central theme of tenacity, which emerges
from *The Bridge of Beyond*. Telumee's home is a cabin that she
has moved to the east and to the west; hers is a 'volcanic and
hurricane-swept' island.

Telumee is the narrator of this fictional autobiography
and begins her story with 'My People' in which she revisits the
women of her family. She starts with her great-grandmother,

Minerva, who had been freed from slavery by the 1848 French emancipation of its colonies. Her grandmother, Toussine was the mother figure who cared for her from the age of ten and who greatly influenced her life. Her own mother, Victory, abandoned her to her grandmother. Telumee's journey is an interior one from childhood to adulthood; from the insecurity of young adulthood to mature confidence. Despite a difficult life in which she has had to be self-sufficient to survive, Telumee gradually learns to seek strength.

Each foremother is important in understanding her story, particularly in how she comes to earn her given name, Telumee Miracle. She is honoured like her grandmother, Toussine, who was given the title 'Queen without a name' by her community. *The Bridge of Beyond* might be considered fictional autobiography, relating the stories of a succession of Lougandor women or maternal ancestors. What makes them special is the secret they have learned about dignity, even in the face of the greatest adversity, and what is passed on about how to live in the light of this knowledge. As in much of the region's most-celebrated writing, this novel is not a linear tale. It circles around the generations and loops back to connections that are ancestral. That is to say, it writes against the Western tradition of individualism. It accepts that there are connections and influences that are not of an individual's making.

Central to the knowledge that is passed on explicitly by Toussine, is an understanding of how to positively relate to their island home, Guadeloupe, and how to embrace the realities of the present. The need for explicit positivity refers to that which is sometimes forgotten, namely that for the Black people enslaved there, this was not their original home. Terrible memories of the trauma of slavery are associated with the island. This makes it all too possible to reject the place and in the process to effectively destroy oneself with negativity as experienced by many of the characters in the villages of L'Abandonné as well as Fond Zombi.

Toussine, however, teaches appreciation of the flora, fauna and natural environment as ways of strengthening the self, as well as becoming attuned to the land. That understanding, reflected in Telumee's opening lines describing her island home, indicates that the lesson has been learned. Telumee, now an old woman reflecting on a life lived positively in the face of great adversity, joyfully contemplates death as the story opens: 'If I could choose, it's here in Guadeloupe that I'd be born again, suffer and die.' In light of the island's history, such a positive perspective is rarely articulated, and for many novels of the region, the protagonist must flee the island. But Telumee's Guadeloupe, with its characteristic flame trees and coconut palms, its small wooden houses, orange trees, hummingbirds and congo canes, is a place to proudly claim her garden space on the island. Her life has been a discovery of the self as one who resists degradation even in the poorest material circumstances. An important part of such positivity lies in a closeness with the landscape of 'field after field' stretching towards 'forest and spirits' she has come to make her own. It is a process that, in turn, she is sharing with others.

Telumee's foremothers: Minerva, Toussine and Victory are key characters who bear witness to their lives and pass their stories down to their children. Telumee tells us it was her mother, Victory, who first acquainted her with her grand-mother Toussine's story, by frequently talking about her with considerable 'reverence' and 'fervor'. At the same time, Schwarz-Bart represents her Lougandor mother figures as being very different from each other. Each enjoys varying degrees of success as nurturers of their children. Victory fails as a nurturer, instead submitting to drink and a new lover, then deserting her daughter. Telumee is then nurtured by her grandmother and goes on to advocate her teaching as a philosophy of life to be shared with all those who 'will strug-gle'. The differentiated characteristics of the mothers point to more than physical mothering. One of the most memo-rable characters, Ma Cia, Toussine's old friend, is described as 'a famous witch' but she devotes considerable time to Telumee and teaches her much about the past that is also her history. Ma Cia is not represented in the context of family life, but as a keeper and sharer for those who appreciate her complex knowledge. This is pertinent, as none of the mothers is schooled, but Telumee, who relays their story for future generations, offers a tale that is culturally rich with Creole values. It seems significant, too, that Telumee is portrayed as virtually unschooled and that she does not herself bear any children and yet she is the custodian of shared knowledge and experience.

The novel's concern with genealogy points to a broader interest in the island's history, itself singularly dominated by the brutalities of colonial slavery. The maternal is important because it links directly to enslaved Caribbean mothers, who were specifically not allowed to function as mothers to their children, being owned by their masters. Linked to the distorted functioning of mothers in such a context, *The Bridge of Beyond* also highlights family breakdown and economic degradation, all of which might be thought of in the context of a broader history. Schwarz-Bart is ground-breaking in her treatment and representation of this bitter history. She allows the women, still embattled in the post-slavery years, not only to speak for themselves, but also to urge a collective response in solidarity.

THE NOVEL

The Bridge of Beyond was first published in French as *Pluie et vent sur Télumée Miracle* by Éditions du Seuil in 1972. It was well received and awarded the Grand Prix des lectrices de Elle in 1973. It was translated into English by Barbara Bray and published by Atheneum Books in the US (1974). It was republished, with a new introduction by Bridget Jones, by Heinemann in 1982.

THE AUTHOR

Simone Schwarz-Bart (1938–) moved to Guadeloupe from France as a young child and later studied in Paris. She is an author and playwright. Her second novel, *Ti Jean L'horizon*, was published in 1979. Her 1987 monodrama, *Your Handsome Captain* (*Ton beau capitaine*) was well received. She co-authored several books with her husband and fellow author, André Schwarz-Bart, such as *A Dish of Pork with Green Bananas* (*Un plat de porc aux bananes vertes*) in 1967 and *In*

Praise of Black Women (*Hommage à la femme noire*) in 1989, a multi-volume encyclopaedic work. In 2006, Schwarz-Bart was awarded the rank of a Commander in the Ordre des Arts et des Lettres. In 2008, she received the Prix Carbet de la Caraïbe et du Tout-Monde (jointly with her co-author) for her lifetime of literary works.

IF YOU LIKE THIS, TRY...

Marie-Elena John's debut novel *Unburnable* (2006) is also multi-generational. Set on the Caribbean island of Dominica and in the US, it draws distinctively on the region's orality. *Unburnable* tells the story of three generations of women over a 50-year period. See also *The Joy Luck Club* (2006) by Amy Tan, which is an intergenerational novel of mothers and daughters – four Chinese women who migrate to the US in 1949 gather to share stories and secrets. *Daylight Come* (2020) by Diana McCaulay is about a mother and daughter who must stick close to each other to survive. It is 2084 and they are on the Caribbean island of Bajucu, which has overheated due to climate change.

A QUESTION
OF POWER

BESSIE HEAD

1974

Mixed-race relationships were illegal during the 1930s in South Africa and, so, when Elizabeth, the novel's protagonist, was born, her family committed her mother to a mental institution for the rest of her life. Elizabeth is placed with foster parents who she believes are her real parents. At the age of 13, Elizabeth is told by the headmistress of her mission boarding school that her mother had been a wealthy white woman and that her father – her mother's lover – was a Black servant.

Her mother arranged funds to cover her daughter's education before she committed suicide. But Elizabeth's headmistress makes her life miserable, inflicting on her the unjust and severe punishment of being locked up for a day whenever there is a disagreement between her and the other children. Once her schoolmates realize this, they bully and beat Elizabeth daily, as they know that if she retaliates, she will be the only one to be punished. Elizabeth exists in this situation until she leaves school at 18. She marries the first man who shows her some affection, but he also shares his affections with every woman he meets. When she receives complaints about his sexual harassment she leaves with their son, answering an advert for trained teachers in Botswana. She goes to live in the village of Motabeng on a one-way exit visa to permanent exile. Her harrowing experiences in South Africa, including an episode where she attends court as a suspected communist, mean that she never wants to return 'home'.

Her troubles continue, however, and after verbally attacking a man in public for no apparent reason, she is asked to leave her teaching job. She seeks help from Eugene, the Afrikaner headmaster of Motabeng Secondary School, who takes her to hospital after the verbal assault. This marks the beginning of her mental breakdown. Workers in a local industries project set up by Eugene build her a new home near to her vegetable garden. This becomes a successful addition to the project and, at first, benefits Elizabeth's mental health.

The story builds slowly, as Elizabeth remembers the moments that led to her breakdown and then her subsequent healing. The author wrote this novel after recovering from a period of mental ill-health, where she felt that she was becoming unwell, yet was unable to prevent it. She is able to look back on this psychotic period to let readers into the mind of a person struggling with their mental health, one who is trying to navigate their day-to-day life, despite the physical and mental pain they experience as they do so.

It is painful for readers to watch Elizabeth's living hell, where she is too scared to sleep because of horrific nightmares, which torment her during the day. Her son senses his mother's instability, and we fear for his security during Elizabeth's black-outs, when unbeknown to her he stays out for days. Yet one of the characters who appears in her nightmares is Dan, who tells her that her son will be dead within days. Head's story is symptomatic of how being solitary can lead to mental ill-health, even if you do enjoy 'being on your own'.

Although *A Question of Power* has been described as an 'autobiographical' novel, it is a sophisticated work of literary fiction which fluidly moves the reader between Elizabeth's real and imaginary worlds. She is tortured by lewd behaviour that she is forced to watch, mixed with prophecies of death. Sometimes she thinks it would be best if she killed her son before killing herself.

When reading the intertwining passages, it can sometimes be difficult to separate the two worlds. The character Sello is prominent in her daytime world and her nightmares, and is a living person, possibly an ex-lover. In her mind he has become both God and Satan. He is joined by Dan, who appears in the second half of the book as a wealthy, beautiful man, who she believes is having a homosexual relationship with Sello. They are all dominated by the presence of 'Medusa' whose power in the novel is described as situated in her many vaginas, rather than her strands of hair.

There are two men in Elizabeth's life whom she can rely on. The first is Tom, the Peace Corps volunteer who visits her regularly for conversation and to eat her wonderful stew. He proves to be a good listener when she needs it most. The second is Eugene, who sees in Elizabeth someone like himself, who wanted to escape the systemic racism in South Africa to raise a child in a healthy environment; one where his son could freely play with Elizabeth's and call each other 'best friend'. In these two men we see the scope of what humanity can be at its best. She can also rely on Kenosi, a fellow garden-worker who, suspecting the inner turmoil that Elizabeth descends into, tells her that she can never leave the garden, as she would not be able to work on it alone. Kenosi does her best to maintain it while Elizabeth is in hospital for seven months, when the abyss of utter darkness that she falls into becomes unmanageable.

A Question of Power takes us on a psychological journey – it is almost as though we see through her eyes, which makes it even more intrusive and exhausting, and yet more intimate. Head enables the reader to be this close even though it is written in the third person. And remember, Elizabeth had to live this.

There are not enough books by Black authors who talk candidly about mental health through their characters, although that is beginning to change. Other themes encountered in the book include the detrimental psychological effects of apartheid and of becoming a refugee, both of which contribute to Elizabeth's mental instability. At the time it was written, creative works such as this by Black South African writers were scarce, and it would have been difficult for the author to get this published while living in South Africa. Instead, readers relied on stories by white South African writers about the lives of Black South Africans living under apartheid. There are few novels from Botswana written in English or translated into English. This is a country with a population that stands today at less than two and a half million – consequently, Head's talent and resilience to write even in her precarious mental state are to be treasured.

THE NOVEL

The first edition was published in 1974 by Davis-Poynter and Random House in the US. It was published in the Heinemann African Writers Series in 1974 and published as a Penguin Classic in 2002. The novel is on the 'Africa's 100 Best Books of the 20th Century' list.

THE AUTHOR

Bessie Head (1937–86) was born in South Africa and moved to Botswana in 1964 with her son. She is regarded as a Motswana writer, having received citizenship there. She was also honoured by her country of birth, and was awarded the Order of Ikhamanga (a South African posthumous award). Head wrote three other novels: *When Rain Clouds Gather* (1968), *Maru* (1971) and *The Collector of Treasures and Other Botswana Village Tales* (1977). She also wrote three short story collections: *Serowe, Village of the Rainwind* (1981), *A Bewitched Crossroad: An African Saga* (1984) and *The Cardinals: With Meditations and Short Stories* (1993), published posthumously.

IF YOU LIKE THIS, TRY...

Freshwater (2008) by Akwaeke Emezi, a dark, controlling story told through the multiple identities of Ada. In *Orange Laughter*

(1999) by Leone Ross, Tony lives in the New York Subway system, showing how easy it is for someone to slip through the net of sanity. *The Salt Eaters* (1980) by Toni Cade Bambara sees the dynamic Velma Henry climb back from her depression and suicide attempt with the support of the community, highlighting the importance of shared cultural identity and spiritual connection. One of the strongest southern African women writers to emerge in the past 15 years is Zukiswa Wanner. In her first novel, *The Madams* (2006), she wrote about the reverse cultural and economic situations post-apartheid, where the Black middle class employ – sometimes white – maids.

IF BEALE STREET
COULD TALK

JAMES BALDWIN

1974

'Skinny little' 19-year-old Tish and 21-year-old Fonny, are in love, having been best friends since childhood. Fonny asks Tish's father, Joseph, for permission to marry his daughter, and he happily says, 'yes'. He knows Fonny to be a polite and gentle soul who has frequented the Rivers's home over the years. They decide to look for a downtown Manhattan loft to live in, as they are not domestic living spaces so they are cheaper to rent than the projects uptown in Harlem and the Bronx. Fonny feels a loft will also make an ideal studio to craft his wood and stone sculptures. They make friends in the area, from the local staff in Spanish restaurant to the Italian-owned grocery store. When Fonny is jailed on a false accusation of raping a 'Porto Rican' (Puerto Rican) woman, the locals and their new wealthy, white American landlord are on his side.

Tish's family have embraced Fonny as their son, so they take the lead on finding and paying for a lawyer to represent him. Sharon, Tish's mother, travels to the Puerto Rican favela to meet and hopefully to encourage the rape victim to tell the truth. Fonny's father, Frank, stands by his son and he and Joseph do what fathers need to do to protect their own. Frank's decision distances himself from his religious wife and two daughters, who shun Fonny, simply for being a young Black male, who is darker than they are, and regard him as worthless.

Set in the early 1970s, the story is told through Tish as the first-person narrator. It is only when Fonny is in jail, that she finds out that she is three months pregnant; it gives both of them the positive reinforcement they need to hold on to in their fight for justice. The Harlem daily grind is seen through her eyes, as are the themes that Baldwin most strongly wants to explore, particularly the dimensions of Black people in love and intimacy.

Religion is another dominant theme shown through different perspectives and voices than those in his previous novels such as his semi-autobiographical, *Go Tell it on the Mountain,* which highlights the dominance of Christianity in Baldwin's life. Two decades later, he examines Black Christian life in this novel, combined with different facets of love. The exploration of Christian love within a family like the Hunts, when not all family members attend church is one example. Mrs Hunt, a woman of the Sanctified Church, has charitable 'agape' love but cannot show affectionate 'philia' love for her son.

She is, as her husband describes it, in love with Jesus and dresses up only for Him, on Sundays. Mrs Hunt has raised her two daughters, now in their twenties, in her image and though they want to be in loving family relationships of their own, they appear unapproachable. Baldwin shows how Christianity can divide as well as unite a family. The strong sibling love and support between Tish and her smart, feisty older sister Ernestine, in their Baptist Church upbringing, is shown in juxtaposition to that of the women in the Hunt family.

Baldwin's ambivalence regarding the way in which Christianity dominates people's lives is reflected in the rich and harsh dialogue in which Frank spares no sensitivity for his wife in his blasphemous attacks, accusing her of 'making out' with Jesus and saying that he himself, unlike God, was not going to crucify his son.

Although Mrs Hunt believes herself to be an upstanding Christian, she curses the baby that Tish is carrying, saying that she hopes the foetus shrivels and dies. Frank reminds her that it is their grandchild she is condemning and strikes her so hard that she falls to the ground. We see in Frank the deterioration of a man who starts out as a loving family man, law-abiding, hard-working, quiet-living, but who becomes a thief to support his son. He also mentally and physically abuses his wife and daughters, eventually sinking into depression and alcoholism, as he feels helpless over the plight of his only son. Black men have a constant juggle to remain invisible, to avoid being apprehended by the police for something they did or did not do. Forced to live in this way, Baldwin makes us consider the difficulty for the Black man to rise and achieve against the odds. It is prominent in the novel through the embedding of the phrase coined by Baldwin: 'He wasn't anybody's nigger. And that's a crime, in this fuckin' free country. You're supposed to be somebody's nigger.' This basic premise, drawn from his observations of race in the US, is reflected on later in the award-winning documentary, *I Am Not Your Negro*, the script based on his unfinished novel, *Remember This House*.

By moving to Manhattan, Fonny was declaring a confidence to do so; that 'he was his own Negro'. However, the police had other ideas, and showed him that it is they who will decide his fate. Fonny knows that if he succumbs to the ravages of prison life – being beaten up, put into isolation and probably being raped like his friend Daniel, who the police pressured so that he could not provide Fonny with an alibi – then that would define him as 'somebody's nigger'. The reader does not discover if or when Fonny gets out of jail, conveying a sense of never-ending uncertainty; a factor of Black life.

The backdrop of institutionalized racism in a pre-Black Lives Matter world, and the mistreatment of Black men by the police and authorities makes their lives bleak; they often feel beaten before they have barely started living. The fact that a disproportionate number of young Black males in the West are stopped on a daily basis by the police for something as simple as walking along the street, makes this story immediately universal and painfully current. This is just one tragic story of many and there could be many more such stories, stoop stories, church stories, prison stories; all reflective of urban world stories. But most of all, in one of America's classic urban love stories, Baldwin wants to show that young Black love is hopeful.

THE NOVEL

First published by The Dial Press in 1974 in the US and Michael Joseph in the UK, this critically acclaimed novel became a Penguin Modern Classic in 1994. It was later adapted for film and released in 2018.

THE AUTHOR

James Baldwin (1924–87) was born in Harlem, New York. He wrote in various genres, publishing six novels, three plays, and seven collections of essays, short stories and poems. He has also had five posthumous collections published. His first novel *Go Tell It on the Mountain,* was published in 1953, although it was his essays *Notes of a Native Son* (1955) and *The Fire Next Time* (1963) that made him an established voice of the US civil rights movement. Baldwin received awards and honours, including a Eugene F. Saxton Memorial Trust Award (1945), a Guggenheim Fellowship (1954), the George Polk Memorial Award (1963), MacDowell Fellowships in 1954, 1958 and 1960, the Foreign Drama Critics Award (1964) and a Commandeur de la Légion d'honneur (1986). He was awarded a number of honorary degrees, including Honorary Doctor of Letters from Morehouse College (1976). Baldwin moved to France in 1948, where he lived until his death in 1987.

IF YOU LIKE THIS, TRY...

The Street by Ann Petry (1946), set in Second World War era Harlem, is a commentary on the social injustices endured by Lutie Johnson, a single Black mother. Walter Mosley's multiple series of books focus on African-American urban life, which include the Easy Rawlins series based in Los Angeles, introduced in *Devil in a Blue Dress* (1990). Other great, non-US, urban stories include *The Scholar* (1997) by Courttia Newland, set on a London council estate; *Harare North* (2010) by Brian

Chikwava, set in London; *Brick Lane* (2003) by Monica Ali, set in London's East London Muslim community; and *Deadly Sacrifice* (2020) by Stella Oni, featuring the first Black woman detective in the UK, moving between London and Lagos. *City of God* (1997) by Paulo Lins is set in the favela in Brazil where he grew up. *Nairobi Heat* (2009) by Mũkoma wa Ngũgĩ is set in Kenya. An unusual, memorable urban love story is *The Consequences of Love* (2008) by Sulaiman Addonia, set in Saudi Arabia.

BETWEEN TWO WORLDS

MIRIAM TLALI

1975

Miriam Tlali's debut novel should be read by everyone. It is concerned with the inhumane system of apartheid to which South Africa clung until the closing decade of the 20th century. *Between Two Worlds* reminds us, decades later, how readily forgotten is man's enduring capacity for inhumanity.

Tlali presents the reader with a microcosm of urban life in apartheid South Africa. The setting is 'Metropolitan Radio' – a radio, furniture and electrical appliances shop within which the characters all interact. The central character is Muriel, a newly employed, young Black woman who is trying to establish herself within the enclosed and cramped world of Metropolitan Radio, which necessarily involves a multiracial clientele. The novel's deceptively simple plot tells of Muriel's journey through that world of employment, from first arrival to leaving her job. Tlali's storytelling strategies are particularly revealing of the complexity of the worlds occupied by the Black and white workers that apartheid was brutally attempting to segregate. The system ensured that one group, Blacks, would have little alternative but to serve the other, whites.

South Africa's apartheid violence assumed many forms, and it is in the workplace, with its exploitative practices built upon white supremacist ideology, that Tlali places Muriel. It is this space, with its demarcated workshop area for repairs, iron-barred cash point and its protected space for white women employees, that Muriel must share – not, initially, with other clerical staff who are white but with the mechanics. This is where the action of the narrative takes place. The nature of Muriel's lived violence at work, while appearing mundane, nonetheless represents a crucial site of struggle. A university graduate and experienced employee who is qualified and skilled in book-keeping, Muriel has recently left one employer. Her former employer's testimonial omits to mention her seniority and experience. In this way, he justifies having routinely underpaid her and ensures that her new employer will continue the practice of exploiting her. Hired as a 'helper' at Metropolitan Radio, Muriel notes on reflection that her first day at the new workplace signalled only that she stood to discover much, 'especially as far as relationships between different races were concerned.'

In her new job, as well as the one she has recently left, it is Muriel's knowledge – or what she is expected to know *as a Black person* – that becomes an issue. This does not simply concern whether she knows both typing and book-keeping; it is assumed that she does *not* have either skill set. Employed as a 'helper' at Metropolitan, she is engaged in tasks such as folding letters and putting them into envelopes. What becomes vitally important at Metropolitan, is what Muriel knows or learns about how the intricate mesh of apartheid rules. These have been designed to control space to the advantage of those defined as white, maintaining their privilege. Thus, on her first training day, when a chair is found for her, its cushion is promptly removed. The cushion-less chair will be hers during her employment at the company. Similarly, in order to maintain the required racial demarcation line demanded by apartheid, Muriel is not allowed to share the same room as the white women employees. For the same reasons, protected by apartheid regulations, Muriel is not allowed to use the one functioning women's toilet and must suffer any related humiliation. Such is the racially hierarchical world of Muriel's workplace, from which vantage point she must observe, interact and learn. Yet, Muriel is no victim.

Despite her awareness of the demands of apartheid to keep her in a lesser place designated for Black people, Muriel speaks up to her white co-workers. She challenges their casual views by showing that she is well informed when she refers, for example, to Botswana – which they still consider Bechuanaland. On the subject of security regulations and their impact upon Black lives, she tells them that it relates to 'cheap labour', undermining 'all law of morality and decency'. Furthermore, it makes a 'nonsense of the concept of the family unit'. She negotiates another job and, though offered more pay, resigns.

Foremost among the characters of *Between Two Worlds* is Muriel's boss, Mr Bloch. His first interaction with a prospective employee as the novel opens is an impatient, 'You! Come here, quick!' and his directives to Black customers include, 'Stand over there!' before he greets white customers with a smiling, 'Can I help you?' Tlali does not present a world in which the Black characters are good and the white characters are bad – far from it. She illustrates that Mr Bloch can be humorous and idiosyncratic and that her characters might all, including Muriel, be considered flawed. Indeed, Tlali represents the titular 'two worlds' as complex entities in and of themselves. Competing dynamics, she shows us, are at play among 'whites', who are primarily English-speaking and Afrikaans-speaking. Equally, 'blacks' are shown to be a complex grouping comprising different linguistic and national groups. Tlali reveals the minutiae of belittling, racialized behaviour seen from the *inside* of apartheid. To outsiders this view of colonial and racialized daily life under apartheid is astonishing – and almost unreal as a depiction of late-20th-century existence.

Realism is the key to Tlali's storytelling. She acknowledges drawing on her own experience of employment in apartheid South Africa, allowing her to render *Between Two Worlds* into a form of autobiographical fiction. The choice of a self-conscious narrator and situating of the action within the tight space of Metropolitan Radio realizes Tlali's clear aim of storytelling that teaches, as it has traditionally done. Alongside telling a story, she simultaneously interrogates the nation's racial politics, itself potentially destructive to all involved. She does so through Muriel's ongoing consideration of herself in relation to other characters, whether it is the elder Johannes, known as the tea-boy, or the cashier referred to as Baas Ponty, or a range of customers and fellow employees, Black or white.

The novel succeeds in generating much-needed reflection on the political, social and moral meanings of a nation foolhardily out of step with the times. Its insistence on racialized servitude was already soundly discredited in earlier times. Furthermore, what appeared to be a slice-of-life narrative on publication, *Between Two Worlds* now increasingly reveals its engagement with history. It also highlights the conditions of writing and publication by women, particularly Black women and Black South Africans in the early 1970s. Given Tlali's details of the tortuous process of publication for this novel – including intervention by foreign church officials and later removal of 'some parts' of the manuscript to render it publishable – *Between Two Worlds* raises the haunting question: what makes literary writing count?

THE NOVEL

An extensively cut version of *Between Two Worlds* was first published in 1975 as *Muriel at Metropolitan* by Ravan Press. When Longman purchased the international publication rights and released the full version in 1979, the novel was banned in South Africa until the late 1980s. The 2004 edition, published by Broadview Press, Canada, contains an introduction by Tlali, shedding light on the novel's history.

THE AUTHOR

Miriam Tlali was the first Black, female South African novelist to be published in English. She is an author of fiction and a playwright. Her publications include *Amandla* (1980) about the events of 16 June 1976 in Soweto, marking the uprising of Black South Africans against the system of apartheid; it was banned in South Africa. Her short story collection *Mihloti* was published in 1984 and *Footprints in the Quag* (1989) was published internationally as *Soweto Stories* (1989). Her play *Crimen Injuria* (1986) was staged in Holland and in the US. Tlali's ground-breaking writing has profoundly influenced the writing of Southern Africa, especially that of women writers.

IF YOU LIKE THIS, TRY...

Baby Kamble's *The Prisons We Broke* (1986), translated from the Marathi book *Jina Amucha* by Maya Pandit (2008). This is an example of Dalit literature, which explores the caste system in India from the point of view of those historically considered the most inferior, much of which offers parallels and comparisons with South Africa's system of apartheid.

WOMAN AT
POINT ZERO

NAWAL EL SAADAWI

1975

There can be no more defiant opening sentence: 'Let me speak. Do not interrupt me. I have no time to listen to you.' In this profound and powerful novel by Nawal El Saadawi, the majestic Firdaus will tolerate no opposition, even from the psychiatrist narrator who she addresses in her last hours of life. A woman at 'point zero', Firdaus has killed a man, turned herself in and will now be killed by the State in Qanatir Prison, Cairo.

Based upon an episode in the author's life, this is a searing tribute to one Egyptian woman's courage and the unwavering spotlight she placed on the source of her lifelong oppression – men. The novel gives voice to feminist resistance and shows how far one woman is willing to go. Firdaus demands that she be executed, but not because she is repentant. After a lifetime of abuse, exploitation and subjugation, Firdaus chooses to have power over her own mortality, to remove herself from any further male oppression, 'which frightens them'.

The terrible trinity of patriarchy, poverty and prostitution circumscribes the life of Firdaus whose name means 'Paradise' in Arabic. The deprivation of education for girls, the violence of male control and the object status of women are the book's recurring themes; what hope is there for finding self-esteem? Men's primacy is reinforced from Firdaus's earliest memory. While her father eats supper every night, his children go hungry and her mother hides the food from them so he can always eat. If a male child dies in the night she is beaten – but he still eats his supper.

El Saadawi was a warrior for women's rights and lifelong campaigner against female genital mutilation (FGM), which she had suffered. In *Woman at Point Zero*, Firdaus remembers the ordeal in the form of the disembodied dark eyes that loom over her at different points in her traumatized life. This is clearly linked to flashbacks of the perpetrator, leaving bodily and psychological scars from which recovery is impossible.

Although Firdaus is intellectually inquisitive she can only access education when her parents die. Her uncle, who has sexually abused her, takes her to live with him in Cairo. At boarding school, there is a brief oasis of nurture but no possibility of going onto university as she is female. The 1973 *infitah* under Anwar Sadat, courted capitalist competition in Egypt, but did not allow wholesale equality for women. A recurring theme during Firdaus's peripatetic journey from the countryside to Cairo is the fact that at every stage of life, irrespective of a woman's class, she will be viewed as an object whose function is to serve men. Subservience endows respectability. Women are the goods to be traded in marriage for material security and virginity is the property asset.

Firdaus expresses the epiphanies in her life through potent symbols of rings, circles, eyes, veils, money and imprisonment. A pivotal moment occurs when, as a sex worker, she realizes that the money she charges buys her a degree of autonomy. She describes a veil dropping from her eyes after a small but significant act of going to a restaurant to eat without being scrutinized for the quantity of food she consumes.

Men are an unrelentingly brutal presence. Firdaus is imprisoned firstly by her family, then within a forced marriage, which she flees. The refuge she finds with a waiter, Bayoumi, becomes a living hell as he beats her and prostitutes her to other men. Firdaus also portrays women who are male enablers, carrying out the oppression of other women. It is her own mother who arranges her FGM, while her uncle's wife marries her off to a brutal elderly relative. In a brief interlude by the River Nile after Firdaus has escaped from Bayoumi, she is saved by Sharifa Salah el Dine who transforms her and offers a haven of luxury, only to find herself again sold for sex, 'every hour a man would come in'. While her body desires physical pleasure in contrast to the degradation she suffers, ultimately the tenderness she yearns for is unachievable.

After fleeing Sharifa's brothel. Firdaus manages her own sex work, gaining some material comfort and independence, until this is punctured by a 'friend' Di'aa, a journalist client who tells her she 'is not respectable'. She uses her secondary school certificate to get a job in an office and hopes to find love and security, but tragically, there begins another reversal of fortune, and finally the descent to point zero.

Throughout Firdaus's life her voice deserts her. She cannot speak up in her defence, speak out at school, nor explain her situation when asked. The reader is privy to this agony of muting as she fails to express herself. Yet, Firdaus exerts subtle power at the end of her life. As an inmate, she haunts and controls the atmosphere of the penitentiary with her silence, unsettling everyone who crosses her path from the prison doctor and the wardens to El Saadawi's first-person narrator, a psychiatrist undertaking research into women inmates.

Readers cannot fail to be affected by Firdaus, whose abilities are crushed in a cruel patriarchal world. Brought to the lowest social point possible, she is morally transcendent. El Saadawi's sobering insight is that Firdaus is far superior to herself in courage. Firdaus becomes indelibly inscribed in El Saadawi's memory. After her own imprisonment by Sadat's regime in 1981, El Saadawi wrote how she scanned the faces of her fellow prisoners for Firdaus, 'I could not bring myself to believe that she had really died.' This is truth-telling, delivered without sentiment. Firdaus remained unbowed and fiercely forthright in naming the reasons for women's oppression, just like her author, Nawal El Saadawi.

THE NOVEL

First published in Arabic as امرأة عند نقطة الصفر, *Emra'a enda noktat el sifr* in 1975, the novel was translated into English by Sherif Hetata and published by Zed Books in 1983.

THE AUTHOR

Nawal El Saadawi (1931–2021) was born into a prosperous family in the Egyptian village of Kafr Tahla. She became Director of Public Health for the Egyptian government, but was dismissed after publishing her first nonfiction book, *Women and Sex* (1972), in which she denounced FGM and the sexual oppression of women. Her writing ranges from fiction to nonfiction. She is the author of 55 books; her first (unpublished) novel was written aged 13. Her work has been translated into more than 40 languages. El Saadawi was a recipient of numerous international awards and honorary degrees. These include: Great Minds of the Twentieth Century Prize (2003) and the 2004 North-South Prize from the Council of Europe. In 2020, she was named one of *Time* magazine's 100 Women of the Year.

IF YOU LIKE THIS, TRY...

Palestinian author Sahar Khalifeh's *My First and Only Love* (2021, English translation by Aida Barnia), an epic story of nationhood from the end of the British Mandate for Palestine (1948) to the 21st century, as seen through the eyes of Nidal. She discovers family secrets and a lost history in a poetically immersive rendering of a resistant nation surviving political turmoil. Salwa Bakr's *The Wiles of Men and Other Stories* (1992, translated from Arabic into English by Denys Johnson Davies) is set in Cairo. Each tale concerns a woman's struggle to thrive within a repressive society and

Bakr can be credited in many ways with writing women's presence into Arab literature.

Leila Abouzeid's 1966 novel *The Last Chapter* (2003, English translation by John Liechety) tells the story of Aisha, a Moroccan woman and her emotional journey through the culture clash of two worlds. She is the first Moroccan woman literary author to be translated into English. Syrian exile Nihad Sirees's *The Silence and the Roar* (2013, English translation by Max Weiss) is a satire on the hubris of an unnamed dictator. It is relayed by banned writer, Fathi Schin, as he is drawn into the humour and horror of a regime's propaganda and display, when he only wants to visit his family. Haitian author Louis-Philippe Dalembert's *The Mediterranean Wall* (2021, English translation by Marjolijn de Jaeger) follows three contemporary women's migration odysseys: Dima fleeing torture in Syria, Semhar escaping conscription in Eritrea, and the Nigerian Shoshana leaving starvation and environmental destruction caused by global warming. Their paths meet as they wait to cross the Mediterranean Sea from Libya, hoping to find safety in Europe.

16

OUR SISTER KILLJOY: OR REFLECTIONS FROM A BLACK-EYED SQUINT

AMA ATA AIDOO

1977

Sissie, a young Ghanaian woman, is our Sister Killjoy. She is selected to visit Europe as part of an educational trip, an event worthy of her photograph appearing in her local newspaper at home in Ghana. An educationalist, Sissie applies for the study abroad programme, hoping to use what she learns in her work when she returns home. She is immediately given a place on the programme and is fêted at the German Embassy before she leaves, first with an invitation to a cocktail party, then a second invitation to a private dinner.

Sissie's main destination is Bavaria in Germany, where she strikes up a friendship with a young, local woman, Marija Sommer. However, it ends abruptly when Sissie and her study group leave for other German cities and Britain, before returning home to Ghana. Marija is a bored housewife and mother to newborn Adolf Jr. Although they cannot speak each other's language, the young women discover a bond. Their new relationship attracts gossip from neighbours and so they meet later in the evening, when it is dark. On one of Sissie's visits, Marija impulsively reaches out and touches Sissie's breast. It is a fleeting moment between them, yet for Sissie, it registers a change in their relationship. For the first time she contemplates the possibilities of a same-sex relationship. She also considers the ease with which relationships form between white women and African men when they move abroad, and the rationality of sexual desire in those travelling for work or study abroad, particularly when loneliness is involved.

Readers will feel some sympathy for Marija at the abrupt termination of the friendship – particularly after we have seen her warmly invite Sissie into her home, and provide light relief from her regimented educational schedule. As Marija plans a special weekend family lunch so that her new friend can meet her husband, Sissie prepares to leave town. Marija's obvious distress appears to be dismissed by Sissie, although she does initially feel guilty about not informing her friend sooner. She suspects that the relationship is based partly on the exoticism of her, an African woman in a small town in Germany, where African people are rarely seen. Marija turns up at the train station the following morning with her usual food parcel for Sissie. After waving goodbye she runs after the train, sharing recommendations for places to visit.

Sissie makes a short diversion through the ex-colonial 'mother country' of Britain. While there, she meets other

Ghanaians, giving her opinion freely about their adopted European status and their shunned African home. She publicly challenges those who have left, particularly those studying on a government scholarship who do not plan to return home, despite promises to do so. Sissie's observations are sometimes naïve rather than arrogant, in presuming that she is giving her fellow Ghanaians a wake-up call. They have heard it all before and have ready answers in response to her accusations.

She kills the joy of fellow Ghanaians living abroad as she accuses them of being sell-outs for preferring the Western life-style to working for the betterment of their own country. Sissie is also a killjoy to diasporans, after assessing their privileged life in the West as really no privilege at all, and pronouncing that they are 'running to stand still'. She sees them as suffering just as much as Africans on the continent, albeit in a different manner. This confirms for her that living at home in Ghana is where she wants to be.

Towards the end of the trip, Sissie writes a letter to the man she loves – 'Her Precious Something' – who is also travelling abroad, but who is not intending to return. This letter is something of a wake-up call to herself, as by now she has conversed with enough Ghanaian men abroad to be able to imagine the kind of free and easy life he will be living. Her letter meanders in her mind and on paper; will she ever see him again? She may never send this letter, but she does end with a new under-standing and wisdom that enables her to come to terms with the possible loss of the man she loves.

Our Sister Killjoy is genre challenging. Aidoo decided to throw out the conventional novel structure, which she interprets as a colonial approach to storytelling in itself, to freely mix writing styles to suit the stories she wants to tell. This experimental writing incorporates fiction, poetry and prose in letter form to create a narrative that tells a contemporary story of African life disrupted by colonization, both on the African continent and within individual lives in the diaspora. Sissie's sharp, unforgiving commentary explores the themes of the African diaspora and the impact of colonialism, particularly the colonization of the mind.

Aidoo is a prominent figure writer in the African community who publishes in all genres. Although written several years ago, many of the underlying issues that she raises here have not changed. These include Black and non-white migrants being treated as second-class citizens, the on-going impact of colonialism and neo-colonialism on Africa, and the challenges – such as racism – faced by Africans in the diaspora. This is the sadness that we are forced to encounter at the end of the book, along with the realization for Sissie, that to some extent she alone cannot change the situation, even in her own relationship.

This short novel appears light, yet it carries a serious message of colonial damage, particularly to those Africans whom Aidoo sees as too often gravitating towards the materialism of Western society. Yet it also shows us what decolonizing the structure of a book can look like. There is unexpected humour in the way that she sometimes describes the struggles, ultimately stating that Africans are all the same, wherever they live, in their experience of heartbreak, joy and dreams.

THE NOVEL

Her debut novel, published by Longman African Writers in 1977, remains one of Aidoo's best-known works. It was voted one of Africa's 100 Best Books of the 20th Century.

THE AUTHOR

Ama Ata Aidoo (1942–) is a highly influential Ghanaian academic and writer of fiction, plays and poetry who has lived and taught around the world. In 1992 she received the Commonwealth Writers' Prize for Best Book (Africa) for her novel *Changes* (1991). Aidoo is the first published African women dramatist and her first play was *The Dilemma of a Ghost* (1965). She also edited the anthology *African Love Stories* (2006).

In 2000, she established the Mbaasem Foundation to support and promote the work of African women writers. The Aidoo-Snyder Book Prize was launched in 2005 for writing which highlights African women's experience. It is awarded by the Women's Caucus of the African Studies Association. The Ama Ata Aidoo Centre for Creative Writing was inaugurated in 2017, at the African University College of Communications (AUCC) in Accra, Adabraka, Ghana. Yaba Badoe, author of *True Murder* (2009) and documentarist, has made an award-winning documentary, '*Art of Ama Ata Aidoo* (2014) about her extraordinary life.

IF YOU LIKE THIS, TRY...

Buchi Emecheta's *Adah's Story* (1983) is two books in one, containing the stories *In the Ditch* (1972) and *Second Class Citizen* (1974). It explores the wretched lives lived by Africans in Britain. Contemporary Ghanaian women writers include Amma Darko, whose semi-autobiographical novel *Beyond the Horizon* (1991) is set in Ghana and Germany. It is about a woman tricked into joining her husband in Germany, where she is forced into prostitution. *The Kaya-Girl* (2012) by Mamle Wolo brings two young girls together from opposite ends of the social scale and they have a profound effect on each other's lives. Yaa Gyasi's *Homegoing* (2016) is a sweeping, rich historical novel that starts in 18th-century Ghana and ends in 20th-century America. Bernardine Evaristo wrote her first, semi-autobiographical novel *Lara* (1997) in a prose-poetry style, and it covers 150 years of family history in Europe, Africa and Brazil.

TERRITORY OF LIGHT

YŪKO TSUSHIMA

1979

What does the future hold for a young mother, deserted by her feckless husband and forced to raise her two-year-old daughter alone in 1970s Tokyo? How will she be judged by those around her when she insists on a divorce, seeks out casual sexual relationships, leaves her daughter home alone to temporarily escape her maternal responsibilities, and finally reaches breaking point?

Mother and daughter move into a new, rented apartment on the fourth floor of an old office building. The title, *Territory of Light*, refers to the intense brightness of the light in their new home, which has windows on all sides and a rooftop terrace. This contrasts starkly with the bleakness she faces in her life, as she gradually slips into despair. The mother uses the unlocked downstairs apartment – which is not yet let – as a refuge from her domestic space.

Tsushima interweaves dreams, memories and flashbacks to slowly reveal the impact of the unnamed mother's struggle with abandonment and full-time employment, as she feels increasingly trapped by her situation. As readers, we follow her in this first 12 months as a single parent and slowly realize that we are being gently immersed into an unflinching, but sensitive portrayal of maternal despair. In a traditional society that centres marriage as the expected way for women to gain security and respectability, Tsushima's subject is a bold departure from convention. In narrating the mother's first-person perspective, she experiments and moves the predominant I-novel or confessional genre of Japanese fiction with which she began her writing career, into new and controversial territory.

In the quietly disturbing chapter, 'Sunday in the Trees', her daughter disappears in the park: 'I could see no sign of my daughter beside the pond, nor on its surface.' Rather than look for her, the mother looks for a bench on which to have a cigarette. Eventually, she finds the girl curled up, having 'cried herself to sleep.' Her evident lack of empathy in merely patting her daughter's shoulder in recognition of the incident is linked to a flashback of her discovery of an injured boy who had hidden himself away in their school hall for half a day; she had walked away, telling no one.

In 'The Earth's Surface' she is on a train one Sunday afternoon: 'My daughter was not at my side.' Her need to lose herself, to be free of her responsibilities, causes her to be irresponsible. We then discover her young lover, Sugiyama, has failed to turn up to their Sunday trysts for a few weeks. This segues into her daughter's increasing fits of anger, crying in the night and a preference for staying with her friend's parents who she begins to call 'mommy' and 'daddy'. The daughter's rejection of the inhospitable space that her mother's unmet emotional needs have created, is seen alongside a sense of injustice that the mother has no one to help her raise her child. This is a story swathed in enigma and punctuated by disconcerting revelations. Our central character appears entirely alone, disconnected from family or friendships. There are occasional references to a problematic relationship with her own mother, who she eventually avoids leaving her toddler with. What has caused such intense emotional isolation?

Tsushima's economical use of language creates delicate and unforgettable moments and an awareness of a world becoming increasingly strange across the 12 chapters. As the woman's sense of freedom and selfhood diminish, she ruminates, 'I wished I could forget I even had a child.' There are shocking moments where the reader is privy to maternal vengeance. She has no social life, resorting to casual sexual encounters in parks or the seduction of another parent's husband. As these men reject her, she turns to alcohol for comfort. She is the target of constant censure from others. We witness the damaging effects on her self-esteem of the cruel and superficial assumptions made about her status as a divorced mother. Yet, Tsushima's narrative never fails to acknowledge the wonderment of the complex attachment between mother and daughter and the anguish of their inevitable separation augured in the child's sleepovers.

While the narrative has a tender and almost wistful quality, all is not what it seems. There is a persistent sense of growing danger throughout the book, portending violence and death. The story begins with mother and daughter wandering around potential apartments, while the estate agent tells her about a family suicide by gas after a divorce battle. Her gradually disintegrating everyday life is set against a backdrop of a series of sharply observed calamitous events: someone throws themselves in front of a train, a boy falls ten storeys to his death, and a chemical factory explodes with many fatalities.

Yet what of the absent husband? Fujino has never provided financially for his daughter and has no intention of doing so. He shows little attachment to her, displaying the immaturity of a child himself. Towards the end of the novel, as he unexpectedly presents the signed divorce papers after nearly a year, he announces that he has more pressing financial priorities. He has a theatre company to start – and cannot disappoint those relying on him – and he wants to fulfil his dreams of making a film. He does however declare that he will bestow custody on her. Tsushima offers a fascinating perspective from Japan of the ubiquity of the single mother's experience. Her female characters remain unnamed as she illuminates how women are so easily confined by child-rearing, while men refuse such hurdles in pursuing their ambitions. How will the young woman respond? Is this one outrage too many?

Readers cannot fail to be moved by the sequence of events revealed in this exquisitely affecting book. Any mother who has ever felt themselves engulfed by child-rearing, estranged from their self-worth and confidence, exhausted and on the edge, will recognize and be touched by the candour of Tsushima's narrative. The author does not shy away from difficult – sometimes taboo – topics, but offers a poetic voice to maternal ambivalence. Throughout this extraordinary book, we appreciate how behaviour that appears ordinary and unremarkable can mask a complicated inner world. Above all, this is a mesmeric and intimate evocation of the secrets that mothers hold close to their hearts and which are so rarely the subject of literature.

THE NOVEL

First published as a novel by Kodansha in 1979 in Japan, 光の領分 – or *Territory of Light* – was originally published in 12 monthly instalments by *Gunzō* literary magazine between 1978–9. It was translated from Japanese into English by Geraldine Harcourt (2018) for Penguin Modern Classics in the UK and Farrar, Straus and Giroux in the US.

THE AUTHOR

Yūko (Satoko) Tsushima (1947–2016) was raised by her mother Mitsuko from an early age after her father, the novelist Osamu Dazai, died by suicide with his lover. Her first collection of short stories was published when she was 24. In her prolific career, Tsushima was the recipient of multiple prestigious awards, including the Women's Literature Prize (1978) and the 2007 Murasaki Shikibu Prize. Her work is only now being more widely read outside Japan, as her posthumous acclaim grows. Most of her books have been translated into English by Geraldine Harcourt: *Child of Fortune* (1978), *Territory of Light* (1979), *Woman Running in the Mountains* (1980), *The Shooting Gallery and Other Stories* (1988) and *Of*

Dogs and Walls (2014). *Laughing Wolf* (2000) was translated by Dennis Washburn for a 2011 English-language edition.

IF YOU LIKE THIS, TRY...

Wiradjuri writer Tara June Winch's *Swallow the Air* (2006) contains poetic interlinked short stories where the tragedy of their mother's suicide sets in motion for teenage siblings, May and Billy, individual routes to coping with loss, and May's odyssey to find her father. Korean author O Chŏnghŭi's *River of Fire* (2012) offers short stories threaded together by the perspectives of their alienated, isolated female protagonists. Nigerian-British author Irenosen Okojie's *Nudibranch* (2019) is a dazzling and shape-shifting collection, interspersing themes of time travel, phantasmagoria and daily life. It hosts a panoply of vivid characters and events, including a goddess, an albino architect, a travelling circus in 1800s Prussia and a lightning strike on a sand dune – all as stunning and unsettling as the nudibranch mollusc of its title.

KINDRED

OCTAVIA E. BUTLER

1979

From the shockwave of its opening sentences, 'I lost an arm on my last trip home […] and much of the comfort and security I had not valued until it was gone', Octavia Butler's masterpiece is a novel of painful and astounding power. What circumstances could have caused such extreme injury and loss? Was the person in an accident? Are they a soldier returning from combat?

It becomes clear that 'seeing is believing' as you read this novel. African-American woman Dana is inexplicably propelled back in time from Los Angeles 1976 to Maryland in the American South of 1815. Dana is 26 years old and married to her white husband Kevin. They are both writers and have just moved into their own home, funded by the proceeds of Kevin's latest novel. Their families have not warmed to their relationship. The premise is striking. While time travel excites imaginations into 'what if' thinking, it also depends *who* travels back to *when* and *where*. Dana is transported back to a Southern plantation to save her ancestor Rufus Wyelin from drowning as a small boy. Saving Rufus enables him to father the child who becomes her direct ancestor. As a Black woman she is catapulted into obvious danger. To Dana's alarm, she discovers Rufus is white and the son of the owner of her relatives, pitiless Tom Wyelin. The time travel device serves a vital narrative function. It enables Butler to recreate and recognize the uninterrupted lineage from past to present, of the twisted and brutal genealogies born out of the institution of enslavement; from which the modern American nation has grown.

Like Toni Morrison's *Beloved* which was published eight years after this novel, Butler crafts an entirely new reading experience, one that articulates the consequences of plantation life and its beyond-belief cruelties towards enslaved African people. While Morrison fashions a whole new literary shape in her model of 'rememory', Butler's 'rite of return' is related in straightforward realist prose. It spills over boundaries between science fiction (due to its time-travel motif) and draws upon the genre of historic 'slave narratives'. A fantasy novel, *Kindred* is unsettling, page-turning reading. It unflinchingly poses moral questions, asking how any enslaved person could have lived through and withstood such horror, and how this survival can be understood as a legacy for descendants.

Dana receives no warning as to when she will find herself back in the 1800s for each episode of her multiple journeys. Her days and months away are registered in mere minutes or hours in 1976 time when she returns. While she is initially alone in the past, a further twist in the plot is introduced when she finds that Kevin has travelled back in time too.

Kindred offers the opportunity to examine how and why the enslavement system could be sustained. At one point Dana and Kevin witness young Black children playing a game of 'auction' through pricing each other's monetary value. Dana shockingly reflects, '*See how easily slaves are made?*' Although Kevin offers some protection to Dana while they live in the antebellum South, there is also an unbreachable gulf in understanding for, as Dana notes, while they are both observers, acting their roles from a 1976 perspective, she is 'drawn all the way into eighteen nineteen'. She is directly implicated in ways he never can be. Unnervingly, Kevin begins to adapt to the white male dominance of the period and Southern ways of life. Will he become another Rufus?

As Dana learns to be part of the 19th century, it becomes her daily present rather than history. She takes various things from 1976 to help her – facsimile freedom papers she copies from her local library, aspirin, sleeping pills and pens that show her applying future knowledge to the past. This is the only concession Butler orchestrates as Dana learns how to survive as an enslaved person while sustaining her resistance to the systematic denial of her humanity. Whenever Rufus's life is threatened she is transferred back in time, and when her life is threatened, she is catapulted back to 1976. Each new episode creates an increase in her bodily injuries from the physical punishments that she withstands, but for how long?

Butler wrote *Kindred* as a stance against presentism, the idea that enslavement history can be consigned neatly to the past. Or that people today would have been able to resist enslavement or not resort to compromise as part of a survival strategy. What her novel achieves is to reinforce how the pernicious, unequal social relations were inescapable norms. It is through Dana's constant reassessments of her historical condition in relation to what she takes for granted that this is so effectively and heart-stoppingly conveyed. At any time, even as a free Black woman in 1815, she is vulnerable to re-enslavement, violence or death at the hands of Southern whites each time she is returned to the past. The way she finally extricates herself from the 19th century will linger on in readers' minds.

Historical novels are as much about the contemporary contexts in which they are produced. This novel dispels any notion that the brutalities of history no longer exist. While *Kindred* makes clear links between the antebellum South and 1970s America, it is also chillingly apt for 2020s social and cultural conditions, where cases abound of white police shooting Black people first and asking questions later. In this respect, *Kindred* remains a vivid reminder of how the assumptions fuelling these killings find their source in enslavement of Black people's bodies as chattel denied humanity and free will, with disposable lives.

'The past is never dead. It's not even past' wrote William Faulkner in *Requiem for a Nun*, and it remains the harsh truth in terms of race relations in the United States and elsewhere today. To read *Kindred* is to find a way into the causes, the consequences and the impact of racism through a suspension of disbelief, but in the knowledge that what Butler so innovatively crafts in her unique novel, is completely and unavoidably true.

THE NOVEL

Published in 1979 by Doubleday to critical acclaim, *Kindred* is Butler's best-selling novel and was hailed by the critic Walter Mosely as 'everything the literature of science fiction can be'. It was conceived as a response by Butler to a young Black activist who expressed shame at the subservience of previous generations who failed to rise up against their enslavers. Butler believed that historical context had to be fully taken into account in order to understand the actions of our predecessors.

THE AUTHOR

Born in Pasadena, California, Octavia Estelle Butler (1947–2006) decided to pursue her career as a writer at ten years of age. Her first novel *Patternmaster* (1976) evolved into a connected sequence of books about people with telepathic powers called 'patternists' in *Mind of My Mind* (1977), *Wild Seed* (1980) and *Clay's Ark* (1984). Butler is the first African-American woman to gain prominence in the genre of science fiction. Her novels blend social critique and African-centred spiritualism with fantasy.

The short story collections *Speech Sounds* (1984) and *Bloodchild and Other Stories* (1995) won Hugo Awards from the World Science Fiction Society. Butler's much-praised Xenogenesis trilogy: *Dawn* (1987), *Adulthood Rites* (1988) and *Imago* (1989) explores genetics and race. This was followed by her Parable series: *Parable of the Sower* (1993) and *Parable of the Talents* (1998). In 1995, Butler became the first science fiction author to receive a 'genius' grant from the MacArthur Foundation. She received a lifetime achievement award from PEN Center West and the Langston Hughes Medal from the City College of New York. Her final novel *Fledgling* was published in 2005.

IF YOU LIKE THIS, TRY...

The Murders of Molly Southbourne (2017), in which British-born Nigerian science fiction author Tade Thompson takes the *doppelganger* genre in a whole new direction in his award-winning horror novella. Molly watches herself constantly dying. However, whenever she bleeds, another Molly manifests herself, identical in every way but seeking to destroy her. Mohsin Hamid's *Exit West: A Novel* (2017) uses a motif of mysterious doorways that provide portals from one country to another in a swirling allegory of war, love, loss, migration and the hostilities faced by the protagonists Nadia and Saeed as they seek safety.

Red Spider White Web (1990) by Misha Nogha reconfigures the white-male-dominated genre of cyberpunk from a First Nation woman's perspective to create a dystopian setting where the city of Mickey-san (a parody of Disney) is sealed off from the tunnels of Dog-ten below and halo-artist Kumo struggles daily to navigate her existence and survival.

THE JOYS OF MOTHERHOOD

BUCHI EMECHETA

1979

Nnu Ego is the cherished daughter of the highly respected and wealthy Igbo Chief, Nwokocha Agbadi. She was the only child he had had with Ona, a strong-headed woman and the daughter of Chief Obi Umunna. Agbadi loved Ona more than any of the wives that he had married or had inherited. Before she died, Ona had agreed with him that if she gave birth to a daughter, she would be raised by her father; she gives birth to Nnu Ego. Years later, Nnu Ego is allowed to marry a husband of her own choosing, Amatokwu, a young farmer. She bears no children for him in their first year of marriage and her father collects her in disgrace. He eventually finds her a new husband through an arranged marriage, four days' travel away in the city of Lagos. The year is 1934.

Nnu Ego's life is reduced to ridicule and poverty with her new husband, Nnaife, who she never really loves or respects – after all he takes pride in his job of washing clothes that includes the underwear for his white employer and his wife.

But Nnu Ego tolerates him, as he is the father of the three sons and four daughters that become her blessings and joy in life.

Emecheta begins the story with a striking scene as Nnu Ego runs erratically through the streets of Lagos, knocking people down and finally reaching Carter Bridge, desperate and determined to end her life. She had discovered the death of her baby son and her life, which initially seemed to be blessed, becomes an ongoing series of tragedies.

The passion between her parents on the night Nnu Ego was conceived was heard throughout the compound by all members of his family. For Agbadi's first senior wife, Agunwa, knowing that even when seriously ill he preferred a woman from outside his marriage to comfort him, caused her so much pain that she became ill and died. It was traditional on the death of a wealthy patron for their slave to accompany them to their burial to take care of them in their next life. Agunwa's young slave girl begged for her life, but was nonetheless buried alongside her as custom decreed. But the spirit of the slave girl lives on as Nnu Ego's *chi*, who distorts her life and needs to be appeased in order for Nnu Ego's life to blossom. Therefore, though cherished by her father, at the same time he unconsciously tainted her life, and she was condemned to struggle until she died.

The novel moves from one tense situation to another in the constant hope that Nnu Ego will finally climb out of poverty, but with each new child and each wife that Nnaife takes, that hope fades. They eventually return to Ibuza, he to his family home with his new wife and their two children, while Nnu Ego returns in disgrace a second time to her family compound, banished by her husband's family. They regard her as evil, blaming her for Nnaife being sent to jail after he attacked a Yoruba man, the prospective father-in-law of Kehinde, one of their daughters. Kehinde was also Nnu Ego's daughter after all and so the fault was hers.

The Joys of Motherhood is important in showing how people get left behind as a country transitions. There is little direct discussion of colonialism; the impact is shown via the life experiences and friendships of the characters that Emecheta tells the story through. For example, we see the contradictions and ambiguities of the British authorities when they ban chiefs in the rural areas from having slaves, saying that it is evil and illegal, yet Nigerians are working hard for the British in the city. This is like another form of slavery, despite being paid work, as it is barely enough to live on and white employers refer to African people as 'baboons'. One of the main issues that Emecheta tackles is the move from rural to city life pre- and post-independence, providing a constant comparison between the different levels of poverty and employment. Lagos becomes the place where people can earn a salary in cash, rather than in crops or cowrie shells; where a bride price is in paper money rather than in live-stock and palm wine. But the old tradition still holds – there is still a price to be paid for a woman – and that is how they are valued.

The different ways in which from birth, boys and girls are regarded in the home and in the community is made all too evident. Her story also highlights the role and status of girls and women in African society, as a woman is valued by the number of male offspring that she can produce. This is one reason why Nnu Ego is so unusual, as neither she nor her mother were judged by these standards.

The Joys of Motherhood is a story that provides a deep understanding of Igbo marriage culture, death rites, marriage rites and parental rites. Yet at the end, is a solemn realization that a woman's loyalty to her family, tradition and culture does not necessarily benefit her. In the circumstances that women like Nnu Ego find themselves in, it is a fight to live independently as a single parent, even if it is ultimately more beneficial for the children. We can see how women's fight for independence can lead to being ostracized as was the case for her co-wife. We also see how colonialism denigrates colonialists, so that their position in the family is challenged and they have to reassert their worth through cash, which is transient, rather than through traditional means such as land or cowrie shells. It enables us to see how traditions and culture change with the imposition of an outside force and how at the same time the balance between livelihoods, lifestyles and status subtly yet permanently changes.

THE NOVEL

First published in the English language by Allison & Busby in 1979, the novel's unflinching, pioneering and honest prose is widely praised to this day. The novel was also published as part of the Heinemann African Writers Series (2008).

THE AUTHOR

Buchi Emecheta (1944–2017) wrote 16 novels and three children's books. She also wrote the BBC television dramas, *A Kind of Marriage* (1976) and *Family Bargain* (1987). Her experience of being a 22-year-old single mother of five in Britain formed the basis of her first semi-autobiographical novels, *In the Ditch* (1972) and *Second Class Citizen* (1974). She received the *New Statesman*'s Jock Campbell Award for *The Slave Girl* (1977). Emecheta wrote the first female account of the civil war in Nigeria, *Destination Biafra* (1982). She published three books: *Double Yoke* (1982), *The Rape of Shavi* (1983) and her autobiography *Head Above Water* (1986) with Ogwugwu Afor, the publishing company she ran with her son, Sylvester. In 1983 she was one of *Granta*'s Best of Young British Novelists, and in 2005 she received an OBE for her services to literature.

IF YOU LIKE THIS, TRY...

Flora Nwapa's *Women Are Different* (1986). Nwapa is acknowledged as the first African woman novelist to be published in the English language, telling the stories of Nigerian women's lives. A generation of exciting Nigerian woman writers have emerged in the past 20 years including, Sefi Atta, whose stories – such as *Everything Good Will Come* (2005) – are about the challenging lifestyles for young Nigerians, both in the country and in their travels outside. *Ghana Must Go* (2014) by Taiye Selasi focuses on the upheavals of one family who live in the US, but end up scattered across the globe.

Lesley Nneka Arimah has produced a blend of Igbo folklore with magic realism in *What it Means When a Man Falls from the Sky* (2017). Books set in northern Nigeria include *The Stillborn* by Zaynab Alkali (1984), the first novel written by a Muslim woman in Nigeria.

SO LONG A LETTER

MARIAMA BÂ

1980

Ramatoulaye and Aissatou are Senegalese friends who married Senegalese men of their own choosing, outside of the arranged marriage protocol, much to the dismay of their families. But they were in love and Senegal was on the cusp of a new era of political independence, which meant freedom from the old colonial French system. In the early 1960s there was change in the air and a move towards exciting societal and cultural transformation of African cultural pride known as 'Négritude'.

Ramatoulaye begins her story 25 years later when their husbands' mid-life crises cause their love to change and both men marry much younger second wives, a custom that is legal in Islamic Senegal. Modou, Ramatoulaye's husband, marries a schoolgirl, Binetou – one of her eldest daughter's closest friends. Mawdo, Aissatou's husband, marries his first cousin Nabou. Neither of the husbands leaves their first wives; they expect them to now become 'head wives'. However, Aissatou decides to get divorced instead; she learns English, secures a high-ranking international post and moves to the US with her four sons.

Ramatoulaye decides to remain married to Modou, yet his obsession with his new wife means that he does not bestow the respect due to Ramatoulaye as a head wife. Pressure from Binetou's family forces him to cut ties with Ramatoulaye and their 12 children. In the end, there does appear to be some poetic justice, as both husbands fare worse than their wives.

So Long a Letter was Mariama Bâ's first novel and written in the form of a letter. Ramatoulaye starts to write after her husband dies of a heart attack at work. During the first months of the official mourning period, she recounts hers and Aissatou's early friendship. She sets this alongside the major events in the country and in their personal lives that were once full of promise, up until her present struggles as a single working mother.

As Modou had been too cowardly to inform Ramatoulaye of his second marriage, he had sent the imam, his elder brother and his best friend to visit Ramatoulaye, after they had attended his wedding. They delivered a message of thanks to her for 25 years of loyal marriage and to inform her that she remained his friend and confidante. It recalls the well-known adage that the wife is always the last to know, in the most extreme sense.

Equally painful is that after Modou's death, when his debts are presented to the family, Ramatoulaye learns that the house that she jointly purchased with him had been remortgaged so that he could pay for a new villa for himself and his new wife, her new car and a house for his mother-in-law. He had also raided their joint bank account to give Binetou a monthly allowance leaving Ramatoulaye almost penniless. In addition, his mother-in-law, Binetou's mother expected Ramatoulaye to continue to provide for her daughter and two children.

These actions provide a better understanding of patriarchy and polygamous practice, where a man can have more than one wife. Culturally and legally, the woman not only relinquishes all her possessions to her husband's family when they marry, but as she is one of the possessions, if another man in her husband's family takes on the 'responsibility' of marrying her after her husband's death, then everything she has, then becomes the property of her new husband. Ramatoulaye maintains a quiet grace and dignity throughout her mourning period until her husband's elder brother visits her again, accompanied by the imam and Mawdo, to claim her as his wife. Ramatoulaye is more valuable to him than Binetou as she has a salary, car and home. But this time, Ramatoulaye says 'no' to custom, and refuses him. Within one page we move from being astounded by such audacity, shaken with rage, screaming at injustice to cheering her bravery. This novel is a roller coaster of emotions from start to finish.

Other themes that the novel deals with include family and community life, religion, death rituals, and Senegalese class hierarchy. One theme delved into deeply is how the cultural system forces women to manipulate other women in order to survive. Aissatou and Ramatoulaye's friendship offers a strong alternative to this. Aissatou buys Ramatoulaye a much-needed car, yet it is also a symbolic purchase of love, support and understanding for her sister-friend; of the freedom of Aissatou's new life alongside her non-judgemental attitude towards Ramatoulaye, who made the decision to remain in a humiliating marriage.

Towards the end of the story, the focus is on the next generation and for the first time, Ramatoulaye names all of her children. Within 20 pages, she shows how she manages inter-generational expectations. It is as though her teenage daughter's pregnancy, her three sons becoming injured by a vehicle on the streets, and discovering three other daughters smoking, makes Ramatoulaye quickly shift out of her own sorrows into the life she has to live for her children. Up until this point, we have only really heard from her eldest daughter, Daba, whose marriage highlights the move of the younger generation to more equality in male–female relationships.

Daba does not find household work a burden. Her husband cooks rice as well as she does; her husband says, 'Daba is my wife. She is not my slave, nor my servant.' In another subtle moment of redress, this modern married couple buy the villa Modou bought for his second wife, alleviating her mother of that debt.

Through the passion and then the pain of marriage break-ups, interfering families and teenage rebellion, Bâ provides us with a profound meditation on marriage and relationships, and a critique on patriarchy. It makes this short book powerful, as many of the situations that Ramatoulaye is forced to deal with in Senegal, can be found in any society, despite this being written about 40 years ago.

THE NOVEL

Originally published in the French language as *Une si longue lettre* by Les Nouvelles Éditions Africaines du Sénégal (1980), the novel was translated by Modupé Bodé-Thomas and published in English by Heinemann African Writers Series (1981). This, Bâ's first book, was internationally acclaimed as soon as it was translated into English and won the 1980 Noma Award for Publishing in Africa. It was voted one of Africa's 100 Best Books of the 20th Century and listed in *500 Great Books by Women: A Reader's Guide* by Erica Bauermeister.

THE AUTHOR

Mariama Bâ (1929–81) was a Senegalese novelist who had been a teacher and a school inspector before becoming a writer. Her book *La Fonction politique des littératures Africaines écrites* (1981) is a treatise on African cultural renaissance and established her as a vocal activist for African girls' and women's rights. She was also a vocal critic against neo-colonialism, a central theme in her books. Her second novel, *Scarlet Song* (1986), also received accolades.

IF YOU LIKE THIS, TRY...

A Dakar Childhood (1982) by Nafissatou Diallo is an autobiographical work, one of the first books about a young female growing up in Senegal. Polygamy, one of the book's central themes is also at the heart of Lola Shoneyin's *The Secret Lives of Baba Segi's Wives* (2011). In Shoneyin's novel, the polygamous marriage of four wives set in Nigeria is humorous with unexpected revelations at the end. *Ways of Dying* (1995) by Zakes Mda tells the tales of poor citizens and their fight against authority, set in South Africa.

Other aspects of Francophone life and the cultural conflicts it creates between Islamic French-African and Westernized French-African life is addressed in the 1961 novel, acclaimed by other African writers, *L'Aventure ambiguë* (*Ambiguous Adventure*) by Cheikh Hamidou Kane. The parents of Samba Diallo, a devout pupil in a Koranic school, send him to Paris to study philosophy.

The important Senegalese woman writer Aminata Sow Fall depicts the daily life of the masses in Francophone Africa in her 1986 novel, *La Grève des bàttu* (*The Beggars' Strike*), in which the poorest citizens go on strike and hold the city to ransom. One of the most dominant 21st-century Francophone women writers is Véronique Tadjo. Her book, *In the Company of Men* (2021), captures accounts of the Ebola epidemic in West Africa.

THE COLOR PURPLE

ALICE WALKER

1982

When *The Color Purple* won the Pulitzer Prize in 1983 demand for the novel took everyone, including Walker's UK publisher The Women's Press, by surprise. Written as a series of letters, mostly addressed to God, it tells the story of an abused, poor and bewildered Black girl, Celie. She makes her plea to God to give her 'a sign' to help her understand her situation and the unfolding of her life after teenage pregnancies and a forced marriage. The novel is set in the first half of the 20th century – the Jim Crow Era – in the Deep South. The pattern of Black lives is seen to be continuing, to all intents and purposes, as if slavery had not ended decades earlier; time seems to be suspended as the novel begins. It is through this pattern that a violent patriarchy is recreated in the lives of the characters.

The book's epistolary form camouflages Walker's intricate plot, which divides the novel into two parts. In the first half, 14-year-old Celie, regularly raped by 'Pa' while her mother becomes increasingly ill, tries to shield her younger sister, Nettie, from similar abuse. She does not know that 'Pa' is her stepfather. Her only possible confidante is God to whom she writes regularly in a largely unschooled vernacular. When their mother dies and a suitor asks to marry Nettie, he is refused and instead, Celie is offered to him. Thereafter, Celie lands in a loveless marriage to a widower with four children. Nettie runs away from home and is briefly reunited with Celie only to be forced to leave. She then disappears from Celie's life after promising to write. In the second half, the action of the novel turns with the help of a female ally Shug, who becomes Celie's lover. Through Shug, Celie discovers a stash of Nettie's letters hidden away by her abusive husband. She learns from Nettie, that she has travelled to West Africa as a missionary and she has news, too, about Celie's children from her teenage pregnancies. Celie writes more to Nettie and less to God until the sisters are reunited some 30 years later. In the course of the novel Celie is transformed through the emotional support of her new friend Sophia and Shug. She leaves her husband and discovers a new independence and a larger community of support.

When Celie is being abused, she feels 'so ashamed' of her life that she believes herself only able to speak to God about her feelings, emotions and the people impacting upon her life. The characters revealed in her letters might be divided into two groups. Women such as Sophia and Shug, are shown as acting upon a clearer understanding of themselves and their humanity. Foremost among the men are those serial male abusers, first, 'Pa', and second, her husband, 'Mr', who rape and beat Celie. Initially, they are not referred to by their first names but by their status. Once Celie's position becomes more secure, they operate on first-name terms and readers come to know them as Alphonso (Pa) and Albert (Mr). Men like this unthinkingly carry the patterns learned through enslaved life into their current relationships. In the process they persistently demean Black women.

Through these male characters, Walker illustrates how sex is routinely used as their means of domination, combined with physical abuse. Thus, asked by his son why he beats Celie, her husband replies matter-of-factly, 'Cause she my wife'. The women, too, similarly brutalized by the physical punishment that slavery demanded, range in their acceptance or rejection of the dominant code, and must pay the price either within the home or in the wider society. Celie advises her stepson Harpo to beat his wife, Sophie, into becoming the desired submissive wife. Sophie refuses the submissive role and pays the price in wider society by being incarcerated. Shug, who appears to be the most liberated, has nonetheless also colluded with men's oppressive behaviour and hurt other women in the process. Nettie, on the other hand, escapes a Southern marriage through her missionary travels and finally sheds light on the missing pieces of Celie's life, specifically her children. When Nettie returns to Celie with her sister's children, who have escaped Southern enslavement, they complete the circle to underscore hope for the future.

For many African-Americans, religion proved to be an important source of emotional support, particularly the Christian religion that missionaries brought to the recently enslaved. Walker's precarious characters, especially Celie, illustrate the need to draw on religion. Celie, for example, in her desperation relies on a God who will at least listen.

Shug's version of God includes an appeal to the erotic. Nettie as a missionary, carries out God's work. Walker suggests that Celie's own limited view of religion imposes its restrictions on her life, while Shug's is more expansive and Nettie's is the more widely informed. Walker refers to her interest in the field of spirituality; Celie learns to be more spiritual as she discovers herself becoming more fully a person in her own right. She comes to see God not simply in church-defined behaviours and practices, but also in nature and beautiful artefacts such as fabrics, as well as the creating of things, such as the clothes that she makes with increasing confidence.

Just as Walker revises the kind of religious ideas held by Celie, centred upon an imposed Christianity and a long-haired white man with large feet, she also revises the patriarchal values imposed through enslavement. She does this by queering expectations principally through her central women characters, Celie and Shug. By the end of the novel, Walker overturns the gendered behaviours that the patriarchal order expects. These are displaced in the novel so that Sophia builds and mends the roof, Harpo allows himself to enjoy cooking and Albert comes to enjoy sewing. The male is no longer dominant, but willing to co-exist rather than coerce. The order of patriarchal control has been disrupted.

THE NOVEL

First published in New York in 1982 by Harcourt Brace Jovanovich in the US, *The Color Purple* won both the Pulitzer Prize for Fiction and the National Book Award for Fiction in

1983. Coinciding with the renaissance of African-American women's writing, the rise of feminism and an explosion of feminist writing, Walker's novel soon became a success. However, following the release of the film adaptation of the book, Walker received considerable criticism for what was considered by some to be her attack on Black family life and a corresponding demonising of the Black male.

THE AUTHOR

Alice Walker (1944–) is an internationally acclaimed African-American poet, fiction writer and essayist, whose writing is widely translated. Though best known for her Pulitzer Prize-winning *The Color Purple*, her prolific writing also includes children's fiction and a memoir. Walker has published as many novels as volumes of poetry, and four short story collections. Her other novels are: *The Third Life of Grange Copeland* (1970), *Meridian* (1976), *The Temple of My Familiar* (1989), *Possessing the Secret of Joy* (1992), *By the Light of My Father's Smile* (1998) and *Now is the Time to Open Your Heart* (2004). Her first poetry collection is *Once* (1968), and following publication of *Revolutionary Petunias and Other Poems* (1973), Walker was a finalist for the National Book Awards for Poetry in 1974. Her short story collections include *In Love and Trouble* (1973), *The Way Forward is with a Broken Heart* (2000) and *You Can't Keep a Good Woman Down* (1981). Walker was awarded the Mahmoud Darwish Literary Prize for Fiction in 2016. *In Search of Our Mother's Gardens: Womanist Prose* (1983) is her most widely known collection of essays.

IF YOU LIKE THIS, TRY...

Toni Morrison's, *Sula* (1973) for a deeply sustained exploration of same-sex friendship. Dionne Brand's debut novel, *In Another Place, Not Here* (1996), centres the complex relationship of two women and is set on a Caribbean island in the grip of political upheaval. Chinelo Okparanta's *Under the Udala Trees* (2015) is a Nigerian-American bildungsroman about Ijeoma's coming of age in an Igbo community during the Biafran War. It celebrates lesbian love and sexuality in the face of violent homophobia.

SEGU

MARYSE CONDÉ

1984

Guadeloupean author-Maryse Condé, turns to West Africa in much of her fiction. This historical epic, *Segu* (and its follow-up, *Children of Segu*) is dedicated to her 'Bambara ancestress' and in it Africa assumes grand proportions. *Segu* is a gripping account of the African perspective of the European slave trade during the late 18th and early 19th centuries. Segu, the capital of the Bambara Kingdom, is a 'vast place' developed along the banks of the Niger River. The city is 'at the height of its glory' when the novel begins. No other place is 'livelier' for miles around. While the kingdom was once feared 'as far away as Timbuktu', drastic change is on its way, as the lives of four of the ten sons fathered by the nobleman, Dousika Traore will reveal. Segu, part of present-day Mali, is their ancestral home – a place of wealth, successful warring, fetish priests and a reliance on indigenous African religious practice. The secret held by Dousika's first-born son, Tiekoro, will not only illuminate the imminent change, it will be central to it. Several plotlines follow the four sons – Tiekoro,

Siga, Naba and Malobali – as they traverse new territories and continents in the wake of change, and the growth of the transatlantic slave trade. The characters change as the focus shifts from one generation to the next.

Tiekoro centres the main conflict in the novel on the escalating hostilities between two opposing world views: of Islam's value systems and the Bambaras' firmly established fetishism. At 15, Tiekoro develops a secret fascination with Islam. On first slipping into a mosque, it is the calligraphy that intrigues him. Thereafter, as he reflects on Bambara culture through the eyes of Islam, he becomes increasingly horrified by his culture's ritual sacrifices and much else. Chaos descends on the Traores' household following the rebellious first-born's declaration in favour of Allah. At the same time, the King, despite his much-vaunted sense of justice and tolerance is facing growing intrigue in his court, while the reality of hostilities press in on the kingdom. In the wake of the intrigue that ensures Dousika's dismissal from the court, Koumare, the Traores' fetish priest, divines that Tiekoro must be sent away to Timbuktu to study Islam and must also take his brother Siga with him. The fate of the four brothers and the survival of their line drives the novel. As Koumare sums up, four sons would need to become 'hostages or scapegoats, to be wantonly ill used by fate' in order to satisfy the gods and the ancestors.

The novel traces the rise of Islam as it impacts upon the demise of the Traores. Yet, though Condé presents Islam as the dominant threat, slavery, too, threatens Segu. Naba, one of the 'scapegoat' brothers beloved by Tiekoro, is kidnapped and lands finally in Brazil. He and his son, Eucharistus, born on a slave plantation are forever lost to the family. Eucharistus, who comes to accept Christianity in the context of Caribbean slavery, grows up with no Bambara cultural memory.

Bambara tradition characterizes Dousika Traore's generation. His status as a nobleman, friend of the king, father of ten sons and patriarch of five families, confirms his authority within society. His wealthy compound reflects this, with the necessary comforts of wives, concubines and servants as well as storehouses of cowrie shells, gold dust and so on. Dousika has an enduring relationship with his trusted fetish priest, Koumare. True to custom, he remains aloof to domestic tensions involving the women of his compound who must attend him depending on his appetites, sexual or otherwise.

The world that *Segu* presents is polygynous and patriarchal. Three generations of Dousika's sons animate the novel. For Tiekoro, the first-born son of Dousika's first wife, Nya – a daughter of the ancient Kulabily ruling family – a marvellous future is foretold. His religious convictions will be lost for some time on his brother, Siga, who is an inferior by birth and must accompany him to Timbuktu. Siga's mother, an unnamed slave-concubine, in desperation, eventually dies by suicide. Considered a crime by the Bambara, this leaves Siga, a servant brother, both disadvantaged and haunted. As a consequence, until he is sent away with Tiekoro, Siga is almost invisible to him. While a similarly negative relationship with Tiekoro is experienced by Malobali, this is not the case for Naba. Tiekoro adores his younger brother, Naba, with whom he shares both a mother and father.

Condé illuminates the fragility of relationships and the power dynamics within the family. Tiekoro's religious fervour and his patriarchal authority determine that his son Muhammed is sent away to a Koranic school. Siga's fate, however, is tied up with his mother's, as is Malobali's. Their mothers do not have the status of wives. Sira, Malobali's mother, plays a mostly passive role with a life that revolves around her sons and husbands. Sira is eventually proactive and escapes the compound to return to her people. Escaping for her own self-respect, she deserts Malobali on the grounds that a son belongs to his father. The third woman to take matters into her own hands in the Traore compound is Nadie, whose life with Tiekoro ends tragically.

The novel itself not only spans over a century in terms of its chronological scope, but it also reaches out geographically across Africa, South America and England – places that will become home, however temporary, to members of the Traore family. Yet, it is on the other side of the Niger River that the explorer and lone white man, Mungo Park is spotted when he arrives in Segu in 1797. Ominously, Dousika's compound is emptied as everyone goes to the river's bank hoping to see the spectacle. Condé draws on real people, places and events to contextualize the saga and add to its richness. Beyond the skilful telling of a complex fiction, *Segu* explores the violent impact of Islam, and its part in the decline of the Bambara Kingdom. *Segu* relates a grand narrative. In the process, Condé reveals the pincered scars suffered by the Bambara Kingdom in the late 18th and early 19th centuries, not only the part played by Islam, but also by the colonial slave trade and Christianity.

These themes are rarely explored alongside each other, but in *Segu* they make compelling reading.

THE NOVEL

Segu, originally published as *Ségou: Les murailles de terre* (1984) by French publishing house Seghers, is a major work and bestselling novel. The English-language version was translated by Barbara Bray and published in 1987 in the Penguin Modern Classics series. The sequel, *The Children of Segu* was originally published as *Ségou: La terre en miettes* (1985) and translated by Linda Coverdale in 1989.

THE AUTHOR

Award-winning Maryse Condé (1937–) is a renowned Caribbean author. She has written novels, plays, children's books and literary essays. She won Le Grand Prix Littéraire de la Femme in 1986 and Le Prix de L'Academie Française in 1988. In 2018 she won The New Academy Prize in Literature, the alternate award to the Nobel Prize in Literature. She was awarded the Cino Del Duca World Prize in 2021. Condé's fiction includes (with original, French-language publication dates): *Heremakhonon* (1976), *A Season in Rihata* (1981), *I,Tituba Black Witch of Salem* 1986) and *Windward Heights* (1995). Condé has held professorships at multiple US universities including Columbia, Harvard, Princeton, Virginia and The University of California, Berkeley.

IF YOU LIKE THIS, TRY...

Ayi Kwei Armah's *Two Thousand Seasons* (1973) recreates the early stages of Euro–Arab contact with pre-colonial Africa at a stage when it is without hereditary rulers. Ousmane Sembène's *God's Bits of Wood* (1962, English translation by Francis Price) explores Senegal's resistance to French colonial rule and the country's struggle for independence.

ANNIE JOHN

JAMAICA KINCAID

1985

We meet Annie immediately, as she is communicating two important points. First, that she has been speaking to no one except her parents, and second, that she is preoccupied with death. This haunting coming-of-age story of a girl growing up on the island of Antigua follows Annie from a seemingly idyllic childhood, where she is worshipped by her parents, towards an uncertain future. Annie, once an indulged only child, especially close to her mother, with whom she experiences a sense of 'paradise', now feels betrayed by her as their relationship turns to one of conflict. Annie's youth and her sheltered experience lend to the novel a sketchy, but also at times contradictory, projection of a life filtered primarily through the first-person narrator.

Annie's reflections on death illustrate the way in which she verifies details of her world through a constant dialogue with her mother and represents it through her nuclear family, a few school friends and other familiars. Atlantic slavery destabilized family life so the extended family is more usual in the Caribbean. Kincaid's choice of a nuclear family for Annie draws attention to coloniality and its impact. This is illustrated by the Red Girl, Annie's friend to whom she becomes devoted precisely because her mother would disapprove. The Red Girl's dirty clothes, filthy nails and rich, unwashed smell are unexplained, but should be aligned with impoverished and insecure colonial conditions. Unlike Annie, the Red Girl does not have a secure home, and her disappearance from Annie's narrative is in line with this. Like Annie's father's story of being brought up by his grandmother, the Red Girl had been sent away to live with her grandmother.

The tradition of storytelling is central to the novel. Annie's mother and her grandmother, Ma Chess, are expert oral storytellers. After her mother's constant sharing of tales with her daughter, Annie comes to master her own story, in effect, reinventing herself. As she matures, Annie attempts to supplant her mother's symbiotic place in her life, with the aim of obliterating festering memories of her mother's crass and – in her eyes – unforgivable rejection. Annie's stories of pubescent sexual discovery involving girls would provoke her mother's censure and increasingly motivate the daughter's actions. Kincaid's narrative style – sometimes referred to as semi-autobiographical because of the way it borrows from her own life – is playful with storytelling, which itself permits Annie's subsequent reinvention. In the process, the narration cuts off full accounts of other characters to afford a stark focus on Annie's life. At the same time, the privileging of the auto-biographical, that allows Annie's determined wrenching away from her mother, unsettles the novel and leaves questions about the extent of Annie's knowledge of her mother.

There is a question that the novel sustains throughout: what does Annie know or what is being withheld from the reader and to what effect? For example, Annie's first stories about her mother portray an idyllic relationship, during a period in which she not only refers all her existential queries to her mother, she also adores her. Annie just as readily finds herself intoxicated with the sound of her mother's voice, her elusive smell – evoking lemons, sage, roses or bay leaf – and is as entranced by her facial movements or her laughter. Identifying at first completely with the mother and effectively rehearsing the stories of her childhood told by her mother, it is Annie's name that forms the title of the novel. Meanwhile, the reader learns towards the end of the narrative that this name is shared, for as the young adult Annie asserts: 'She was my mother Annie; I was her daughter, Annie.'

Annie has much to learn about Caribbean girlhood. As she discovers, the 'paradise' of her early maternal relationship will ground the gendered story that she must shape for herself, irrespective of any realization that her role as a female within society seems pre-determined. Within her own home, the gender story is symbolized by her mother's travel trunk, in which she has stored mementoes of Annie's life, and is thoroughly rehearsed so that Annie knows both the script and characters by heart, and tells of female devotion to domesticity. The mother's crafting – embroidered flowers, smocking, scallop edging – simultaneously represents maternal care resulting in the child's paradise. Equally, the trunk signifies the possibility of escape from the inevitable, by moving abroad. It also questions the extent to which the elder Annie's flight from patriarchy might be considered a success.

As young Annie acknowledges, her girlhood is spent mostly in school, a space for able girls, where those considered 'dunces' are routinely humiliated. Annie sees that power lies in words, both spoken and written, as well as in a hierarchy of colonial action that is determined abroad. Colonial power at home is dictated by schooling but also by the church, which regulates not only school but also wider society. In school, as Annie notes, Black girls can achieve agency only through the written word and only within the parameters allowed by coloniality. Out of school, female role models, like her mother and grandmother, remain constrained by the patriarchal order, irrespective of any resistance. One danger is a circularity built into the colonial order and reinforced by the education system, requiring Annie finally to act upon the knowledge that her mother's attempted escape at a similar age affords one of the few options available to her.

In her colonial classroom with its exercise books featuring the 'wrinkled-up' face of Queen Victoria, Annie cannot know that colonial practice had long set in motion the makings of a docile workforce. Linked to this, the emphasis on civilizing through religious and moral education has led to the distorted focus on 'the young-lady business', as Annie experiences it, taught through outmoded English manners, preferably by colonials. Yet Kincaid's *Annie John*, focused on the protagonist's growing desire for a life distinct from her mother's, painstakingly sketches into this disarming tale, key signifiers of the larger, colonial picture. However, a different course is suggested for Annie who, like her mother, reads and thinks. Unlike her mother, Annie's rebellion signals an ominous rejection of coloniality.

Kincaid's genre-breaking novels often confound review-ers and bookshops alike, and this novel can be read in two ways. The first, and perhaps most obvious, is as a bildungs-roman, or exploration of the moral and psychological growth of the protagonist, placing it within a white, male, European tradition that has only recently begun to accommodate women, including Black women. A second psychoanalytic reading focuses on the intense mother–daughter bond and painful separation narrative. Alternatively, the novel's distinct concerns with gender, culture and history specific to the Caribbean are fruitful, and render *Annie John* an uneasy fit as either a coming-of-age story or a dyadic tale of separation. This gendered tale also sheds light on Kincaid's masking. Her deployment of the 'I' or first-person narration throughout the book – with its distinctive restricting and focusing of the reader's attention – will, at times, subvert the narrative, even as it relates Annie's story. Annie is characterized both as a storyteller and interested in *how* to tell a tale; she is prone to revising her narrative for the effect on her audience. This unsettling plays throughout the novel, requiring the reader to make sense, with Annie, not only of the world she has inher-ited, but also of the ways in which she revises her accounts through different versions of stories about that world.

THE NOVEL

First published in English (1985) by Farrar, Straus and Giroux in the US, *Annie John* was well received by critics, who were particularly interested in the mother–daughter bond. The novel was foremost within the first wave of Caribbean women's writing to attract critical attention outside the region.

THE AUTHOR

Jamaica Kincaid (1949–) was born in Antigua and emigrated to the US in 1965. She wrote for *The New Yorker* from 1976 and several of her early pieces focused on the Caribbean were later included in her Morton Dauwen Zabel award-winning collection, *At the Bottom of the River* (1983). Her short stories have also been published in *Harper's*, *Rolling Stone* and *The Paris Review*. Kincaid's nonfiction includes *A Small Place* (1988), *My Brother* (1997) and *My Garden Book* (1999). She was awarded the Anisfield-Wolf Book Award for fiction for *Autobiography of My Mother* (1996). Novels include *Lucy* (1990), *Mr Potter* (2002) and *See Now, Then* (2013). Kincaid teaches at Harvard as Professor-in-Residence of African and American Studies.

IF YOU LIKE THIS, TRY...

Merle Hodge's *Crick Crack, Monkey* (1981) is a coming-of-age novel focused on Cynthia (Tee) whose childhood without a mother similarly leads to migration, from Trinidad to England. Hodge's narrative strategies differ from Kincaid's to include an omniscient narrator, thereby affording a more rounded account of the protagonist's life. Sandra Cisneros's *The House on Mango Street* (1984) is set in the US and similarly focuses on a girl protagonist, Esperanza, and the girl's Mexican-Chicana community, one that she may well leave, but not desert.

BELOVED

TONI MORRISON

1987

Beloved is spellbinding fiction that translates the taboo subjects of infanticide and Black slave motherhood for our times. Morrison's ground-breaking novel was inspired by her discovery in 1973 of an account of the 19th-century fugitive Margaret Garner who killed her baby daughter, rather than hand her over to slave catchers. Garner's intention was to kill her children and herself, but she was seized before she could fully execute her desperate plan.

Morrison waited a decade to revisit Garner's story, which raises such profound questions about Black motherhood and Atlantic slavery. In this fictionalized retelling, the creation of the protagonist Sethe is inspired by Garner and her struggle. Sethe is a young mother, who flees slavery with her four children, but is forever haunted by the deadly choice she felt compelled to make.

When the story begins, the novel's central character, Sethe, lives with her daughter, Denver, at a home where they had arrived as a runaway family 18 years earlier. Referred to by its address,

124 Bluestone Road is a 'spiteful' home and readers are immediately curious to find out why. As Sethe recalls, she was then
'big, and deep and wide' in terms of maternal possibilities for her
children she considered saved from slavery. In despair she had
killed her baby, Beloved, been jailed and seen her two boys desert
the home. Haunted, and with memories of Beloved enmeshed
in those of her own lack of mothering, Sethe embraces a second
chance to mother Beloved when she appears to have returned.
A distraught Denver is reduced to observing Sethe's increasingly
desperate attempts at meeting Beloved's demands. Welcomed
initially by the local community, they are now isolated.

Morrison's skilfully crafted fiction weaves a powerfully
haunting novel centred on three characters: the young mother
Sethe; Denver, her daughter who through a lifetime of trauma
grows up with her mother; and the eponymous Beloved, who
dialogues with the hidden histories of similar stories in the
archives. Through a process Morrison calls 'rememorying', she
reconstitutes Garner's tale so that it can be brought fully to life
through the quality of creative mediation that she applies.

Set in Ohio in the years following the Civil War, it is 124
that is central to the story and becomes a place of memories for
its isolated characters. As Sethe rememories every mention of
the plantation, ironically named 'Sweet Home', she evokes the
painful enslaved past, especially being held down and having
her baby's milk sucked from her breasts. 124 overlooks The
Clearing, a space of spirituality within which her mother-in-
law, Baby Suggs, once preached and supported the community.

Sethe's intense tale of loss centres around her 'best thing',
her two-year-old, who she attempts to save from the trauma

of slavery by killing. At the same time, Morrison keeps us guessing about who or what Beloved is in the novel. Is she a stranger they have taken into their home or the ghost of the murdered child? Or does she represent Atlantic slavery itself, returning in one guise or another to haunt humans? As the enigma of Beloved runs its course, the novel poses complex questions about the impact of racialized slavery and its far-reaching legacy.

The novel's concern with haunting is compelling. Sethe is haunted by the horrific deed of infanticide that finally defines her and holds her in its grip. Meanwhile, large questions loom in the novel concerning the role of history and mankind's racialized and terminally distorted understanding of humanity; specifically, its capacity to dehumanize on racial grounds and to refuse recognition of the suffering that ensues. The novel insists upon remembering not only the atrocities of Sethe's personal history, but also the further violence implicated in the overwhelming pressure to diminish, deny and dismiss them. As a result, the past, present and future become implicated in ways that strongly resonate today, so that the mirror that Morrison's *Beloved* holds up to us invites a much-overdue resistance to the structures of power that collude towards maintaining the racial power dynamics fuelling Sethe's desperate act. Morrison's uncompromising probing has led to the novel being banned from time to time; it was listed during 2007–16, as among 'The Top 10 Most Challenged Books', as part of the American Libraries Association 'Banned Books' project.

Beloved certainly narrates a bitter story of slavery. As the speech patterns and lived experience represented in the novel signify, *Beloved*'s characters are unmistakably African-American. Furthermore, the history that the novel reconstructs is, without doubt, African-American. Yet, in the globalized context that readers increasingly have come to understand, there is a growing awareness that Atlantic slavery's atrocities were similarly experienced much more widely than in the US. Morrison's dedication page reference to 'Sixty Million and more' reminds us of the wider global context of slavery.

Much has been written about the novel in relation to its pointed reconfiguring of history and its nuanced portrayal, particularly of women. It is important to appreciate that with this novel, Morrison has bequeathed a new literary genre, that of the neo-slave narrative. This differs from the original slave narrative in its insistence upon revealing the interiority of the enslaved. *Beloved* has inspired literary writers across the globe to imagine anew the lives of those once enslaved. Atlantic slavery was an outcome of European colonial practices in regions of Africa, South, Central and North America, as well as the Caribbean; this informs the novel's global reach. Sethe's resonant, human story is transgressive in its breaking of a long-held silence concerning the trauma resulting from the dehumanizing of the enslaved.

The recent explosion of international publications within the neo-slave narrative genre is an indication of Morrison's status among contemporary writers and her reach in shaping literary culture. This impact can be traced in the US and UK through to Africa, as well as the Francophone, Lusophone and Hispanic areas of the Americas and the Caribbean. Examples include Laura Fish's *Strange Music* (2008) and Ana Maria Gonçalves's *A Colour Defect* (*Um defeito de cor*) (2005).

Morrison's ground-breaking *Beloved*, in reclaiming, (re)presenting and centring the enslaved as fully human, has been extraordinarily influential in subsequently inspiring many books and other forms of writing from poetry to theatre. To borrow from Morrison, such new writing serves to 'fill in the blanks that the slave narrative left.'

THE NOVEL

First published in 1987 by Alfred A. Knopf in the US and Chatto & Windus in the UK, the novel won both the Pulitzer Prize and the American Book Award in 1988.

Beloved has been widely translated and is a popular choice for reading groups and book clubs, contributing to its extensive readership. The novel's scholarly reception has proved to be phenomenal. It was adapted into a film, starring among others, Oprah Winfrey and Thandiwe Newton. Additionally, the libretto for the opera, 'Margaret Garner' was written by Toni Morrison with a score by Richard Danielpour and premiered in 2005. In 2006 the *New York Times* nominated *Beloved* the best novel in 25 years.

THE AUTHOR

Toni Morrison (1931–2019) was born in Lorain, Ohio, in the United States. She was the first Black woman to become an editor at Random House (from 1967 to 1983). In 1977, Morrison won the National Book Critics Circle Award for *Song of Solomon*. She received the Nobel Prize in Literature in 1993 and was honoured with the Presidential Medal of Freedom in 2012, as well as the Ivan Sandrof Lifetime Achievement Award in 2015. As a Creative Writing professor, Morrison retired from Princeton University as Robert F Goheen Chair in the Humanities in 2006. Her oeuvre spans five decades and includes children's fiction, adult novels, nonfiction, cultural criticism and edited collections. Author of 11 novels, Morrison's fiction includes *The Bluest Eye* (1970), *Song of Solomon* (1977) and later works, *A Mercy* (2008), *Home* (2012) and *God Help the Child* (2015).

IF YOU LIKE THIS, TRY...

Andrea Levy's *The Long Song* (2010) which is set in 19th-century Jamaica and foregrounds women's experiences in slavery through the central narrator called July. Booker-longlisted novel (2021), *The Sweetness of Water* (2021) by Nathan Harris is set in Georgia. Taking place in the wake of the American Civil War, this lyrical novel follows two very different routes as two formerly enslaved brothers hope freedom will let them find their mother, and two Confederate soldiers must conceal their love for each other from the outside world.

NERVOUS CONDITIONS

TSITSI DANGAREMBGA

1988

Dangarembga takes us to Rhodesia in the 1970s for this powerful coming-of-age story, set against the backdrop of the oppressive British colonial system. The colonizers' dominant education structure was designed to impress on young minds – like Tambudzai's – that learning everything in English was for their own salvation. Tambu, as she is known, is a bright and feisty 14-year-old, and she is the narrator of this intense story. Tambu lives on a rural homestead with her parents and three siblings and is determined to continue her schooling, even if she has to earn the money to pay her school fees herself. She is unexpectedly granted her brother Nhamo's place at the mission school 20 miles away after he dies of mumps. So begins the change in her life that she refers to as, 'the period of my reincarnation'. A British education will lead to a well-paid job that will help to raise her family out of poverty. Tambu wins a scholarship to the Young Ladies College of the Sacred Heart, but discovers there is a price to pay once British culture replaces an indigenous one.

Early on in the book, we witness Tambu's frustration as her brother and father try to thwart her entrepreneurial efforts to pay for her school fees. Her father considers that paying for her schooling is a waste of money as once she is married, everything she earns and owns will belong to her husband. The mealies (corn) that she grows to sell at the market, suddenly start to disappear. Her brother, Nhamo, has been trying to impress the girls at school by giving them her mealies to roast. When Tambu confronts Nhamo, she lunges at him and tries to beat him up. She is so upset that she can barely speak when a teacher breaks up their fight and demands an explanation from Tambu, who is pointed out as the perpetrator.

Tambu moves to live with her paternal uncle, Babamukuru, when she takes her brother's place as he is also the headmaster of the mission school and patriarch of the family. She consciously humbles herself as a 'paragon of feminine decorum', compared to her 'volatile and strong-willed' cousin Nyasha, Babamukuru's daughter. Tambu initially believes that Nyasha is arrogant since they have barely spoken since the return of her family from Britain. Yet their friendship is rekindled and sisterly love becomes strong, so that when Tambu is punished by her uncle and has to do the maid's household chores, Nyasha insists on helping her. Similarly, Tambu supports Nyasha when she and her father get into a physical fight after Nyasha comes home late from a school dance. It is a tense and harrowing scene that is difficult to forget. As they sit outside, Nyasha tries to calm down by smoking a forbidden cigarette. Tambu realizes that despite the difference in their upbringing, she and her cousin are forever bonded as victims of 'femaleness' and that all of their difficulties are solely a consequence of being female in a male-dominated society and nothing will ever change that.

One major difference between them though, is the state of distress that Nyasha is locked in, caused by 'double conscious-ness', described by Sartre as producing a 'nervous condition'. This is one of the main themes of the book, as we see Nyasha and Nhamo struggle with the effects and tragic consequences of being in this state of mind. Dangarembga shows this through Nyasha's loss of her mother tongue and her strenuous attempts to re-learn her Shona language so as not to be alienated from her school mates. Nyasha's is the heart-breaking story that is rarely told of the child who is forced to straddle two cultures over two continents at a formative age.

Nhamo's double consciousness results from his decision to dissociate himself from the Shona language. At the start of the novel Nhamo returns to the homestead during his first school vacation and boasts of his inability to speak or under-stand Shona, he taunts his sisters and his mother as if they are inferior to him. He has embraced British culture as his own. Dangarembga deftly balances the debates around mother tongue as she weaves into her narrative words from the Shona language that have no direct English translation. Other terms highlight cultural experiences such as *nhodo,* a children's street game like jacks. In doing so, she offers a subtle reminder that there is a richness in retaining mother tongue that cannot be replaced by the colonizers' language and which helps to rein-force your own sense of identity and worth.

Nervous Conditions is not a typical coming-of-age novel. It is deceptively simple yet encompasses several layers and themes that must be navigated and revisited. There are the overarching themes and context of the hierarchical and patriarchal family system in Rhodesia, which denigrates African women. This was combined with a British colonial system that was more akin to apartheid before Rhodesia became politically independent in 1980 and renamed Zimbabwe. Issues of family dynamics include the complexity of father–daughter relationships, as seen between Nyasha and the over-protective Babamukuru. This is contrasted, almost humorously, with Tambu's irresponsible and lazy father. Dangarembga's observational skills are evident in her cleverly structured debut novel as she delves into matters that are at once local and global within the two-year period that this story covers.

Tambu's mother Mainini, uneducated and married at 15, is the character who conveys the prophetic words that clarify the emotional destruction of a colonial education, double conscious-ness and family fragmentation, 'what will I your mother say to you when you come home a stranger full of white ways and ideas? It will be English, English all the time'. Mainini experi-ences mental and physical deterioration after Babamukuru takes first her son, then her daughter to live with him.

Dangarembga was the first woman novelist in Africa to boldly detail the pervasiveness of patriarchy and gender inequality, and the consequences of colonialism with its under-mining of oppressed people psychologically and economically. In Tambu, we have a young girl protagonist who challenged, head on, the differences in treatment of men and women. We meet her again in the second and third novels that make up the widely acclaimed Tambudzai trilogy.

THE NOVEL

Originally published in the English language by The Women's Press in 1988, the novel's current publisher is Faber & Faber (2021). Dangarembga wrote this, her debut, at the age of 25 and it was hailed by Doris Lessing as one of the most important novels of the 20th century. The novel has been voted one of Africa's 100 Best Books of the 20th Century and one of the BBC's Top 100 books that Changed the World (2018). It also won the Commonwealth Writers' Prize in 1989 and is featured in *500 Great Books by Women: A Reader's Guide* by Erica Bauermeister.

THE AUTHOR

Tsitsi Dangarembga (1959–) is a novelist, playwright, activist and filmmaker. Her second novel in the Tambudzai trilogy was *The Book of Not* (2006), where Tambu attends a predominantly white secondary school and starts her first job. In her third novel, *This Mournable Body* (2018), we follow the older Tambu through difficult times; this was shortlisted for The Booker Prize in 2020. Together with *Nervous Conditions* they make up a trilogy published by Faber & Faber in the UK and Graywolf Press in the US. Dangarembga was awarded the Peace Prize for Literature from the German Publishers and Booksellers Association (2021).

She founded the Institute of Creative Arts for Progress in Africa (ICAPA) in 2014 and *A Family Portrait*, a collection of short stories, which includes her story, 'The Brick', was produced by ICAPA Publishing in the same year. Her next book is *Sai-Sai, Watermaker*, a dystopic speculative fiction novel for young adults.

IF YOU LIKE THIS, TRY...

Books by Yvonne Vera, a prolific Zimbabwean woman writer who covers challenging themes, particularly women's issues, as explicitly as Dangarembga. Chimamanda Ngozi Adichie's coming-of-age debut novel *Purple Hibiscus* (2003) is much preferred by many African women readers to her bestselling novel, *Half of a Yellow Sun* (2006). *26a* (2005) by Diana Evans is a coming-of-age story of mixed-race twins Bessie and Georgia Hunter, growing up in an interracial family between Britain and Nigeria. *A Man Who Is Not a Man* (2010) by Thando Mgqolozana recounts the story of a South African boy who goes through circumcision rites; it does not go well. *We Need New Names* (2013) is a very different, but equally thought-provoking, coming-of-age novel by Zimbabwean writer NoViolet Bulawayo.

WOMAN HOLLERING CREEK AND OTHER STORIES

SANDRA CISNEROS

1991

In the title story, 'Woman Hollering Creek', Juan Pedro Martínez Sánchez requests permission from Don Serafín to marry his daughter, Cleófilas Enriqueta DeLeón Hernández. Juan Pedro is in a rush as he needs to return to work and so the wedding takes place within two weeks of the couple meeting. Once married, they head back to the US in his new pick-up truck. Home for Cleófilas is now on the other side of the Mexican border in the US, a place where she has neither family nor friends.

Cleófilas had been glad to leave Mexico where she took care of her six brothers and her father. She had been looking forward to having only one man to look after, having her own home and raising a family. However, she soon wishes she was back in Mexico as the daily routine in her new home involves her husband beating her. Cleófilas' tears and begging for forgiveness have no effect on him. She longs to escape and return to Mexico, but she knows this would bring disgrace on herself and her family.

Although she is due at a pre-natal health appointment for her second child, she has to beg her husband to drive her there. The doctor recognizes her as another young Mexican woman caught in the US–Mexico marriage border trap. She speaks no English and the doctor notices how badly she has been beaten. He is determined to help her and so books a follow-up pre-natal appointment and arranges for a female friend to drive her to the Mexican border to escape her abusive husband. On the way, Cleófilas is driven over the creek and her driver reminisces on the well-known Mexican folktale of 'La Llorona' ('The Weeping Woman') who drowned her two children when she saw her husband with another woman. The variations of the La Llorona folktale are of women drowning, women drowning children and women crying – drowning in tears – because of the loss of their children. Readers are also bound up in the La Llorona tale as we weep for Cleófilas, who is caught in the trap of being a woman subjected to either extreme physical abuse from her husband or enduring the abuse and shame of becoming a divorced one. Other stories included in this collection are reflective of La Llorona's tale, whether they are to do with unfaithful men, children suffering or stories that incorporate an association with water.

The 'Eyes of Zapata' is a mesmerizing folk tale set against the Zapatista uprising, which started in Chiapas, Mexico in 1994 and was inspired by Emiliano Zapata, the revolutionary leader of the land reform movement. It is a story of love and betrayal: the love between Inés and Miliano, and between

Miliano and his country. They run away to his hometown as her father disapproves of their relationship. Inés is convinced that he loves her deeply as he woos her with promises, such as building her a brick house with tiles instead of thatch. But Miliano loves his country more than Inés and he is voted in as town councillor, because he has vowed to fight the government for local people to be able to retain their land rights. In his role of rebel of the state, he eventually becomes an outlaw fighting around the country, leaving Inés and their children in the home that he builds for her on the edge of his hometown.

In their quest to find and destroy Miliano, the authorities raid every village, stealing whatever is of value, leaving the villagers destitute. Inés is blamed, and called a witch, even though she suffers as much as they do. She is betrayed by Miliano as he persists in travelling around the countryside wooing women in his traditional Mexican garb. Inés can see into the future and she knows about Miliano's infidelities before anyone tells her as she is able to 'fly' and hover over the country. She sees him in bed with other women but, despite this, she does not love him any less. He has one woman in particular who cannot have children. Again, Inés and her jealousy are blamed for this and Miliano takes their son to live with his sister where he becomes a pawn and is kidnapped by the authorities. It is an experience the boy never forgets and in the end he betrays his father. On Milano's last return to Inés, he is visibly worn out, as are the loyal town folk who once supported their hero. The tension in the story increases as we sense a dramatic end, as seen through Inés's flight to see what the future holds for them.

Cisneros is adept at changing the tone of her prose to suit the tale. From the initial warm stories that reminisce of childhood, her lyrical voice tells the story of 'My Lucy Friend Who Smells Like Corn', and childhood wisdom in 'Eleven'. But as the female characters become older and get married, their suffering begins. Between the stories are liberal sprinklings of vignettes, the most captivating being 'Little Miracles, Kept Promises', concerning the blessings and miracles that people take to their church to be granted by the Virgin Mary or a patron saint. These convey so much of Mexican life, working-class life, the nature of human beings and their relationship with their maker. Some brief one-liners are the foundations of stories in themselves. Some requests beg for pimples to disappear, another asks the 'Miraculous Black Christ of Esquipulas': 'Please make our grandson to be nice to us and stay away from drugs. Save him to find a job and move away from us. Thank you.'

Together, this series of tales from both sides of the border of Mexico provides an intimate insight into family life. Cisneros reminds us of the universality of childhood, as families watch Mexican films in a local cinema, and children wander off and find other amusement or curl up, using the armrest of the cinema chair as a pillow.

The in-between life as 'mericans' is reinforced by the way Cisneros moves in and out of writing in English, using Spanish words and phrases where it feels most natural to do so. Her writing is detailed and authentic, even her heroines are not spared their faults. Factual news reports on disappearing Mexican women suddenly become chillingly real in these revealing stories, where we see that there is no safety net for Mexican women from violence or from poverty.

THE COLLECTION

First published in 1991 by Random House in English, this collection of short stories won the Anisfield-Wolf Award in 1993.

THE AUTHOR

Sandra Cisneros (1954–) is a Mexican-American poet, short story writer, novelist, essayist, performer, visual artist and literary activist. She focuses on the variety of life experiences and struggles of Hispanic girls and women in her writing. She has written five books of fiction, the most popular being her coming-of-age novel, *The House on Mango Street* (1984), along with two collections of poems and a memoir.

Accolades include NEA fellowships in poetry and fiction, the Texas Medal of the Arts Award, a MacArthur Fellowship (1995), a Ford Foundation's Art of Change Fellowship, several honorary doctorates and recognition in The Frederick Douglass 200. Book awards include Chicago's Fifth Star Award, the PEN Center USA Literary Award, the Fairfax Prize and the National Medal of the Arts, awarded to her by President Obama in 2016, and the PEN/Nabokov Award for Achievement in International Literature (2019).

IF YOU LIKE THIS, TRY...

Vintage Cisneros (2004), which is a compact edition of excerpts of her books and a useful introduction to her writing. Other short story specialists include, Jacob Ross's *Tell No-One About This* (2017) and Olive Senior's *Summer Lightning and Other Stories* (1986). Short story collections are often the first book to have been written by emerging award-winning writers, including *Interpreter of Maladies* (1999) by Jhumpa Lahiri, *Gorilla, My Love* (1972) by Toni Cade Bambara, *Reef* (1994) by Romesh Gunesekera, *Drinking Coffee Elsewhere* by Z Z Packer (2003), *Drown* by Junot Díaz (1996) and *Krik? Krak!* by Edwidge Danticat. Irenosen Ikojie has emerged as one of the most exciting short story writers in Britain with *Speak Gigantular* (2016). *Under African Skies* (1997) edited by Charles Larson is one of the best ways to explore the short fiction written by the most well-known African writers of the period.

TEXACO

PATRICK CHAMOISEAU

1992

'Literature in a place that breathes is to be taken in alive' is an opening retort that sets the tone of *Texaco*. In many ways, the novel insists on a clear break with tradition, especially in its privileging of Francophone Creole – applauded by some and viewed as contentious by others – as a literary language. Here, the orality of storytelling in the author's birthplace underpins the literary art upon which the novel is structured.

Within the witty and nuanced narrative, Chamoiseau treats the reader to writing that interlinks space, time and memory to bring to life a vibrant community of characters. Among them is a Haitian 'man of letters', a much-anticipated urban planner, an isolated old medicine man, the journal-keeping protagonist Marie-Sophie Laborieux, whose 'only weapon' is words, and the Word-Scratcher or author, himself. The author is occasionally addressed by selected characters and responds readily to them in the local Creole language, in preference to French. In its original French-language edition, the language play – between French and Francophone Creole – would be particularly striking. The space of competing languages is of special concern in the novel, within which Creole-ness, signified through language use, is heightened. The physical space on which the novel is focused is Martinique, the island in the Francophone Caribbean where Chamoiseau was born and still lives.

The main setting for the novel is City, and more precisely, at the centre of the novel lies Texaco, the squatter district located on the edge of Martinique's capital Fort-de-France. Affluent outsiders view Texaco as a shantytown and want an end to its growth. This is key to the tension of the fictitious district, itself built upon Marie-Sophie's written and oral accounts. Chamoiseau's crafting is richly deceptive, reflecting the piecing together of Marie-Sophie's discovery of both herself and her relationship to the space that Texaco, with its 'piled-up hutches', represents. In a similar fashion, the sections of the novel that are drawn from Marie-Sophie's fabricated series of notebooks and memory become key to both the patterning and substance of the narrative that the novel gradually reveals. The name, Texaco, draws directly from the well-known oil refinery and also refers to land acquired by the multinational company. This land is partially reclaimed as the site upon which Marie-Sophie repeatedly rebuilds her fragile, makeshift home, alongside her community. Their plight urges the reader to question why this group squatting within Texaco is privileged to have their story told, and why this industrial space is equally privileged in the novel.

In considering this question, attention is drawn to the problem announced early in the novel, namely that those dispossessed – through enslavement – of land among other

things, will eventually shun the countryside and its plantations, due to having been so thoroughly dehumanized there.
Yet, their experience of City catapults Texaco's would-be
inhabitants into further exploitation since the central city also
exposes them to unfamiliar political battles along class, colour,
caste and neo-colonial lines. In fleeing City's exploitative practices, Texaco begins to be realized as the possibility of a new
type of community. Despite a history of having continuously
been denied resources, the group summon sufficient resilience
to challenge the established order by building sustainably.
It seems meaningful that it is from Texaco's contentious site
that time is revealed as the history of the island told from the
vantage point of those dispossessed by both the old order of
colonial slavery and the neo-colonial order.

The narrative that unfolds is calibrated in milestones or
what the author calls 'ages' related to the possibility of being
human in one's own right and providing housing for oneself.
The disempowered were first housed in longhouses and *ajoupas*
(Indigenous-style huts) and they only gradually come to share
new-found knowledge about building with straw, crate wood,
asbestos and, finally, concrete. While the use of such fragile and
sometimes dangerous building materials signifies their designated place in the ordering of humanity, they also reflect the
storytelling strategies that are brought to bear on this narrative.

Drawing on oral forms of storytelling and the wisdom of
elders, Chamoiseau introduces the figure of the urban planner to open up contemporary debates about questions of care,
ecological boundaries and the rebuilding of community through
attachment to urban spaces. The author's playfulness with

language sometimes camouflages and at other times enhances his re-humanizing of the Black characters. Either way, it reminds us that whether dehumanized through Atlantic slavery, as represented in the 19th-century opening of the novel, a central goal is to grant the characters full humanity. Furthermore, the pages of the novel lay bare an assemblage signifying the author's process, the collective nature of the narrative and expectations of fragmentation. It soon becomes evident, though, that the narrative is composed of memories. Memory is deployed as the main strategy through which an orally transmitted history emerges. The history is substantiated by notebook entries and tape recordings; the fragments indicated on the page account for the lives of three generations of Marie-Sophie's family. It is within these memories that her father, Esternome, a slave-baby at the beginning of the novel, is shown to recover his humanity, albeit through a rather haphazard process. At the same time, his story is vital to Marie-Sophie and Texaco in that he provides the model and, most importantly, the critical survival skills necessary for the next generation to discover their own humanity.

While Marie-Sophie's memories include those of her father, this novel is less about individuals and more about community. On one level, there is the piecing together of a family history, on another, the story of Texaco itself is revealed. At the same time, the fictionalized history of Martinique remains central to the novel. It poignantly illustrates the direct relationship between the escape from slavery and colonization by the island's 'black slaves and mulattos', followed by an abandonment of the plantations 'to throw themselves into the conquest of the cities.' In the process, the novel raises an array of questions concerning the nature of freedom. Can one human give freedom to another (perhaps by saving their life) when the giver is also responsible for the lifetime deprivation of the other's liberty? Also, how might freedom, supposedly given by another be realized? The latter teasing question lies at the heart of Chamoiseau's *Texaco* and its humanizing of the shantytown dwellers. Above all, this is a nuanced political novel celebrating humans relearning the skills of community and how to be inclusive.

THE NOVEL

Texaco was first published by Gallimard in French in 1992 and was awarded France's highest literary honour, the Prix Goncourt. This award attracted some controversy, which seemed almost inevitable given that Chamoiseau was only the second Black writer to achieve such recognition within French letters. It was translated by Rose-Myriam Réjouis and Val Vinokur for an English-language edition published by Granta in 1997 in the UK and Random House (1997) in the US. *Texaco* was received with critical acclaim and was a *New York Times* Notable Book of the Year. Despite the linguistic challenges set by this novel, *Texaco* has been translated into many languages, including Japanese and Korean.

THE AUTHOR

Patrick Chamoiseau (1953–) was born in Martinique, an island located in the eastern Caribbean and an overseas depart-ment of France since 1946. His publications span a range of genres, including literary fiction, essays, film scripts and children's fiction. Chamoiseau's writing highlights the tensions concerning the Francophone Caribbean. He has been known as an activist and creolist since his co-publication, *In Praise of Creoleness (Éloge de la Créolité)*, with Jean Bernabe and Raphael Confiant in 1989. As his 1997 essay 'Writing in a Dominated Land' ('Écrire en pays dominé') confirms, politics is integral to Chamoiseau's literary art. Acknowledging particularly the influence of poet, philosopher and fellow-Martinican, Édouard Glissant, his writing probes questions of relationality or relatedness, integral to which is the diverse network of cultures that formed the Caribbean. Titles translated into English include *Solibo Magnificent* in 1999 and *Slave Old Man* in 2018.

IF YOU LIKE THIS, TRY...

Jacob Ross's award-winning crime novel, *Black Rain Falling* (2020) is also set in the eastern Caribbean, though in the English-speaking area of Grenada and Carriacou. Ross shares similar concerns with the region's history, Creole language diversity and questions of community.

28

BREATH, EYES, MEMORY

EDWIDGE DANTICAT

1994

Breath, Eyes, Memory moves between Haiti and New York, following the story of Sophie Coco, who was born to her 16-year-old mother after a violent sexual assault. We meet 12-year-old Sophie at the start of the novel as she is living in the small town of Croix-des-Rosets in Haiti with Tante Atie, her mother's elder sister; she had lived there since she was a baby. Her mother Martine sends a plane ticket to her sister with a message asking her to send Sophie to join her in New York. From the day she arrives in her new home in the rough Brooklyn neighbourhood, Sophie realizes that her mother is deeply disturbed by nightmares. An obedient child, she attends school, studies hard to become the doctor that her mother wants her to be, then returns home to cook dinner for herself and her mother.

One night, Martine returns home from work early to find the now 18-year-old Sophie is not at home. Suspecting her daughter has a boyfriend and to preserve her virginity, she subjects Sophie to the same humiliating weekly 'tests' that she and her sister, Atie suffered at the hands of their own mother. Martine is unaware that it is their African-American neighbour Joseph, a musician, who has fallen in love with Sophie. He asks her to marry him and in an act of retaliation to break the bond with her mother, Sophie inflicts harm on herself to break her hymen. Although she elopes and has a baby with Joseph, she is not mentally 'free', and so she retreats with her baby daughter to her old family home in the village of La Nouvelle Dame Marie to be with Tante Atie and her grandmother, Ifé. Her mother follows Sophie to take her back to her husband and to organize important family matters in advance of death, such as land and burials. Returning home also enables mother and daughter to rebuild their relationship. Martine has not remained in touch with her mother since she moved to New York. But Martine is pushed to the edge of sanity when she herself becomes pregnant. It takes a final visit to La Nouvelle Dame Marie for Martine and Sophie to break their bondages, and to set themselves mentally and physically free of their memories.

From the opening scene, we are drawn to the warmth of the small town where Sophie lives with her aunt. Danticat describes the communal preparation of the *konbit* potluck dinners, from children drying out leaves for the fire to the trail of adults bringing out trays of plantain, sweet potato and other foods to be cooked on the fire, with ginger tea handed out to all. 'It was a way to get together, eat, and celebrate life.' *Konbit*, a Haitian Kreyol term that encapsulates the essence of community and unity, provides both backdrop and a security net for Sophie's early life. But soon after this gathering, her life changes and in an attempt to break their emotional bond and recast herself as Sophie's carer, Tante Atie returns Sophie's Mother's Day card, insisting that she gives it to her biological mother in New York instead. That this was not easy for Atie becomes apparent as the story plays out.

The communal tradition of *konbit* continues to underpin Haitian migrant life in New York. The connections to home, family and friends are maintained by sending cassette tapes through the Haiti Express store, situating the story firmly in the pre-smartphone era. Conversations in local restaurants centre on American oppression and the dangerous boat crossings to escape poverty. It's all *konbit*.

Danticat moves the reader between the parallel existence of Haitians at home and in New York around the streets of Flatbush Avenue, which remind Sophie of home – where people 'walk and talk in Creole and play dominoes on the stoop.' The political violence against Haiti citizens carried out by the vicious militia group, the Tonton Macoutes, is presented alongside New York schoolchildren being beaten by their peers for not speaking fluent English; they were also taunted with the four H's: only Heroin addicts, Haemophiliacs, Homosexuals and Haitians have AIDS.

The novel is written in four parts: Sophie as a child and her move from Haiti to New York, Sophie at 18 living in New York, Sophie escaping to her village of La Nouvelle Dame Marie, and Sophie and Martine returning to New York together. Short chapters propel the story forward, making it unputdownable as we want to know if and how these women survive. Behind closed doors, this is a dark tale of self-destruction. The disturbing act of 'mother love' which tests a daughter's virginity is nothing short of sexual assault and is never spoken of openly. What we cannot fail to realize by the end, is that it is not only the danger, mental and physical suffering that women endure, but also the violence inflicted on women by other women, with the objective of satisfying men's desires. Sophie joins a sexual phobia group, where other women of colour struggle to reclaim and free themselves from acts of genital female mutilation and incestuous rape. Yet they are also determined to find the strength in their adversity to be free of the mental pain which they endure.

What makes *Breath, Eyes, Memory* so distinctive and memorable is Danticat's ability to weave together traditional and contemporary modes of storytelling and her presentation of the supernatural as seemingly natural. Similarly, she enables us to understand how Haitian culture remains intrinsically African, through the use of phrases and beliefs, such as talking of going to Guinea as a kind of spiritual passage to heaven. The third part of the book ends with a sense of foreboding as Atie looks wistfully into the distance at the hill she calls Guinea, this is where all the women in the family would eventually meet at the end of their life journeys. Danticat shows how myth, the folk tale and speculative fiction are seamlessly woven into tales of our everyday lives.

THE NOVEL

First published by Soho Press in the US (1994) and in the UK (1995) by Abacus. The novel was featured on Oprah's Book Club and won two awards: the 2018 Neustadt International Prize and 2019 St. Louis Literary Award.

THE AUTHOR

Edwidge Danticat's (1969–) first book was *Krik? Krak!* (1995), a collection of short stories which was a National Book Award finalist. Other titles include the novels: *The Farming of Bones* (1998), *The Dew Breaker* (2004) and *Everything Inside: Stories* (2019). She has written seven books for children and young adults, and a travel narrative. Her memoir, *Brother, I'm Dying* (2007) was a 2007 finalist for the National Book Award and a 2008 winner of the National Book Critics Circle Award. She was editor of *100 Best American Essays* (2011). Danticat was awarded the 2009 MacArthur Fellowship and 2018 Ford Foundation 'The Art of Change' Fellowship.

IF YOU LIKE THIS, TRY...

Danticat's anthologies are essential reading as introductions and explorations of Haitian and Haitian-American writers. These include: *The Butterfly's Way: Voices from the Haitian Dyaspora in the United States* (2001), *Haiti Noir* (2010) and *Haiti Noir 2* (2013). Maryse Condé, from the Caribbean island of Guadeloupe, is acknowledged as a master storyteller in a different style. Her dark tale, *The Wondrous and Tragic Life of Ivan and Ivana* (2017, with English translation in 2020) is set in the 21st century and filled with dramatic tension, incorporating themes that reflect societal ills from terrorism to neo-colonialism.

Danticat gently introduced the topic of same-sex relationships between Atie and Louise. Other writers who imaginatively explore this theme are *Sections of an Orange* (2009) by Anton Nimblett. Yulisa Pat Amadu Maddy was one of the first authors to explore homosexuality in West Africa in his novel, *No Past, No Present, No Future* (1997), in which three young male friends explore their sexuality. Open discussions of same-sex relationships have increasingly entered the stories of writers of African and Caribbean descent, helping to break down the taboo of talking about this publicly.

29

DISCERNER OF HEARTS AND OTHER STORIES

OLIVE SENIOR

1995

Since her prize-winning *Summer Lightning* (1986), Olive Senior has led the field of Caribbean short fiction. Her distinctive, lyrical voice resonates in the stories that make up *Discerner of Hearts*. The secret lies in an alchemy of both writerly Standard English and spoken Jamaican Creole. Her stories are set mainly in rural Jamaica from the early 20th century onwards, demonstrating the range of Senior's voice and her deft control of several language registers. Just as the pitch of Senior's nuanced voice is varied, so too is the focus of each narrative and the point of view.

Together, these stories take us into a world peopled by dispossessed Black characters, others invested in colonial values and children rejected by biological parents. The background to these intimate stories is one of hidden poverty, racial hierarchy, social and racial inequities, and competing cultural and religious values. These tales are also haunted by the ghosts of Atlantic slavery. Those explored below fall within four themes: racialized relationships, social change, masculinities and mental health.

The stories – 'Discerner of Hearts', 'Zig-Zag' and 'Window' – share the first theme: racialized relationships signifying coloniality. For Senior, the knowledge that historically, proximity to whiteness afforded the possibility of upward mobility contributes to such exploration. 'Discerner' opens with young Theresa's actions as she embarks on an unspoken mission to petition Cissy's (her family's Black live-in maid) spiritual healer, 'Father' Burnham, on Cissy's behalf. Theresa is a middle child, acutely timid and a misfit within her 'backra' or 'turn-skin' (near-white) family. Her close relationship with Cissy motivates her to undertake this quest. She is undeterred by her parents' dismissal of Burnham's practice as evil or obeah. Moreover, observing the balmyard or space of healing that is meaningful to Cissy, Theresa's understanding of Cissy's world grows, and she discovers a new confidence. Cissy's voice is integrated so her hope surfaces that 'one day the world going spin the other way.' That is, that the Black majority will have access to more opportunity.

The title of 'Zig-Zag' evokes hair patterning that reveals racial mixedness. This story highlights interracial tensions within the domestic space. It centres the special relationship of the 'backra pickney' child, Sadie, with the family's Black maid, Desrine. Sadie senses racial division linked to her own 'coarse and curly' hair and overhears her family expressing fears that she was destined 'to turn *down*' or adopt undesirable

behaviours attributed to Black people. The markers of difference fuelling racial division in this Black and white family
include her straight-haired sister, Muffet, 'always turning red'
and their 'Mother Dear's' loaded references to their white,
English mother. Muffet is selected to live with high-ranking
relatives in Kingston in preparation for university and an illus-
trious future. Meanwhile, as Sadie discovers herself to have
skin 'darker than Papa's even', Aunt Mim whispers about 'when
blood gets mixed', and Sadie recognizes that even in her friendship with Desrine's daughter, race played its part.

'Window' is set in the early 20th century period of
Caribbean workers returning home from the Panama Canal
project. Racialized slavery becomes interlinked through the
plantation setting, in which two generations – old Ma Lou and
her mother – had served. On Dev's return to the plantation
with his hard-earned savings, we see the now-ruined plantation through his eyes, and in the light of his new wealth and
skills as a craftsman. When he proposes a solution to everyone's problem, namely that he buys the plantation, repairs it
and marries Brid(get), the mistress' younger daughter, his
grandmother is outraged. Having been trained into a system
in which Black people are subservient to whites, Ma Lou's
distress at the idea turns to fear that it could kill the mistress,
Miss Carmen. The perspectives of Dev and Brid suggest an
opening up to change as Brid finds the courage to open the
shutters that would allow eye contact with Dev.

'The Lizardy Man and His Lady' incorporate two of Senior's
favoured storytelling strategies: writing 'for the listener', and
presenting the child's view of events, which leaves the reader

continually reassessing the sparse details that are made available. Along with 'The Chocho Vine', these tales best illustrate the theme of socio-political change in Jamaican society. The narrator of the 'The Lizardy Man' is the servant, Gatha, whose charge is Shelly-Ann. The story begins with child characters, Shelly-Ann and Roger, whose violent play foreshadows the events that follow. The reader eavesdrops in order to follow the turn of events as Gatha gossips. The violent finale represents not just domestic tragedy, but presents a fragment of the crack-cocaine and drug wars – signalling a disturbing shift in national affairs.

'The Chocho Vine' also points to national change. The setting is Miss Evadney's garden, first planted when she was a new bride after the First World War. Now an old, bad-tempered widow, she has suffered many family disappointments. Her devotion to the chocho plant 'flourishing' in her garden and her only source of income, is key to the story. After her squatter and ganja farmer neighbours steal her chochos and she retaliates, her plant is deliberately cut. Miss Evadney connects this with the destruction of mountains caused by the mining of bauxite exported to America. The neighbour's warning, 'Socialist time now' and 'nothing nuh belong to you one any more', hangs over the story. It is suggested that within such political change, man's destruction of nature and the environment relates to colonial and national history, as well as the hurt inflicted on humans.

A third theme, masculinities, informs 'Swimming in the Ba'ma Grass'. Here, the narrator is the distraught wife, Miss Lynn, whose story – unknown to her – brings the two male characters fatally together. Her husband, Arnold, is a fisherman, amenable and humorous. The gun-toting policeman Shannon, known as the 'Enforcer', has a national reputation for violence. When at work in the police station, Shannon is sexually suggestive to Lynn, and she slaps him. An increasingly unhappy Lynn confides in her husband, without revealing the sexual harassment involved. Arnold's complaint to Shannon's superior provokes vengeance. While patriarchal society forms the larger context, Senior is noticeably writing against the grain of stereotyping that has applied to Jamaican men.

Finally, madness is central to 'You Think I Mad, Miss?', and the youthful character Isabella Francina Myrtella Jones. She has plenty to say and her narration becomes a dramatic monologue in the Jamaican vernacular. At the traffic lights on a busy road, she waits to address drivers forced to stop. In full flow, she bares her grievances about her betrayal by a lover, leading to disruption of her studies, loss of their baby and her detainment in a mental health institution. Questions concerning the truth of the story remain with the reader.

These intricate and diverse stories suggest a world being tested anew. Much of the richness of the writing lies in what is inferred and relate to the island's colonial history.

THE COLLECTION

This is Senior's third short story collection, published by Canadian publisher McClelland & Stewart in 1995. Many of these stories were also published in international journals. This collection, widely reviewed and well received, extends Senior's range with many tales focused squarely on adult protagonists.

THE AUTHOR

Olive Senior (1938–) is an award-winning Jamaican poet, fiction writer and editor. Her short fiction includes the Commonwealth Prize-winning *Summer Lightning* (1986) and *Arrival of the Snake Woman* (1989). Her poetry includes *Talking of Trees* (1986), *Gardening in the Tropics* (1994) and *Over the Roofs of the World* (2005). Her awards include the Jamaica Centenary Medal for creative writing; the Institute of Jamaica's Musgrave Gold Medal for her contributions to literature; Canada's Writers' Trust Matt Cohen Award for Lifetime Achievement; the OCM Bocas Prize for Caribbean Literature; and Poet Laureate of Jamaica. Her writing is widely translated.

IF YOU LIKE THIS, TRY...

Erna Brodber's *Myal* (1988) is a novel that fully treats the question of spiritual healing as explored in Senior's title story. Carmen Esteves and Lisbeth Paravisini-Gebert's anthology, *Green Cane and Juicy Flotsam* (1991), features women writers from across the Caribbean, translated from the many languages of the region.

SALT

EARL LOVELACE

1996

Alford George does not speak until he is six years old. As a late learner, he grows up as an outsider. Therefore, it is no surprise to the rural community where he lives that he plans to go to Britain to further his education. As the time for his departure draws near, he discovers that his parents are about to be evicted from their home as his father, Dixon, never purchased the land, despite having purchased bricks to build a home. Alford realizes that the money he had set aside to leave Trinidad, would now need to be used to buy the land to enable his father to finally build the house he had promised his long-suffering mother before she dies.

We follow the rise and fall of Alford from highly respected schoolteacher, a man who lost the love of his life – causing a mental breakdown – to respected, then demoted politician. He had worked hard to be a people's politician, but his intentions were misconstrued. His story is interwoven with those of other men, also outsiders in their families, who become involved in different levels of Trinidad politics from the national party and the opposition party, to local politics and community politics.

The story covers 19th-century Britain declaring Emancipation for African slaves transported to the Caribbean, yet their freedom was conditional. Lovelace traces the history of those who stayed in the Caribbean, but also those who tried to return to Africa, like Guinea John, who placed corn under his arms and jumped off the cliff to fly home. It is important for Africans not to eat salt if they have any hope of being able to one day fly home.

Despite all Lovelace's protagonists being male, there are women with strong characters who are catalysts for change in the lives of the male protagonists. Alford George loses fellow schoolteacher, Miss Ollivera, as he noticed her potential and encouraged her to leave Trinidad. She reluctantly leaves him behind, although equally frustrated that he decides not to go with her, as he believes his new role in life must be to nurture schoolchildren. As he enters politics, he falls into a relationship with Florence, who has waited for several years on her cousin's verandah for the right man to appear in her life. When Alford walks by one Easter Sunday, it is love at first sight for Florence and she slips into his life by pretending she needs a tutor, becoming the regular minute-taker at the meetings he holds to form a new political party. Another woman with a central role in her man's life is Myrtle, Bango's wife who has supported him through his self-financing of young people's marches for local holidays. It is Alford's commitment to provide Bango with public validation that leads to the downfall of his political career.

There is no specific career path for a successful politician and so it is with our odd mixture of politicians in *Salt* who all have good intentions and believe that Alford is their candidate to lead their new party. At the same time, we see the history of Trinidad through the eyes of different characters and perspectives, including the Indian indentured worker and the white plantation owner.

The beauty of the Caribbean combined with the complexity of its politics is wonderfully crafted and contrasted in this novel. *Salt* is the grounding of Pan-Africanism in the Caribbean as Lovelace reveals its origins in the first chapter and continues to weave Pan-African history, colonial history and slave history through the chapters, often subtly depicted through paintings. Salt is itself a symbol of the interconnectedness of Caribbean and African history.

Lovelace reflects the fears of all the ethnic groups on the island, and how they can be so easily divided to create an environment that produces uncertainty between each of them. Although Carnival is the one element in Trinidad that can bring people of different backgrounds together, here, it is twisted and used by a white priest to divide the people, and he initially succeeds. The plague of uncertainty is a dominant force, which runs through both individuals' lives and the development of a burgeoning nation.

One of the most important themes explored in *Salt* is the understanding and history of indentured labour, enslavement and colonialism. Britain is a main catalyst in these processes, as well as the British authorities' actions in which they presumed to repair past damages through reparations and political independence.

The impact of the Black Power movement of the 1970s is awak-
ened in Trinidad through the demand for lifestyle changes, such
as natural-hair styles, which filtered down, even to the villages.

Lovelace brings Trinidad to life through distinct language,
music and colour. The rhythms of the story unfold in the
combination of Trinidad English with Standard English, so
we can hear, as we read, the musicality of the tone, accent and
dialect of Trinidad. Music selections are played in the street
by shopkeepers to entice customers into their stores. Vibrant
colours of the vegetation are everywhere, even at Bango
Durity's ramshackle house in Cascadu, 'planted with bougain-
villea trees and red hibiscus fencing, orchids were growing on
tree stumps, ixora plants, a calabash tree and two coconut trees
near enough to string a hammock in between.'

Most of all, this story is about the Caribbean finding itself
as a nation; about Caribbean people recognizing their origins
and using this knowledge as a means to progress their country.
Lovelace hints that it was the Arawak and Carib, those who
were pushed to live in the hills when outsiders arrived, who
were the indigenous people on the island – and the only people
not making demands.

Despite being specifically about Trinidad, this story is reflective of other Caribbean islands with a multi-ethnic make-up
that is predominantly of African and Indian descent. By focusing on events that took place in history, to relate the period
of the novel, it determines Trinidad history as well as African
diaspora history. It is about acknowledging and embracing your
past and using the strength of that knowledge to enable a people
and a nation to move forward into a strong future.

THE NOVEL

Published by Faber & Faber in 1996, *Salt* received the
Commonwealth Writers' Prize in 1997 and was shortlisted for
the IMPAC Dublin Literary Award (1998).

THE AUTHOR

Earl Lovelace (1935–) is a Trinidadian author of six novels,
nine plays and musicals, a collection of essays and a collection
of short stories. His first novel *While Gods Are Falling* (1963)
won the BP Independence Award and *Is Just a Movie* (2011)
won the OCM Bocas Prize for Caribbean Literature (for fiction
and overall winner). His novel, *The Dragon Can't Dance* (1979)
is considered a classic. Some of his works have been produced
as films by his children. Lovelace has won several other awards,
including a Guggenheim Fellowship (1980) and a National
Endowment for the Humanities grant (1988). Other awards
include a Lifetime Literary Award from the National Library
and Information System, Trinidad (2012) and Honorary
Doctorate of Letters from UWI, St Augustine in Trinidad and
Tobago (2002).

IF YOU LIKE THIS, TRY...

A basic knowledge of Calypso is needed to understand
Trinidad and Tobago society, which *Kitch* (2018) by Anthony
Joseph provides. It is presented in a fictional biography of
the great Calypsonian Lord Kitchener, whose lyrics were

at the centre of the African diaspora in Britain, reflecting the Pan-Africanism that Lovelace unfolds in *Salt*. *The Ten Incarnations of Adam Avatar* (2005) by Kevin Baldeosingh explores Caribbean political history through Adam Avatar's 'past lives', which change every 50 years. *In the Castle of My Skin* by George Lamming (1953) concerns the politics of Blackness and exile. The richness of Trinidad Creole and dialect is distinct in books such as *The Mermaid of Black Conch* (2020) by Monique Roffey and the tragi-comic *Miguel Street* (1959) by V S Naipaul. The first novel to be published by a Caribbean writer of African descent was by one of the most well-known Caribbean writers and intellectuals of the 20th century, C L R James who wrote *Minty Alley* (1936). *Minty Alley* has been reprinted in the series curated by Bernardine Evaristo, 'Black Britain, Writing Back' (2021).

31

THE GOD OF SMALL THINGS

ARUNDHATI ROY

1997

Rahel and Esthappen are seven-year-old fraternal twins who are forcibly separated after a tragedy during the Christmas of 1969 at their grandparents' home in Ayemenem in southern India. Estha is 'returned' to live with his father in Calcutta while Rahel remains with Ammu, her mother. The twins do not see or hear from each other for almost 25 years, until Rahel arrives back at the family home after she is informed that her brother has 're-Returned' to their grandparents' home. Estha does not speak to anyone; he has shut out all of the noise in his head and goes for long walks. Ammu had returned to her parents' home after she left their alcoholic father. He beat her for refusing to have sex with his boss in order for him to keep his job. She is not welcome, as her father cannot believe that a white man would want to sleep with his daughter.

The children become friendly with Velutha, a Paravan ('untouchable'), who is of the lowest caste in their society. Velutha is a hardworking and talented carpenter at their pickle factory and is favoured by the family. Believing that as a divorcee, she has nothing to look forward to in the future, Ammu begins an affair with Velutha. It lasts for less than two weeks, until his father, Vellya Paapen, finds out and sets out to stop their liaison. The caste system is so pervasive and corrosive that Vellya, as a loyal Paravan to the family, would rather kill his son, than destroy the family name of his bene-factor. When Vellya Paapen reveals news of this affair, the grandmother and grand-aunt are so horrified at the shame and disgrace of Ammu allowing herself to be touched by a Paraven that they lock her in her room. Meanwhile, the twins run away, not realizing that their visiting cousin Sophie has followed them.

The depth of the closeness of the twins goes unnoticed, even by their mother. When Ammu castigates one, she is not aware of how deeply it affects the other and so when Rahel is rude to her mother at the cinema and she lashes out at her daughter that these hurtful words will make her love Rahel a little less, it leads to Estha keeping to himself the sexual abuse he has endured at the cinema, in the fear that his mother will love him a little less. They internalize every-thing she says in anger and their actions based on what she says, have tragic consequences.

Meanwhile, Ammu's spoiled elder brother Chacko, a former Rhodes Scholar at Oxford, has returned home to teach at the Madras Christian College. Before he left Britain he married Margaret, who left him for Joe soon after their daughter Sophie was born, but they remain on friendly terms. After Joe dies in an accident, Chako invites his ex-wife and Sophie to spend Christmas with his family in India. In another terrible accident, Sophie drowns when she follows the twins, while her parents are on a short trip to confirm their return flight to Britain.

The antagonist is their grand-aunt whose pet (family) name, ironically, is Baby; yet her actions are far from innocent as she coerces family members to turn against each other. She is the perpetrator who fabricates the story to the police that results in Velutha being arrested for kidnapping the twins, murdering Sophie and attempting to rape Ammu. When Baby's lies are discovered, she intimidates the twins into backing up her story and so betraying their friend, Velutha.

Another dominant theme which Roy explores is the plight of women through the structure of patriarchy and misogyny. When Ammu dies alone at a lodge, the refusal to bury her is 'for various reasons', including being a divorcee and allowing a Parven to touch her intimately. Domestic abuse is treated as an accepted part of married life and not a reason for leaving a husband. Ammu witnessed her mother being regularly beaten with a vase, leaving permanent scars on her head.

Arundhati Roy's distinctive style and voice make this novel memorable. Her lyrical descriptions of India's flora and fauna are lush and engaging. She enriches the narrative by weaving together Indian and Hindu culture. She also uses repetition to great effect. 'Things can change in a day' is a constant refrain, one that hints of what is to come and the change it will make in the lives of all concerned, leaving two dead and two children changed forever. It is often the small happenings that can change our lives.

Roy writes convincingly from the inner sanctum of the special psyche of twins, their special names for each other – Estha is 'Elvis the Pelvis' and Rahel is 'Refugee Stick Insect' – and children's made-up games, such as reading notices backwards to affect a different language. Up until the time that they reconnect with each other, Rahel has wandered through her marriage, to the extent that her husband who first thought her persona enthralling, finally found it perplexing and they divorce. Meanwhile, Esthappen wanders on his feet – taking long walks – and also in his mind, not speaking to anyone while walking nor when he reaches home, until he sees Rahel again.

The trauma that the twins suffer is a reminder of the fragility and impressionability of children in an adult world, but their reconnection enables them to become one again. Whether or not their re-joining at the end is incestual, is deliberately ambiguous.

Within the context of Indian history, politics and culture, Roy explains the complexity of the caste system in Kerala, which is different from the rest of the country and defines the levels of contact that Parvens could have with the rest of society. Her depiction of fundamental human rights issues and how they operate on an individual, family and national basis are explicitly, yet not overtly, explored through this story and this includes the fundamental right of being able to love who you want – and the consequences of that decision.

THE NOVEL

First published by India Ink in New Delhi (1997), Fourth Estate in the UK and Flamingo Books in the US, *The God of*

Small Things won Roy The Booker Prize in 1997. In 2019 it was included in the BBC Arts list as one of the 100 most influential novels in the past 300 years. It has been translated into many languages, and was released as a Bengali language film in 2017, receiving several international film awards.

THE AUTHOR

Arundhati Roy (1961–) has written two novels. Her second, *The Ministry of Utmost Happiness* (2017), was long-listed for the Man Booker Prize. Roy has also published nonfiction, including collections of interviews and essays, such as *The End of Imagination* (1998). She has received awards and honours for her activism work and socio-political writings, including The Lannan Foundation Cultural Freedom Award (2002), The Sydney Peace Prize (2004), The Sahitya Akademi Award from the government of India (2006) and the Norman Mailer Prize for Distinguished Writing (2011). She lives in India and was designated as one of the 100 Most Influential People in the World (2014).

IF YOU LIKE THIS, TRY...

Other books from women writers of South Asian descent include *The Things We Thought We Knew* (2017) by Mahsuda Snaith, which also involves close childhood friendships and the death of one of them. *Fasting, Feasting* (1999) by Anita Desai contrasts the traditional fates of girl and boy children raised in India alongside the dysfunction of Indian and American families. *The Inheritance of Loss* (2006) by Kiran Desai follows two generations of immigrants who try to simultaneously settle into the home that they return to and the new country that they reside in. *Kartography* (2001) by Kamila Shamsie, is a love story between best friends set in Pakistan. Books from other cultures that steep their writing in the tradition of their roots include *Kintu* (2014) by Jennifer Nansubuga Makumbi and *Tale of the Blue Bird* (2009) by Nii Ayikwei Parkes, who locates his story of a clash of cultures in Ghanaian village life, which has become exposed to modern technology.

TRUMPET

JACKIE KAY

1998

'Animals are luckier; they can bury their heads in the sand, hide their heads under their coats, pretend they have no head at all.' The unidentified narrator shares this with readers in the opening moments of this ground-breaking love story, *Trumpet*. Apparently under siege in their own home, they are being harassed by photographers, accompanied by a sound 'like the assault of a machine gun.' Who is this person? Why do they flee to rural Scotland, like a fugitive?

We learn that a shocking reversal of fortune has occurred. The family life shared by Millie, her husband, the virtuoso 20th-century British jazz trumpeter, Joss Moody, and their adopted son Colman is changed forever at Joss's death. It turns out that the secret Joss and Millie have kept throughout their long marriage is made public – Joss's body is biologically female.

This debut novel by Kay, is set in three locations: Glasgow, London and Kepper. *Trumpet* begins with Joss's death in 1997. His life is narrated from the viewpoints of Millie, Colman and Sophie Stones, the reporter and the book's third-person narrator. Millie's is the most prominent narration, beginning in Glasgow in 1955 when she first meets Joss. Although her family at first react with prejudice about her marrying a Black man, they turn up at the wedding anyway. This attitude to interracial couples is returned to towards the end of the book, when Edith Moore, Joss's mother, is introduced as an elderly woman who is losing her memory. Edith proudly displays her photograph of her Black husband, Joss's father, to a shocked home help. Millie's and Joss's marriage is one of a monogamous relationship with conservative gender roles. They are all they could ever want from each other.

Kay's inspiration for her transgender protagonist, Joss, was Billy Tipton, a white American jazz musician and the sensational publicity around his death. When he died in 1989, it was discovered that his body was female, although Tipton had lived as a man; at least five women considered themselves to have been his wife. Kay also combines themes of mixedness and adoption that are central to her famous poetry collection *The Adoption Papers* (1991) and adds another distinctive dimension to celebrate under-represented transgender lives.

Her telling of this sweeping love story mirrors the improvisational qualities of the jazz Joss plays in its radical, revisionary momentum and in his reconfiguring of sounds and rhythms. Joss's existence as a mixed-race, trans man and father transcends categorization, but heteronormativity is quickly reinstated by bureaucracy in processing his death. A doctor crosses out 'male' and writes 'female' on Joss's medical certificate. The Registrar, however, records 'Joss Moody' and not 'Josephine

Moore' on the death certificate. When the undertaker shows Colman his naked father's bodily 'truth' in the funeral parlour, this ignites the son's odyssey into toxic masculinity. Colman's rejection of his father turns to courting revenge for what he sees as his parents' betrayal of him, all tied up in a ghost-written book deal.

A barometer of Colman's journey to discover what it is to be a man, to be male, in the light of his father's body not being so, is the journalist–ghostwriter Sophie Stones. As she crassly ponders their book's likely success, she argues, 'Transvestite has a nice pervy ring to it' and then proceeds to run roughshod over Joss's life and legacy.

Joss's mixedness and queerness is evidence of an unregu-lated body, metaphorically and literally. In the face of the inev-itable public backlash, Millie valiantly struggles to keep alive her authentic memory of their marriage. Kay provides inti-mate portraits of the couple's life, including their daily ritual to bind Joss's breasts and dress his female form to become a man. Yet Kay allows the reader only certain, limited information to maintain her subject's privacy. This approach counteracts the journalist Stones' tabloid gaze and investigative prying. Stones locates Joss's mother, then sends Colman for a visit to extract a photograph of 'Josephine' for their book. However, this visit, reverses his planned revenge as he seeks redemption and reconciliation with his mother, and with the private and public worlds of Joss Moody and his legacy.

Trumpet is a tribute to the reach of diasporic history across gender boundaries. It reforms the expected limits to paternal, maternal and marital relationships. The novel is narrated from every perspective except Joss's, that is, until the final chapter. Joss leaves a letter to be read by Colman after his death, but his son has avoided this for the entire book. In the letter, Joss relates the origins of his father. The shadow of Scottish amnesia regarding its grim colonial legacy and the racism enacted on interracial relationships provide clear historical echoes. Naming Joss Moody's father, John Moore, recalls links to 'Moor', the Renaissance umbrella term that referred to anyone who was not white. When Colman finally reads his father's letter – the first time the reader 'hears' Joss's own voice – he learns about a portrait of Joss's father. This was painted by a local Scottish artist and titled 'Mumbo Jumbo' typical of the derogatory captions of many historical paintings of Black people. Joss writes that this title makes him 'more angry than anything I can remember' and so he passes on the resistance to racism to Colman.

The central characters' fidelity to each other ultimately weathers the storms of external judgement. Kay creates understanding, admiration and acceptance of individual lives, lived on 'their' own terms. *Trumpet* was adapted into a play for the Citizens Theatre Glasgow (2005) featuring Cathy Tyson as Joss and toured nationally. Attending rehearsals, Kay commented, 'It was particularly strange because the person playing Joss looks exactly as I imagined her in my head when I was writing the book. I was really scared to talk to her.'

THE NOVEL

Trumpet was first published by Picador in 1998 and Pantheon/ Random House in the US. It won the *Guardian* Fiction Prize

(1998), the Author's Club First Novel Award (2000) and the Transgender category, Lambda Literary Awards (2000). It was also shortlisted for the IMPAC Award in 2000.

THE AUTHOR

Jackie Kay (1961–) was Makar of Scotland (2016–21). Her highly praised volumes of poetry include: *The Adoption Papers* (1991), winner of the Forward Poetry Prize for best single poem in 1992; *Other Lovers* (1993), winner of the Somerset Maugham Award; *Off Colour* (1998); *Life Mask* (2005); *Fiere* (2011) and *Bantam* (2017).

Her fiction includes: *Why Don't You Stop Talking?* (2002), *Wish I Was Here* (2006) and *Reality, Reality* (2011). Her life writing includes a biography, *Bessie Smith* (1997) and a memoir *Red Dust Road* (2010), which was dramatized by Tanika Gupta (2019). Her plays include: *Chiaroscuro* (1986) revived at the Bush Theatre, London (2019) and the enslavement poem 'The Lamplighter' (2020), broadcast as a radio play. Professor of Creative Writing at Newcastle University, Jackie Kay was appointed MBE in 2006 and CBE in the 2020 New Year's Honours list for services to literature.

IF YOU LIKE THIS, TRY...

Luke Sutherland's *Jelly Roll* (1998), which examines the fluidity of race, sexuality and national identities. Liam, a gay, Black, Irish saxophonist joins a Glaswegian jazz band. The violence of the 'hard man' figure, racism and homophobia are unsparingly portrayed. Of Mununjali and Dutch heritage, queer Indigenous writer Ellen van Neerven's short stories *Heat and Light* (2014) represent young queer female, urban, experiences in Australia, by weaving together mystical and mythical voices and multiple perspectives and time-frames. The theme of Kei Miller's short story collection, *Fear of Stones* (2006), is that of being an outcast in an antagonistic social context. With hilarity and directness, he represents repression and homophobia alongside the characters' quests for love. Paul Mendez's *Rainbow Milk* (2020) is a trailblazing coming-of-age novel about race, class and sexuality as Jesse McCarthy flees his Jehovah's Witness upbringing in Wolverhampton after being 'outed', to immerse himself in 1990s London life.

THE YEARS WITH LAURA DÍAZ

CARLOS FUENTES

1999

This is rich fiction on a grand scale. Laura Díaz, born in 1898, is a Mexican granddaughter, daughter, wife, lover, political activist, companion of Frida Kahlo and much more. Telling the story of Laura through her great-grandson, Fuentes infuses the narrative with Mexico's 20th-century history, interlinked as it is with Europe and the US. The novel, which begins and ends in the US, speaks directly to some of the tensions of our times at a moment when the question of borders between the two countries remains fraught. This extraordinary fictional biography of an everywoman renders her contemporary story truly memorable.

It is 1999 and a Mexican photographer, Santiago Lopez-Alfaro, has arrived in Detroit. His assignment is to film a documentary about Mexican muralists in the US. Studying Diego Rivera's subversive mural at the Detroit Institute of Arts, he recognizes in one of the frescoes or wall-paintings, not only the face of Rivera's wife, the artist, Frida Kahlo, but also that of his great-grandmother, known only through family photographs. He describes Laura's eyes as 'mestizo, between European and Mexican.' In other words, he recognizes the interracial mix that typifies Latin America as, like him, Laura is Mexican.

Laura's life is reinvented through Santiago, remembering what Laura would remember, from early childhood with her German grandparents who settled in Mexico in the mid-1800s, to her experience of the Mexican Revolution. While historical events provide some impetus for what happens next in the narrative, key to the plot is the impact on Laura's life of four characters, each called Santiago. While the influence of her half-brother, the first Santiago, dominates much of her life, it is the fourth Santiago who (re)discovers Laura. What emerges is Laura's growing confidence in taking charge of her life, particularly in her later years. Crucially, the violence suffered by her grandmother, Cosima, when four of her fingers are cut off by a bandit demanding her rings, hangs over Laura's familial past. Violence also stretches into her future, principally through the political events that intrude on her family's life.

In contrast to her depiction in Rivera's mural in which she, like Frida, is male, Laura is the pivotal character who comes into her own as a woman in Fuentes' novel. Her life is portrayed from an aristocratic childhood on a coffee plantation headed by emigrants, Cosima and Felipe (Philip) Kelsen. Leticia, Laura's mother, is the couple's youngest daughter. In contrast to her sisters, Hilda and Virginia, Leticia does not look to her parents' homeland, Germany, for her future. The family includes Maria de La O, who is mixed-race. Together with Hilda and Virginia, they are Laura's three aunts who live together and contribute to

her stability. Their family saga is dominated by Cosima's stage-
coach incident. At 16, Leticia marries a widower, Fernando
Diaz, who already has a son, Santiago. Family is important in
this novel and as fortunes change, Laura's aunts play a support-
ive role, as much through her childhood as through the rocky
marriage that she makes.

It is only when Laura moves home at the age of 12, from the
plantation to the city, that she lives with her father and gets to
know her brilliant and intriguing, older half-brother, Santiago,
who is poised to begin university life. Their relationship is
deepened by his revolutionary leanings, which prove the more
alluring for having been made a binding secret between them.
The devastating impact of Santiago's youthful death by a firing
squad execution paves the way for Laura's search in life for
idealism within which activist politics is at play. When Laura
marries, it is to a prominent union leader, Juan Francisco.
Though his job confirms a commitment to the working classes
and the revolution, Laura becomes disillusioned with their
marriage. When she leaves the marital home, their children,
Santiago and Danton, are left with Leticia. Laura will find, in
the boarding house where her mother and aunts have relocated, the renegade priest, Elzevir Almonte. His connection as
secret matchmaker for her husband is revealed after his death.
Leticia will later persuade Laura to return to Juan Francisco. It
is in the wake of her first love affair, with Orlando, the furtive
friend of her half-brother, that Laura flees Mexico City. It is
only after Orlando has forced her to see the misery of the
City, that Laura becomes aware of a need 'to invent a world
for herself', one that not only comprises society ladies like her

friend, Elizabeth, whose hospitality she accepts. Watching Rivera at work and becoming involved with Rivera and Frida stems directly from this need to find a new world. She soon becomes Frida's companion and travels with them to Detroit.

The bohemian world that Laura cultivates includes artists and thinkers, poets, anarchists and revolutionaries as well as some, later in her life, fleeing from McCarthyism. At the same time, her lovers are influential men whose energies she draws upon as she comes to an increasing realization of herself and her needs. Deserted by her second lover, the Spanish exile, Jorge Maura, Laura's attention turns to her sons. Santiago, the namesake of her half-brother and with whom she shares a particular empathy and love of art, is frail and destined to die young. This is in direct contrast to her younger son, Danton, whose determination and avarice indirectly leads to further tragedy – the shooting of his son, who was named after his brother. Through all of this, Laura grows, first as a woman and later as a photographer.

The novel is set primarily within Mexico, with Leticia and Laura moving away from the Catemaco plantation because of marriage. Laura is 12 when they transfer to Veracruz. Though Detroit, Los Angeles and Lanzarote also feature in the novel, it is Mexico's 20th-century historical context that is important to the narrative. Her half-brother's 'bullet-pierced body in the living room', not only places Laura dangerously close to the Mexican Revolution of 1910, it transforms her life. Thereafter, decade after decade, Laura becomes witness in Mexico City to the modernization process that Mexico undergoes. Her marriage to Juan Francisco affords some eavesdropping at meetings. She harbours Carmela, the presidential assassin, and recognizes some of the faction fighting and the uncertainty of the outcomes involved. Laura's grandson, the third Santiago, dies as government forces fire on students at Tlatelolco, an event that Laura photographs in October 1968. Intriguingly, Laura emerges through her great-grandson's eyes as a contemporary champion, even as he is learning to negotiate the world beyond the country of his birth. That the two, decades apart, share a passion for photography is only partially why he holds her dear. Bloodline apart, she has negotiated change in ways that speak directly to another generation.

THE NOVEL

First published in Spanish by Alfaguara, Mexico, as *Los años con Laura Díaz* in 1999, the book was published in the English language in 2000 by Farrar, Straus and Giroux (translated by Alfred MacAdam). It was published in the UK by Bloomsbury (2002).

THE AUTHOR

Carlos Fuentes (1928–2012) is one of the most important and widely translated fiction writers in Mexico. His many novels and other works include *The Death of Artemio Cruz* (1962) and *Terra nostra* (1975), regarded as a masterpiece. His numerous awards range from the Mexican Writers' Center Fellowship of 1956 to the Miguel de Cervantes Prize, 1987; and the American Academy and Institute of Arts and Letters, 1986.

Fuentes, writing about the novel, asserts that he speaks 'as a writer in the Spanish language from a continent that is Iberian, Indian and mestizo, Black and mixed-race, Atlantic and Pacific, Mediterranean and Caribbean, Christian, Arab and Jewish, Greek and Latin.' His writing reflects the 'meeting place' of this culture which he claims, often through strategies of magic realism, which bring concerns with history into the present. His writing addresses what Walter D. Mignolo calls 'the darker side of Western modernity', with Latin American scholar, Susan Reid identifying Fuentes' work as 'signalling decolonial options' as 'roads towards the future'.

IF YOU LIKE THIS, TRY...

Michelle Cliff's, *Into the Interior* (2010), in which the female protagonist's travels far away from home allow her to explore not only her bisexuality, but a range of transnational relationships while she develops as an art historian, and Jorge Luis Borges' 1949 short story collection, *The Aleph* (Penguin Modern Classics, 2000).

THE BEST OF ALBERT WENDT'S SHORT STORIES

ALBERT WENDT

1999

Many of Wendt's stories in this collection concern Samoans, who live in Samoa or New Zealand. Wendt's traditional folk-tales and contemporary urban tales often include Samoan words without translation and as they re-occur, they become part of a new reading vocabulary.

'Heat' is the story of Maualuga, a traditional Samoan folk-tale, which warns young women of the risk of losing their virginity before marriage; they can simply be made to disappear. Maualuga is beautiful, a role model for other young women and adored by the children in her village. She shows no interest in any man who is interested in her, until a performance troupe pass through the village and a musician in the group seems to seduce her mind and body. After the troupe leave, her parents tell the village that Maualuga has to assist in a ceremony of funeral rites in another village. She is never seen again. As in other societies, when a woman is punished for making one mistake, she is erased from memory so that she does not taint anyone else.

In 'The Bird', Iona and his siblings have lost their parents in a car crash. He is determined that his grandparents' sacrifices in taking care of them in Auckland are repaid in full by making sure that they have all the comforts they need in their own home. Iona becomes a young patriarch and respected 'godfather' who keeps the extended family together, while building an empire so that second and third generation Samoan family members will not live in poverty. Iona castigates his sister for not contacting their grandparents, reminding her to contribute to their upkeep and instructing his younger brothers to change out of their stylish black fashion into less distinctive clothes. In other cultures, the owl is both a symbol of the underworld and of a spiritual connection to ancestors – all connections that can be linked to Iona in enabling the family to be economically and spiritually strong and unified. At the end of the story this is signified by Iona holding the owl aloft – connecting with past family and protecting those still living.

Although some stories are not specifically located within Samoan culture, they still highlight family dysfunction or the keeping of a secret within a family. In 'A Family Again', Paul returns home after almost a year away on one of his work trips and says he will never leave again. His son, Michael, hugs him in relief, knowing not to ask where he has been. The key to this secret is Paul's – and now Michael's – music teacher. She gives Michael a cassette tape and says it is their music repertoire but that he must promise not to play it until she instructs him to.

Hints from his father, about being able to tell him everything soon, leaves Michael in limbo, sensing the unease and the unknown as he waits, patiently.

In another story, 'Deliver us from Alice', a loving wife and husband prepare for an annual memorial for their daughter who died of leukaemia. John decides to celebrate her life instead of mourning it and, so, they always lay a place setting for Alice at the family meal to celebrate her birthday. Although it helped him to handle the grief in the early years, his wife wants this commemoration to stop. She tells him this after the dinner and he turns on her in intense anger, speaking to his wife in the same tone and using similar threatening words as he had done with his father 40 years before, when he saw him beat his mother. Janet fears for her life. Ironically, this action also seems to have evoked the change in John that she had been hoping for, in order for him to 'let go' – but for Janet, it is too late.

Stories set around family, especially those that take people to their breaking point, are stories that Wendt tells well. Patterns of misogyny and racism, prevalent in all cultures, are themes he also includes. The role of Christianity is often seen as a distortion of the indigenous Samoan culture.

Another story that does this, is 'The Eyes Have It' about Fiavaai who had been offered redundancy payment from his job. His wife, two daughters and his mother are confident that he will get another job easily. However, after 26 years of being a skilled worker at Sleeplite, the racist and patronizing reactions towards him when attending interviews are so humiliating that he prefers to settle into the role of house husband at home. He eventually feels redundant, 'like a woman'. One morning while making breakfast his coping mechanism deserts him and his temper snaps. From this point on, his family see him through different eyes.

Wendt's cast of characters resemble everyone's family, friends and neighbours, unlimited in age, gender and status. Something from earlier in their lives or something that is about to happen, erupts. This forever changes the way that their loved ones see them and they experience this in circumstances of navigating change between home, adopted home and new worlds. Equally, having created curiosity or mystery, Wendt knows the point at which the story should end.

Wendt's multi-layered short stories are important not only because of the knowledge of island culture that he shares, but equally for his demonstration that the full melting pot of lived experience is a shared one that it is often hard to forgive, forget and let go. Whether this is in the retelling of traditional tales or in contemporary family narratives, the breadth of his stories highlights Wendt as a master short storyteller.

THE COLLECTION

This book, published by Random House New Zealand in 1999, combines a series of works (some of which are written in patois): two short story collections, *Flying Fox in a Freedom Tree* (1974) and *The Birth and Death of the Miracle Man* (1986); two stories published in literary journals, 'A Genealogy of Women' (1991) and 'The Don'ts of Whistling' (1992), and six previously unpublished stories.

THE AUTHOR

Albert Wendt (1939–) is known as the godfather of Oceanic Literature. His novel, *Sons for the Return Home* (1973) is referred to as the first Pacific novel. He has written 12 novels, and a number of short story collections, poetry collections and anthologies of Pacific writing. Wendt has received several awards in recognition for his work in the creative arts including: the Goodman Fielder Wattie Book Award for *Leaves of the Banyan Tree* (1979) amd the Commonwealth Writers' Prize (Asia Pacific Region) for *Adventures of Vela* (2009). Other awards include the New Zealand Order of Merit for Services to Literature (2001), the Nikkei Asia Prize for Culture (2004), the Prime Minister's Award for Literary Achievement for Fiction (2012), Member of The Order of New Zealand (2013) and the Icon Award from the New Zealand Arts Foundation (2018).

IF YOU LIKE THIS, TRY...

Beyond the Rice Fields (2017 English edition) by Naivo and *Return to the Enchanted Island* (2019 English edition) by Johary Ravaloson were both translated by Allison M Charette. These are the first two novels by Malagasy writers to be published in English. Naivo's novel is set in 19th-century Madagascar and told through twin narratives of a slave and his master's daughter. Rovaloson's novel is a contemporary retelling of Madagascar's origin story.

   Eve Out of Her Ruins by Ananda Devi (2016, English edition translated by Jeffrey Zuckerman), follows the lives of four teenagers in a poor suburb of the capital of Mauritius, as they deal with issues of identity and sexuality in a world not seen by tourists. *This Is Paradise: Stories* by Kristiana Kahakauwila (2013) explores the realities of life in Hawaii and tensions between residents and tourists. *Island of Shattered Dreams* by Chantal Spitz (2013, English edition translated by Jean Anderson), presents a family saga during the period leading up to France using French Polynesia for nuclear testing in the mid-1960s. It is the first published novel by an indigenous Tahitian writer.

MONKEY BEACH

EDEN ROBINSON

2000

'We have an overdue vessel' crackles the Prince Rupert Coast Guard emergency radio channel, a message every family in a fishing community dreads to hear. For Lisamarie Hill and her parents the vast geographical size of Turtle Island – the First Nations' name for Canada and North America, and the remoteness of ancestral regions in the Pacific Northwest, compounds their fears about finding her younger brother. Seventeen-year-old champion swimmer Jimmy had reported boat engine trouble earlier and has now disappeared.

From the disquieting opening, readers are held in wonderful suspense as the narrative folds back into Lisa's reminiscences about her Kwakwaka'wakw or Haisla childhood and her family's seemingly erratic behaviour. This provides both humour and a sense of life's harsh realities, as viewed from a child's perspective. A heart-warming book, the first novel ever published by a Haisla writer, *Monkey Beach* is set on an Indian reservation in Kitamaat territory. The story is told through one extended family, Lisa and Jimmy, their Mum and Dad, Aunts Trudy and Kate and their children, Uncle Mick, Ma-ma-oo (their maternal grandmother), Great Uncle Geordie and his wife Edith.

Lisa's parents continually negotiate the disconnection between contemporary Canadian and Indian societies with Ma-ma-oo being a pivotal character. The mixing of the dominant culture with Indian ways is shared across generations, and Robinson ironically illustrates this hybrid lifestyle, 'We spent the last of the good weather tromping through bushes, picking berries and watching *Dynasty*.' As a holder of knowledge about what has been lost, precious childhood days are spent in Ma-ma-oo's company, learning the Haisla words for the many kinds of blueberries, 'pipxs'm' or 'sya'k°nalh'. Like the majority of readers, Lisa is unfamiliar with Haisla and so Robinson reinforces the point about the loss of indigenous languages and the accompanying loss of traditions and customs. As Lisa laments, 'even at one word a day, that was only 365 words a year, so I'd be an old woman by the time I could put sentences together.'

Charismatic Uncle Mick is her adored uncle, member of the American Indian Movement (AIM), Elvis Presley obsessed and deeply caring of his niece's welfare. He nicknames her 'monster' and encourages all kinds of resistance to authority – parents and otherwise. Lisa rebels at school when she is asked to read a history book claiming her Indian ancestors ate people as 'religious sacrifices', correcting it by quoting Ma-ma-oo, who had said it was as real as 'drinking Christ's blood at Communion'. Taken to the principal's office she fights back, singing one of her uncle's revolutionary songs and Mick frames the rebuking note that the teacher sends home.

Comedic aspects of a child's resistance to colonial values are charming, but interwoven with an edginess. Robinson makes further parodic references to cannibalism when Lisa sinks her teeth into the schoolyard bully during a fight, even drawing blood – but this is also a precursor to something more chilling, as Lisa later describes sexually abused and sexual abuser Josh.

The enchantment of *Monkey Beach* is in no small part attributable to the way in which Robinson renders the spiritual understanding of origins and history through her characters' relationships with fauna, flora and land as being intrinsic to wellbeing. However, the industrialized world changes maps and environments. This means the adaptations of the Haisla people increasingly become compromises, as successive Canadian governments fail to maintain treaties and protect ancestral territories and inhabitants. Holding onto the precious natural ecology and holding onto indigenous languages and customs go hand in hand. The impending signs of threat are everywhere: the Haisla's staple diet the oolichan fish have almost disappeared from the rivers, the logging industry has submerged the best crab beds and the Alcan aluminium smelter detrimentally affects the ecosystem.

Lisa grows up in a loving home, but she spirals down into drug and alcohol dependency in Vancouver after the tragedy of Uncle Mick's death. However, there is something special that marks Lisa out from everyone else. She has premonitions, sees spirits and communes with her dead relatives. A recurring figure who visits her is a small man with red hair, voices of ghosts and birds speak to her. The mythical B'gwus 'the wild man of the woods' is ever-present in her aura.

Yet while Lisa can prophesy death, she has no access to the old songs and ways of the medicine people that have been lost. She understands that she must be mediator between her people and the spirits, and yet, as Ma-ma-oo counsels her on the dangers – without cultural guidance and knowledge, will she survive her gift?

Robinson's novel points to what is not recoverable, as much as to the joy of present-day kinship bonds for the Haisla people. Lisa is determined to find Jimmy – or his body – and the plot twists and turns, back and forth, as each new piece in the puzzle is exposed. This is a story that sparkles with those exquisite childhood moments that become understood from a different perspective as an adult. While we have the evocation of an arcadia, modern encroachments fringe the perimeter of that awareness. The novel has been described as a psychological thriller tinged with supernatural elements, but is it simply this? Robinson throws down the challenge to view the world through a Haisla mystical lens, and the rewards for doing so are many and memorable.

The film of *Monkey Beach* directed by Cree woman Loretta Todd with an all-Indigenous cast, premiered at the Vancouver International Film Festival in 2020 and, like Robinson's literature, is considered a landmark for Indigenous film-making. She presents a call to halt the destruction of biodiverse environments and celebrates the traditional custodians of the land, as they attempt collective repair from the rapaciousness of colonial history which they have survived.

THE NOVEL

Published by Little, Brown Book Group in 2000, it was short-listed for The Scotia Giller Prize and the Governor General's Literary Awards (2000). The novel was also voted a *New York Times* Notable Book of the Year (2000) and the winner of the Ethel Wilson Fiction Prize (2001).

THE AUTHOR

Eden (Victoria Lena) Robinson is a member of the Haisla and Heiltsuk First Nations of Turtle Island, Canada, due to her mixed parentage. Her debut collection of stories, *Traplines* was awarded the 1996 Winifred Holtby Memorial Prize (UK). Her novels include: *Blood Sports* (2006); a memoir, *Sasquatch at Home* (2011); a trilogy: *Son of a Trickster* (2017), shortlisted for the 2017 Scotia Giller Prize and adapted as a television series for CBC television in 2020, *Trickster Drift* (2018) and *Return of the Trickster* (2021). She is recipient of the 2016 Writers' Trust Engel/ Findley Award and lives in Kitamaat Village, British Columbia.

IF YOU LIKE THIS, TRY...

Member of the Stó:lō Nation, Lee Maracle's autobiography *Bobbi Lee: Indian Rebel* (1975) was one of the first Indigenous works published in Canada. In her novel *Ravensong* (1993), set in the 1950s Pacific Northwest, teenager Stacey is caught between traditional life and white-dominant society, and the trickster, 'Raven' is a bridge for communication and reconciliation.

Cree writer and registered member of the Barren Lands First Nation, Tomson Highway's *Kiss of the Fur Queen* (1998) tells of two Cree brothers: Champion and Ooneemeetoo Okimasis. Victims of Canada's notorious Indian Residential Schools programme, they are removed from their family, forbidden to speak their language, abused by the priests and their names are changed. The brothers try to build a future in Winnipeg in the dominant culture's terms, watched throughout their lives by the trickster figure, the Fur Queen. Treaty 1 Territory, Red River Métis author Katherena Vermette's *The Break* (2016) is a story passed between its characters. Stella, a Métis woman, witnesses a violent crime from her window in a desolate borderland area known as The Break. The narrative draws in 11 different perspectives to unfold a moving tale of how a community's women survive violence.

Joshua Whitehead is an Oji-Cree member of the Peguis First Nation in Manitoba and author of Indigiqueer novel *Jonny Appleseed* (2018). Jonny, a cybersex worker, pursues a frantic existence until the week before he returns home for his grandfather's funeral, when he pieces together the mosaic of his life inspired by his beloved *kokum* (grandmother).

36

THE EMPEROR'S BABE: A NOVEL

BERNARDINE EVARISTO

2001

Fittingly prefaced by Oscar Wilde's aphorism 'the one duty we owe to history is to rewrite it', this is a tragic but exhilarating tale, told as a novel in verse, charting the misadventures of the go-getting young Nubian-Roman woman Zuleika from her childhood to her death. Set in 3rd-century Britannia, we meet Zuleika in the weeks before she turns 19. Written from an African-Roman perspective, Evaristo portrays an ancient moment of colonization – where Britannia is merely part of the Roman Empire – well before the later four centuries of the British Empire.

Archaeological findings of African women, such as the Beachy Head Lady in Sussex or the high-born Ivory Bangle Lady buried in York, have turned the 'Romans in Britain' story on its head. So too does *The Emperor's Babe*, gloriously and uproariously rewrite any notion of multicultural Britain as a post-war phenomenon. This ancient classical setting purposefully revises the known narratives of enslavement, colonization and post-war migration as being inevitable motifs for Black British writers.

Zuleika's parents had migrated from another region of the Roman Empire, from what is now Sudan, to improve their prospects. In a world where husbands were free to treat their wives as they pleased, sometimes with terrible consequences, we soon find out that every girl has her price as currency in marriage. We follow Zuleika's short trajectory from sexual innocence to marital violation, at 11 years of age, to Senator Lucius Aurelius Felix, three decades her senior; from poverty to wealth; from semi-literacy to high culture, and ultimately, to catching the eye of Emperor Septimius Severus himself. It might not end well, but along the way we meet a cavalcade of memorable characters: with Alba, Zuleika's best friend as 'the wild girls of Londinium', her Celtic slaves who constantly undermine her, Zuleika's minder – the duplicitous Tranio, appointed by Felix to spy on her, and the outrageous drag club owner Venus, a transgender entrepreneur who stages poetry slams.

The novel begins with Zuleika already married and deserted for months on end by Felix, who is in another part of the empire with his mistress and children. It traces, through Zuleika's perspective, how this young girl from a family so poor that she wears rags on her feet during winter is elevated to the wife of a senator. Zuleika has ambitions to being a poet, has elocution lessons, wears the finest clothes, but something is missing – love. Evaristo offers a panoply of Roman cultural spaces: the villa, the baths, the theatre, the gladiatorial arena, and Zuleika experiences them all. Her comet-like existence achieves the heights of being the Emperor's mistress, but crashes to earth when she refuses her Celtic slaves, Aemilia and Valeria, manumission and they reveal her adultery to Felix. From that point Zuleika's fate is sealed.

According to Tacitus's *Annals*, Londinium in Britannia Superior was renowned for its riches, and trade. Evaristo represents such internationalism derived from Roman conquests spanning 'Roma, Neapolis, Alexandria, Antoch, Carthage, Jerusalem', as well as a gateway to local life, Thameside.

Not only does *The Emperor's Babe* imaginatively excavate a hidden history, but it also upends just what to expect in reading a historical novel by propelling it into new territories, armed with the dynamics of spoken-word poetry, dramatic monologue and monodrama. Eighty per cent of English is derived from Latin roots. In using the fundamental elements of Latin that any English speaker can grasp, the book offers a reminder of what lies beneath the great colonizing and neo-colonizing language of English by means of its ancestor, which remains embedded in what is said and read. Evaristo's witty use of colloquialisms, slang, doggerel and graffiti dissolves Latin's elitist associations to craft an exuberant fusion of ancient and contemporary voices.

The design of the text is as varied as the heroine's fortunes. The typeface is Times Roman (naturally), and visual puns abound with 'roman' numerals. Capitalized chapter titles such as 'ABYSSUS ABYSSUM' ('One Depravity Leads to Another') or text-speak tattoos create an ongoing shared joke with those who can spot the references such as, *'Mi & Tu: IV Ever II Gether'*.

The irreverent mixing of vernacular and slang below, parodies gentility and pretention, and simultaneously ventriloquizes the socially elevated, but unprepared, Zuleika. It implies a provocative subtext of the 'Anglo-Nigerian' 'woman' author, satirically trespassing on hallowed classical territory:

> *Zuleika accepta est.*
> *Zuleika delicata est.*
> *Zuleika bloody goody-two shoes est.*

The joyful impudence also confronts the weighty subject matter of child brides, rape within marriage, transgender lives, the female as commodity and femicide. Zuleika's vulnerability because she is female is central to the tale. While the register is deceptively light-hearted, Evaristo never lets readers forget the tragedy of girls' bodies harmed throughout history as Zuleika reflects more than once in the novel on being a child-bride.

The droll and acerbic moments are many, even in gory situations. Zuleika's visit to the gladiatorial games creates a series of reality checks, beginning with her fantasy of being publicly acknowledged by her lover Severus, which is denied. She is disillusioned by the gladiators: 'I had expected the famous Uber-hunks with pumped-up biceps and sex-packs', whereas, in fact those before her are poor, old and starving. Pregnant women are fed to the lions in an episode that cannot fail to horrify contemporary readers.

Ultimately, Evaristo constructs a wry counterpoint to the 'Lady' graves. Zuleika will never be accepted as a lady despite her elocution, education and grooming – a fact of which she is unfailingly reminded. Yet at her orders, she will be buried ennobled in exquisite violet robes with braided hair threaded with gold. She demands, 'don't forget my jet afro pick, tweezers and nail file.' She could have the hypothetical last laugh about any future interpretations archaeologists might make about her remains. *The Emperor's Babe* is a unique literary treatment of African diasporic heritage, a novel in the service of irretrievable history, relayed by an unforgettable heroine.

THE NOVEL

First published in English by Hamish Hamilton in 2001, the novel was also winner of the NESTA Fellowship 2003, named Book of the Year by the *Sunday Times* and *Telegraph*, and included in *The Times*'s 100 Best Books of the Decade, 2009.

THE AUTHOR

Bernardine Evaristo MBE, OBE is a British-born woman of Nigerian (Yoruba), Brazilian, white English, Irish and German descent. On the back cover of her landmark 2019 Booker Prize-winning novel, *Girl, Woman, Other* (2019) she describes herself as 'Anglo-Nigerian'. She grew up in Woolwich, south London and after drama training at Rose Bruford College (she is now President), she co-founded Theatre of Black Women. Initially a poet and playwright, Evaristo is author of seven novels (two in verse) including *Lara* (1997), *Soul Tourists* (2005), *Blonde Roots* (2008) and *Mr Loverman* (2013), as well as a poetry collection: *Island of Abraham* (1996). She is co-editor of *TEN:*

New Poets (2010) and a prolific book reviews writer. She is Professor of Creative Writing at Brunel University, London and her memoir, *Manifesto: On Never Giving Up* was published in 2021.

IF YOU LIKE THIS, TRY...

Two verse narratives that grip the heartstrings with uncharacteristic perspectives on growing up in Britain are Yrsa Daley-Ward's *The Terrible* (2018) and Rahila Gupta's *Don't Wake Me: The Ballad of Nihal Armstrong* (2019). These offer tales of bravura and striving against the odds in dazzling poetic prose. Fred D'Aguiar's *Bloodlines* (2000) represents an interracial relationship in America's Civil War and S I Martin's novel *Incomparable World* (1996) is a rollicking adventure featuring Buckram, a Black soldier from the losing British side in the American War of Independence living by his wits in late-18th-century London. Sara Collins's magnetic Gothic novel *The Confessions of Frannie Langton* (2019) charts the fortunes of an enslaved girl, relocated from Jamaica to Georgian London, straight into a new household with a mesmeric Madame. Frannie then finds herself on trial for a double murder she cannot remember committing.

37

DOGSIDE STORY

PATRICIA GRACE

2001

For ancient Indigenous cultures, emotional and environmental realities are indistinguishable from each other. *Dogside Story* places the distinct Māori and Pākehā understandings of the world in a constellation of identities and histories. These are shown as being forced together in the colonial aftershock of contemporary Aotearoa (the Maori name for the islands named New Zealand under British colonization). Set at the beginning of the second millennium, the date 2000 represents a symbolic threshold for the remote rural region, Dogside, whose way of life is threatened by tourism and development.

Patricia Grace heartrendingly conjures the difficult negotiations between the compromise of traditions and the maintenance of personal integrity over economic gains. These negotiations relate to themes of settler land appropriation versus Māori cultural preservation, and the taboo topic of incest. Her precise prose style interweaves the scars of survival from past battles with the challenges her characters face in the present.

Opening with an epic origin story, we learn how two coastal tidal river communities formed. Northside is conservative and competitive, known as Godside due to its number of churches, while Southside is fun-seeking and resourceful, known as Dogside due to the number of dogs. We discover that Dogside evolved out of an age-old quarrel between two sisters, Ngarua and Mareanohonoho, over the custodianship of their late brother's canoe. The narrator sets out the personal beginnings of a historic feud, that becomes a sustained community rivalry, and declares, 'From now on the story becomes one-sided. It favours Dogside.'

Grace establishes reader allegiances early on in the novel in anticipation of the plot's shock lines. The purpose of this is to forestall judgement, to create an understanding of the motives of the elders Tini, Wai, Arch and Atawhai, the following gener-ations, Amiria and Babs (the Sisters), their nephew Te Rua and his daughter Kiri, known as 'Kid' and her mother, his sister, Ani Wainoa. We gradually find out the various perspectives around Kid's birth, first revealed through the eyes of 14-year-old Rua and later in Arch's remorse at the community's neglect of two siblings living remotely with old Blind that led to it happening.

Twenty-four-year-old Rua is the novel's central conscious-ness, but the story is told through an omniscient narrator who is involved with the communities, an insider who also offers various angles upon the events. Consumed with grief over his mother's death and the loss of his leg, which has been ampu-tated, the story begins with Rua assuming his paternal respon-sibility for his daughter Kiri, born ten years before. Kiri's mother disappeared after her birth and lives 'on the other side of the world'. However, his mission to claim Kiri back from his neglectful and litigious aunts – the Sisters – who have been raising her, requires him to reveal a terrible secret that could tear apart his community. Meanwhile, Grace has a surprise in store. Readers cannot fail to be moved by the love, care and determination Rua shows and the candour with which he relates the origins of Kiri's birth, even though this might be shocking. At the revelation Wai concludes, 'we know, but it can't be told' and the elders work to protect Rua's fatherhood of his daughter in the light of its circumstances.

While the Sisters take the custody case to the Pākehā courts, the community hold a *hui*, or assembly, to declare support for Rua and to tell the Sisters to stop. Tini gives weighty advice, 'Don't carry the bruises or pass on the bruises.' The ensuing revelations about the Sisters' mother and their brutal upbringing demonstrates the power of the *hui* as a unique Māori compassion-led decision-making process that tries to understand longstanding reasons behind a person's behaviour and achieve consensus. Disabled characters are central presences in Grace's novels, they are portrayed as full participants in their communities; a contrast to the ableist settler attitudes and hierarchies of competition.

Dogside Story represents the important power of the land as a connective force for each individual family, where humans and non-humans are bound together, 'People long for the earth. Even if it's concreted over.' British colonization imposed systems of governance, land acquisition and treaties that ruptured the functioning of Māori life, and were fortified by Christianity and religious conversions. 'The deep-rooted connections across generations of passing on land along with the profound ties between kinship groups are shown in contrast with the modern paperwork of Pākehā 'ownership' as being risible in comparison. Tini notes, 'Before all the new laws were made land was for everyone.'

Grace intentionally omits a glossary as a resistant stance towards the culturally dominant English, allowing readers to encounter the book on its own terms. Māori people were punished for speaking their language by the colonizing British. By the time of the author's generation, it had become a foreign language in its own land. Learning Māori as an adult, Grace's language activism is most clearly evident in her landmark novel *Potiki* (1986). After its publication, Māori became an official language of New Zealand.

Shame was a key component of colonial rule, through the denigration of Indigenous customs and the imposition of English 'civilizing' systems upon colonized people. Grace unflinchingly represents the damage that internalized shame inflicts upon her Māori characters, and how this is inherited across generations. Humour and absurdity in the novel help convey an unsentimental testimony of the strategies and adaptions that characters make to survive and maintain the unity of the *whanau* – the extended family. It leaves us with hope and admiration for the resilience that has enabled contemporary reclamations and assertions of Māori culture to centrally define the nation's future.

THE NOVEL

First published in English by Penguin Books in 2001, Grace's novel was longlisted for the Man Booker Prize (2001), the *Guardian* Book Prize (2002) and the IMPAC International Literary Prize (2002). It was also shortlisted for the Montana New Zealand Book Awards (2002) and was winner of the Kiriyama Pacific Rim Fiction Prize (2001).

THE AUTHOR

Patricia Grace (1937–) is of Ngati Toa, Ngati Raukawa and Te Ati Awa descent. She occupies a unique position in post-invasion Aotearoa's literary history as the first female Māori writer to have her fiction published. She has written more than 20 books across genres. Her debut short story collection *Waiariki* (1975) won the PEN/ Hubert Church Award for Best First Book of Fiction.

Her second novel *Potiki* was translated into a number of languages and won the 1987 New Zealand Book Award for Fiction and the German LiBeraturpreis in 1994. It was republished as a Penguin Modern Classic in 2020. *Tu* (2004) won the Deutz Medal for Fiction and Montana Award in 2005. *Chappy* (2015) was translated into French in 2018. She has received international recognition and numerous honours including the Queen's Service Order in 1988, and an honorary D.Litt from Victoria University in 1989. In 2007, Grace received a Distinguished Companion of the New Zealand Order of Merit for her services to literature and was named the 2008 laureate of the Neustadt International Prize for Literature.

IF YOU LIKE THIS, TRY...

Keri Hulme's 1985 Booker Prize-winning *The Bone People* (1983), which infuses a Māori sensibility into the European novel form. She is of English, Scottish and Kāi Tahu descent. Her novel shows how the bleakest of human intimacies grounded in trauma and abuse can be redeemed through love and spiritual recognition drawn from Māori myth and legend. *Rangatira* (2011) by Paula Morris (of Ngāti Wai and English descent) restores Māori presences in imperial history. Her novel evocatively reimagines Ngāti Wai chief Paratene Te Manu who, while having his portrait painted, recalls his visit to London in 1863 to meet Queen Victoria, a true event which is magically retold in fiction.

Tahitian author Célestine Hitiura Vaite's *Frangipani* (2006) vividly and wittily renders cross-generational differences between Materina and her daughter amid fears that traditional Tahitian ways are becoming irrelevant to young people's lives. The poetic, dream-like prose of Samoan author Sia Fiegal's prize-winning *Where We Once Belonged* (1996) sees the teenage protagonist Alofa come to terms with cultural clashes and generational differences. This is an uncompromising coming-of-age tale of Samoan womanhood in a close-knit community, and debunks white anthropological 'knowledge' about Polynesian customs once and for all.

SHELL SHAKER

LEANNE HOWE

2001

Two violent deaths, over two centuries apart, form an unsolved mystery, which is the backbone of this gripping novel. The parallel stories about leadership, greed and corruption focus on the fates of two Choctaw chiefs, Red Shoes killed in 1747 and Redford McAlester killed in 1991. At the heart of both chronicles is the Billy family, whose women have been the anchors of the Choctaw nation for centuries as peacemakers, who 'make things even'. However, Susan Billy, mother to Adair the stockbroker, Auda the academic activist and Tema the actor, has together with Auda admitted to murdering McAlester.

LeAnne Howe opens a window on Choctaw life, her people's language and spiritual power sustained across the generations in the face of annihilating settler politics. She also portrays the beauty of bonds and traditions that equip people for leading successful lives in the contemporary world. By implication, mainstream systems could learn much from First Nations peoples' governance and counsel.

Shell Shaker is composed of chapters of events from these two separate periods to carry readers into Native American sensibility. It charts the adaptation of customs and rituals, and the realities of living in a land catastrophically transformed by invading Europeans. This is a tale of survival and transcendence of these consequences, and of strength derived from original kinship ties, human and non-human. The narrative immerses us in ceremonies ranging from bone picking to shell shaking, within a context of traditions, lineages and communal responsibilities.

Howe's novel opens in 1738 during a period of warfare. We immediately understand the women's peacemaker roles in the Inholahta Choctaw clan. Shakbatina tells of her grandfather; Tuscalusa prepares to entrap the enemy, the Osano who are led by Hispano de Soto (blood sucker). Meanwhile, Tuscalusa's grandmother becomes the first Shell Shaker, dancing for four days and nights with turtle-shell anklets until the ground is stained with her blood. The spirit of the Autumnal Equinox, Itilauichi, recognizes her sacrifice and saves her people, while Tuscalusa's deception having failed, the men are slaughtered and mutilated by the Osano clan.

Howe explores the ways in which the Choctaw nation's election of leaders can produce an individual who fails to withstand the corrupting forces they need to engage with for survival, sometimes even contributing to his own people's eradication. The chiefs who become corrupted are punished. Red Shoes became Osano-like in his mind and was murdered in 1747; this links to McAlester who seeks Mafia money to establish a casino and is murdered in 1991. It is the cross-generational power of the Shell Shaker women who will solve the mysteries of the two chiefs' deaths.

Unforgettable characters populate this novel, including real historic figures such as the founder of New Orleans, Jean Baptiste Le Moyne Sieur de Bienville. The late-18th-century chapters are unsparing in their detail of gruesome practices and derail any notion of settler claims of Indian 'savagery'. These practices are shown to be the result of longstanding processes of negotiation and customs that are clearly understood and shared by the people of each Native American clan community, not reactive acts of settler violence and dispossession.

Ilapintabi performs an Osano execution on a dead body, accompanied by a song, so the clan can have advance notice of what to expect if captured, to cleanse them of fear. Shakbatina witnesses this and later offers herself up to the Red Fox village to save her daughter who is accused of murdering a Red Fox woman. She seeks the agreement of her community first. They must sanction her action as a judicious means of preventing warfare for their collective future. As a Shell Shaker woman, Shakbatina offers her life to keep peace between the clans.

After being killed, Shakbatina narrates her last moments, as her 'thoughts escape into the wind'. She travels as a witness across six generations, 'marking time, daughter by daughter' until 1991. Howe invites readers to consider the limits of interpretation and alternative cosmologies. Rationalist European thought cannot explain the time travelling and belief in multiple embodiments of people across periods and places.

The two pivotal deaths intersect through dreams, visitations and spirits. Howe's representation of the fluid relationship between Choctaw past and present avoids the cliché of redemptive pre-contact society and its functioning as simply the alternative to white settlement. Instead, she helps us understand how the heritages of First Nations peoples are central to different groups mixing without conflict, not as marginal or ahistoric.

But co-citizenry is not the equivalent to de-colonial thinking. The Choctaw people, uprooted and dispossessed of their lands in what was renamed as Louisiana, were relocated under the 'Indian Removal Act' in 1830 to what is contemporary Oklahoma creating 'The Trail of Tears', so named after thousands of Choctaw deaths from starvation and disease.

Howe infuses her text with Choctaw language, frequently untranslated to emphasize the existence of two universes. It keeps non-speakers on their interpretive toes, always on the boundary of a culture to which they might not belong – yet immersed in the story and involved in the characters' fates.

The genealogy of kinship, human and non-human, is wrought in detail in a context where rupture, killing and dispersal were enacted by white settlers, so 'The spirits moved away, shed their skin that bound land and people together.' In 1991 the spirits are thought to have returned, 'to pick a fight', as a 50-mile-long prairie fire destroys farms, churches, highways and other evidence of white occupancy. This is a universe that exists beyond European imported and imposed controls of laws and property ownership.

Howe's plot pits Western European rationalism against Choctaw received wisdom. To what degree will a contemporary reader assert one worldview over the other? Can both co-exist? How can First Nations sovereignty be acknowledged and applied to modern life, especially in care for the environment? Prepare to be gripped by a tale of how justice is sought in a novel encompassing past and future, when 'day and night were in perfect balance, and Indians had all the luck.'

THE NOVEL

Published by Aunt Lute Books, San Francisco in 2001, the novel's accolades include winning the Before Columbus Foundation's American Book Award (2002).

THE AUTHOR

LeAnne Howe (1951–) is an enrolled citizen of the Choctaw nation. Her documentary screenplay *Indian Country Diaries: Spiral of Fire* aired on PBS in 2006. *Evidence of Red: Poems and Prose* (2005) won the Oklahoma Book Award. Her memoir, *Choctalking on Other Realites* (2013), won the Modern Languages Association (MLA) Prize for Studies in Native American Literatures, Cultures, and Languages. In 2020, Howe co-authored a trilingual (English, Irish and Choctaw) chapbook of poems, *Singing, Still: A Libretto for the 1847 Choctaw Gift to the Irish for Famine Relief* with Doireann Ní Ghríofa. She is Eidson Distinguished Professor of American Literature, University of Georgia.

IF YOU LIKE THIS, TRY...

Anishinaabe descendant Carter Meland's novel, *Stories for a Lost Child* (2017) in which the mysterious gift of a box of writing by her grandfather enables teenager, Fiona, to trace her Anishinaabe heritage through the weight of family silence, finding a route back to cultural belonging.

Louise Erdrich, an enrolled member of the Turtle Mountain band of Chippewa Indians won the Pulitzer Prize in 2021 for *The Night Watchman: A Novel*. It is set in the 1950s in the shadow of US Congress's new 'emancipation' bill that threatens Native American rights and overturns treaties. The novel centres on the actions of Thomas, a Chippewa council member, and Patrice, determined to find her sister in Minneapolis, in the context of their impoverished reservation community.

José Maria Arguedas is of Spanish and Quechua Indigenous descent, and represents Andean life in Peru from the perspective of oppressed communities. *Los rios profundas* (1958) was translated into English as *Deep Rivers* (1978). The novel traces Andean culture through the travels of Ernesto and his quest to reclaim Quechua culture and Inca heritage.

39

THE KITE RUNNER

KHALED HOSSEINI

2003

Amir and Hassan grew up together in the same Kabul house-hold as childhood friends, despite being from different ethnic backgrounds. Amir, from the dominant Pashtun group, lives with his father Baba in the newly affluent Wazir Akbar Khan district. Baba's servant Ali, of the Hazar ethnic group was adopted by Baba's father as an orphan, is disabled and lives in the servant quarters, with his son Hassan.

Born a year apart, both boys lost their mothers at birth. Amir's mother died in childbirth, while Hassan's mother ran off five days after giving birth to him, to join a travelling troupe of performance artists. Still, Ali feels blessed that he has a son. The story manoeuvres us through a series of traumatic departures. Ali and Hassan move from the only home they have known to live with a cousin in the north of the country, Baba and Amir escape from Afghanistan to a new life in the US, and finally, Hassan's son Sohrab, who departs from Afghanistan with Amir.

Baba is like the genial godfather in his community. He is Amir's role model and hero, and Amir dislikes having to share the precious time he has with him, particularly with Hassan. As Hassan was Amir's servant and companion, Baba ensured that he treated him almost like his own son at times. Amir's pain is so deep at not feeling that he is good enough for his father, that he is willing to sacrifice Hassan to make Baba proud of him. Hassan senses this and in his loyalty to Amir, as he is the best 'kite runner' in town, assures Amir that he will run and capture the last kite flying as a trophy at any cost, and he does – at a severe cost to himself. Kite flying, or 'gudiparan bazi', is a significant feature of Afghani culture, and becomes a symbol of love and loyalty – a key factor at the end of the book which signifies change for the future.

To his father's dismay Amir is more like his intellectual mother, as he enjoys reading books more than watching sport. Amir decides from a young age to be a writer, unwittingly helped in this decision by Hassan who enjoys the storytelling time they spend together, sitting under a tree, on top of the hill. His father's closest friend Ramir Khan, who Amir finds easier to relate to than his father, gives him a leather notebook for his 13th birthday, in which he writes his first stories. It is one of Amir's most precious belongings and travels with him on his harrowing journey in a petrol tanker, first to Pakistan and finally to the US.

The skill that Hosseini implements is heightened by dramatic tensions and successive hints that there are more challenges to come. The first 100 pages of *The Kite Runner* could be a book in its own right, as Hosseini takes us on so many emotional roller coasters, it is sometimes too difficult to pick up, yet in the same manner impossible to put down. The

sequence of short chapters moves us swiftly to the next scene
to find out if Amir owns up to his misdeeds, if Hassan surren-
ders his loyalty, if Baba finally accepts his son, if…

The book is driven by themes that re-occur at momen-
tous times and are highlighted by recurring phrases. The one
reiterated the most and which is so memorable, we first hear
when Amir asks Hassan if he would eat dirt for him. Hassan
says, yes, 'A thousand times over.' A simple exaggerated phrase,
which represents love and loyalty, and one which Amir finds
himself saying to Sohrab at the end of the book.

Amir's loyalty is constantly tested with Hassan, yet he
fails his friend more than once and compounds his disloyalty
through his own fears. When he sees Hassan being raped, he
does not try to help him and his guilt means that he can hardly
bear to be around him and so he plants false evidence to impli-
cate Hassan as a thief, knowing that stealing is the one thing
that his father will not tolerate.

It is when Amir and Baba settle in California that they are
able to find a way to bond. Baba buys an old van in which he
and Amir travel around to buy from garage sales on Saturdays
and sell at the San Jose flea market on Sundays. 'Godfather'
Baba brings the Afghan community together through creating their own area at the market. Amir meets Soraya here and
they marry before Baba dies. We sense, Hosseini-style, that
the rest of this extraordinary story is to come when Khan
contacts Amir.

Loyalty is tested again, mid-life, when Amir visits Rahim
Khan in Pakistan as he is dying. Khan reveals secrets that
make Amir doubt everything that he held sacred from his

childhood. Khan asks him to go to Kabul to rescue Hassan's son who has been orphaned by the Taliban. He is being held by Assef who has wreaked revenge on Hassan for humiliating him when they were children, by executing him and his wife. An admirer of Hitler, Assef believes in the ethnic cleansing of the Hazar. Assef, the antagonist in the story, then abducts Hassan's son, Sohrab, to use as a sex plaything, clearly relishing the persona of murderer and paedophile. When Amir goes to rescue Sohrab, the boy saves Amir's life by knocking out Assef's eyeball with a sling – the same weapon Hassan used to protect Amir from Assef when they were children.

The Kite Runner challenges our conscience regarding refugees and asks the question about our individual responses on the issue of human rights. It reminds us of the consequences of war, particularly for women and children. It also asks us to consider big life questions such as our responses to lies and betrayal. It is also about forgiveness, of ourselves and those closest to us. The importance of community is centred too; Baba thrived in his community yet outside it, in the US, he died in his 50s of cancer. Hosseini writes movingly about the Afghan refugee community, yet it is also part of the global refugee community, a 'Refugee Diaspora' in its own right.

THE NOVEL

First published by Riverhead Books in the US in 2003, it was number one in the *New York Times* bestseller list for two years. The 2007 film adaptation was banned in Afghanistan.

THE AUTHOR

Khaled Hosseini (1965–) was born in Afghanistan. In 1976, the Foreign Ministry relocated the Hosseini family to Paris and they were granted political asylum in the US in September 1980. Hosseini began writing *The Kite Runner* in March 2001, while practising medicine. He has since written three more novels: *A Thousand Splendid Suns* (2007), also a number one *New York Times* bestseller; *And the Mountains Echoed* (2013); together, these three mentioned above, have sold more than 55 million copies worldwide. *Sea Prayer* (2018) is an illustrated book for all ages. Hosseini was appointed a Goodwill Ambassador for UNHCR, the UN Refugee Agency (2006).

IF YOU LIKE THIS, TRY...

Earth and Ashes (1999) by Atiq Rahimi, a story told by an old man to his grandson, set in Afghanistan during the Russian occupation. Ethiopia was similarly occupied by communists after the overthrow of the monarchy and *Notes from the Hyena's Belly: An Ethiopian Boyhood* (2000) by Nega Mezlekia is his memoir of that period. *No Place to Call Home* (2018) by J J Bola finds Congolese refugee children struggling to integrate into British society, while trying to hold on to their roots and culture. In *Grace* by Natashia Deón (2016), mothers and daughters are violated in this multi-generational saga about runaway slaves, set during the American Civil War era.

Shatila Stories (2018) is a collaboratively written novel by nine Syrian and Palestinian refugee writers. *The Boat People*

(2018) by Sharon Bala is about Tamil refugees seeking asylum in Canada. *Refugee Boy* (2001) by Benjamin Zephaniah sees 14-year-old Alem left in London by his Ethiopian father to be cared for by the Refugee Council.

SMALL ISLAND

ANDREA LEVY

2004

The Windrush era is reimagined in *Small Island* to tell the story
of England's post-war reception of British-Caribbean subjects.
In her fourth novel, Levy unsettles and ultimately complicates
the more familiar Windrush narrative. This is the narrative of
the enlisted Black male answering the empire's call to war, only
to experience rejection and racial abuse in the post-war years.

Instead, Levy shifts the male focus by placing at the centre
of the novel an ambitious and independent Black female
protagonist, Hortense. This haughty young woman, despite
having only recently conceived of an English 'homecoming',
nonetheless successfully makes it to London in 1948. Schooled
in colonial Jamaica to appreciate, uncritically, all things
English, Hortense carries with her to the imperial motherland
a sense of belonging. Yet, as she discovers, British subjecthood
is serially challenged on British soil if one is Black. Her new
husband, Gilbert, already appreciates this from his wartime
experience; the identity he took for granted and which qualified him to serve in the British Army did not carry much

weight after the war. Deploying a range of narrative skills and humour, Levy unfailingly directs our attention to questions of belonging and conflicting meanings.

Division is at the core of the conflict represented in the novel, based on persistent colonial ideas about racial and cultural superiority, which Levy presents through a disarming narrative structure. She pairs dissonant characters such as the Jamaicans Hortense and Gilbert, who are of differing social groups, brought together in a marriage of convenience, with the white English couple Queenie and Bernard, who are similarly in a loveless marriage. The story unfolds from their diverse perspectives. Despite superficial national and racial similarities, it soon becomes clear that, though each is a British subject and both men have recently returned from serving King and country, each character experiences British citizenship differently. Being Black and British is itself replete with inequality. It is by means of each character's dilemmas that the reader comes to negotiate multiple views of the characters, as well as issues of race, class positions and gender. The tension between the protagonists is heightened by placing them under the same roof, where the reader can observe the desires which drive them. These characters reveal their flaws at close range. Not the least of these is Queenie's fear for her extra-maritally conceived Jamaican-English baby, shaped by the taboo of inter-racial mixing, and concealed for much of the novel.

Levy tells a familial story in *Small Island*, in that her father was among those arriving on the *Empire Windrush* in 1948. Her female characters highlight family relationships to reveal fault-lines embedded in hierarchies of gender. Queenie, for example, grew up a butcher's daughter and, though 'a cut above the miners' children', is nevertheless constrained by class and gender roles that can only be escaped through marriage. She is groomed for an elevated place in society by being removed from her restrictive home environment, a place of severely limited social possibilities. It is her aunt who guides her through elocution lessons, dress and self-presentation in order to prepare for her an upwardly mobile match with Bernard Bligh. His gentlemanly status and desirability as a suitor is signalled by his daily purchase of *The Times*. In the Caribbean, Hortense's grooming also involves being removed from her home to better her prospects. However, her situation is further complicated by racialized colonial dynamics. The father from whom Hortense gains her honeyed complexion, is a white colonial who abandons the impregnated servant girl who becomes her mother. Hortense's understanding of her precarious social standing, racial heritage and family circumstances is, at best, partial. Arguably, much of the wry humour of the novel rests on misunderstood and unstable colonial foundation, grounded less in 1948 than the 'Before' chapters – the Victorian peak of the British Empire.

The humour in *Small Island* might best be considered as irony and perhaps specifically British irony, which ranges from mischievous to teetering on the tragic. Levy deploys irony to open up spaces in the text for the reader to contemplate the novel's overall concern with the British Empire and its aftermath. For example, the irony of Hortense's position within the home of her high-status cousins, foreshadows the fall she will experience in status and material circumstances when she moves to London, especially when the signifiers of her closeness to empire, such as her light skin, are not recognized. Her identity is instead read as merely another Black person and lesser being who should step off the pavement if white women require the space. In another ironic twist, Queenie takes the Jamaican RAF serviceman, Michael, as a lover in Bernard's absence, forcing comparison between her lover and her husband to the detriment of the latter. It throws into relief Hortense's secret love for Michael and, most importantly, the relationship between Queenie and Michael echoes the circumstances of Hortense's own birth. The consequences of the resulting pregnancy reverberate throughout the novel and beyond, challenging the survival of Queenie's marriage to the bigoted Bernard.

In comparison, Gilbert's reference to laughter as his contribution to the war effort might be considered light-touch irony compared to Hortense's humiliation, which is compounded when she finds herself in the broom cupboard after a particularly belittling interview for a teaching job. Levy holds up a mirror to cultural practices that characters, Black and white, would prefer not to have reflected back. *Small Island* translates, for readers, Britain's colonial past and its wide-ranging meanings for the present. Perhaps the underlying irony is that it has taken a Black British writer – woefully underrepresented as a group at the time of the novel's publication – to successfully undertake this necessary task.

Beyond its prestigious publication awards, the success of this novel continues to grow. In 2007 it was selected for 'the largest mass-reading project to have taken place in Britain.' Linked to the commemoration in 2007 of the 200th anniversary of the abolition of Britain's slave trade, the project brought

Small Island to even greater national attention and into the homes of project participants across the UK. In 2009, the novel was made into a two-part drama for BBC television. Helen Edmundson's theatre adaptation of the novel premiered at London's National Theatre in 2019, to considerable acclaim.

THE NOVEL

Small Island was first published in English by Headline Review in 2004. It was awarded the Orange Prize for Fiction (2004), the Whitbread Novel of the Year and the Commonwealth Writers' Prize: Best of the Best (2005). With its many adaptations and mass readings, the tidal change achieved by this novel continues to impact not only individual readers, but also literary institutions.

THE AUTHOR

Andrea Levy (1956–2019) was born in London to Jamaican parents. *Small Island* is her fourth novel. She has written frankly about the difficulties of reconciling her identity as belonging both to Jamaica and to England. Levy's fiction returns to these concerns and to connections between Britain and its Caribbean colonies, particularly Jamaica. Her first novels, *Every Light in the House Burnin'* (1994) and *Never Far from Nowhere* (1996) are coming-of-age novels, focusing on the renegotiation of identities fundamental to migration itself and to the children of migrants. In contrast, *The Long Song* (2010) is a neo-slave narrative with a greater historical scope portraying the complexity of life on a plantation in early 19th-century Jamaica. In this novel, Levy interrogates the colour-class society or plantocracy that the system of colonial slavery enforced with brutal and far-reaching consequences.

IF YOU LIKE THIS, TRY...

Beryl Gilroy's *In Praise of Love and Children* was written many years before its publication in 2007 by Peepal Tree Press, reflecting the difficulties that Black women have experienced in having their stories published. Gilroy's novel with its female teacher protagonist, trained in the colonies, offers a direct comparison to Levy's *Small Island*. An understanding of post-1948 Black Britishness is incomplete without a reading of Joan Riley's *Waiting in the Twilight* (Women's Press, 1987). This focuses upon post-war migration to Britain and concerns itself especially with the experience of women.

DANCING IN THE DARK

CARYL PHILLIPS

2005

Bert Williams is driven by the desire to perform, above all else, and why not? With his vaudeville comedy partner George Walker, he achieves the heights of Broadway stardom. They transform the American musical with their own uproarious shows, filled with songs and much-imitated dances playing to full houses in early 20th-century New York. Their revue *In Dahomey*, the first all-Black American musical comedy to be performed on Broadway, toured internationally including a London West End season and a command performance at Buckingham Palace for Edward VII.

Although comedy is at the heart of this story, it strikes a tragic note and leaves a haunting aftermath. Bert's stellar career comes at great cost. While his audiences laugh and applaud, his fame relies upon him performing in a grotesque distortion of his humanity in blackface.

This fictionalized account of the highest paid performer of his era, is a mesmeric and moving novel that mirrors the experience of theatre itself. Chapters follow a classical play structure of Prologue, three Acts (1873–1903), (1903–1911), (1911–1922) and an Epilogue. There are four narrative perspectives: Bert, George and those of their wives Lottie and Aida, who perform in their revues. We are taken into the heart of a theatre season with script excerpts, reviews, playbills, rehearsal descriptions and acting techniques.

Phillips prefaces his book with the enigma of Bert in the epigram, 'Nobody in America knows my real name and, if I can prevent it, nobody ever will'. Accessing Williams's truth in the full glare of the spotlight, metaphorically and culturally, creates a beguiling tale of ambiguity. Gradually, we enter Bert's private sphere through subtle disclosures by other characters. Unlike George, Bert is not born in the US but in part of Britain's colonial empire, the Bahamas. Phillips traces a migratory route from the Caribbean to Bert's family's relocation to the US. Bert's pursuit of the 'American Dream' is recalibrated in a nation defined and ruled by a colour line, through segregation and Jim Crow. Bert at 11 understands he has 'to learn the role that America had set aside for him to play.'

The contrast between Bert and George, who first meet as street performers aged 20, is central to their act. Bert tall and angular, George shorter and heavily built extends to their personalities. As a subversion of the expectations of Black performers, they claim superiority over the white minstrels and their mockery of Blackness by advertising themselves as better performers. They invert expectations that the performer with darker skin (George) would be the butt of the joke and instead Bert with lighter skin applies burned cork and a wig to mask himself and become George's character's scapegoat.

Bert is a master of illusion, creating a bumbling, raggedy figure alongside the dapper George. He becomes increasingly resistant to blackface performance, but Bert knows their success is dependent upon his hyperawareness of the unspoken agreement between the Black performer and the white audience. Phillips focuses upon depicting the psychological effects on Bert from maintaining this self-distortion. In taking a bow after a performance of *In Dahomey*, Bert's heart is 'heavy with shame'. There are layers of mystery to Bert concerning his sexuality, his feelings about his career and his marriage to Lottie, whom he calls 'mother'. While George is serially unfaithful to the vivacious and talented Aida and will die from syphilis, Bert becomes more physically distanced from Lottie, to the point of not even changing his clothes in front of her. Aida is long suffering regarding George's attraction to white chorus girls, but Lottie suffers longer as Bert increasingly withdraws from their marriage.

Even though Williams and Walker changed theatre forever with their innovative staging, especially in bringing West African performing traditions into the acts they wrote, produced and acted, they were confined within the strict limits of white supremacist expectations of Black performers.

Casting was a segregating process in that Black people could not play leading roles on the white stage, while contact between Black men and white women was taboo. Theatre unions excluded Black people from membership and many white actors refused to share the stage with a Black actor.

Lottie first sees Bert's performance from the faraway seats, where Black people were forced to sit. Aida is known as the 'Queen of the Cakewalk Dance', which New York high society emulated, a version of a dance that travelled from Africa to the US plantations during enslavement. In the London season of *In Dahomey* the cakewalk was omitted on opening night, only to be reinstated after there was pressure from the English press.

How could a blackface performer have survived psychologically? What exactly were the white audiences laughing at? The better Bert performs, the worse it is for him as a person. Bert becomes increasingly depressed and haunted by the made-up face that stares back at him in his dressing room mirror. He is a troubling figure in theatre history as his acclaim and plaudits from white audiences were built upon fulfilling racist stereotypes and performance techniques.

But racist theatricality did not begin in the early 20th century. From the medieval period onwards, a grim repertoire of white people representing Blackness became cemented in European performance traditions. White actors applied make-up and accessories to portray Blackness to audiences. The legacy of this racialized, prosthetic technique exported with colonization remained entrenched in British culture, most especially through the cosmetics of blackface minstrelsy in mainstream productions until the 1980s. While Phillips focuses upon an American performer, his tale holds true in any context where 'blacking up' occurred and still occurs. For what makes people today from prime ministers to celebrities think it is acceptable to adopt blacking up for a party persona?

Although produced 50 years later, Smokey Robinson's lyrics for his and Stevie Wonder's collaboration, 'Tears of a Clown' captures the kernel of Bert Williams's career; a man whom W C Fields described as the 'The funniest man I ever saw, and the saddest man I ever knew.'

THE NOVEL

Dancing in the Dark was first published by Secker & Warburg in 2005 and was named winner of the PEN/Open Book Award in 2006.

THE AUTHOR

Caryl Phillips (1958–) was born in St Kitts, but was raised in Leeds from the age of four months. A graduate of Cambridge University, he has written 11 novels including *Crossing the River* (1993) which was shortlisted for the 1993 Booker Prize, *A Distant Shore* (2003) which won the Commonwealth Writers' Prize 2004, an intertext *The Lost Child* (2015) which responds to *Wuthering Heights* and was a finalist in the Hurston/Wright Legacy Award, and a biographical novel of the life of Jean Rhys, *A View of the Empire at Sunset* (2018).

His five nonfiction books, two anthologies, two screenplays and four plays testify to his influential reach across genres, and his work has been translated into 14 languages. A Fellow of the Royal Society of Literature, Phillips has been awarded six honorary degrees from universities around the world and is Professor of English at Yale.

IF YOU LIKE THIS, TRY...

Corregidora by Gayl Jones (1975) focuses on the life of Ursa, a bisexual blues singer who ends her first marriage rather than capitulate to her violent husband's attempts to stop her singing. Jones traces her character's matrilineal trajectory back three generations to enslavement, and Ursa sings out through love, pain and loss.

Mishima Yukio's short story, 'Onnagata' (1957) in Death in Midsummer (1966, English translation by Edward G Seidensticker) represents an actor in Kabuki theatre who plays the woman-role. Hidden truths and unsettling ambiguous feelings regarding sex and sexuality also underpin Yukio's 1963 classic, The Sailor Who Fell from Grace with the Sea (1965, English translation by John Nathan). This latter book weaves together idealization and disillusionment as experienced through the perspective of adolescent boy Noboro who spies on his mother and her lover the sailor Ryuji leading to dramatically unexpected revenge.

Sirena Selena vestida de pena (2000) by African-Puerto Rican writer, Mayra Santos-Febres was translated into English by Stephen Lytle as Sirena, Selena (2001) and centres on drag queen Sirena Selena and their journey from surviving childhood abuse to street hustling in San Juan to becoming a cabaret star. Their beauty and voice enchants a married wealthy and powerful businessman and their life is changed forever.

HALF OF A YELLOW SUN

CHIMAMANDA NGOZI ADICHIE

2006

The story follows the lives of twin sisters, Olanna and Kainene from the mid-1960s, just before two coups took place in rapid succession and throughout the Biafran War of 1967–70. We are introduced to them at their dining room table at home with their mother and father – self-made man, Chief Ozobia. The culturally conscious Olanna is considered the beauty of the two sisters, and is often used as bait by her father when negotiating lucrative government contracts with lascivious ministers, the latest being Chief Okonji who has joined them for dinner. Olanna, having just returned from Europe, had already planned to escape at the weekend to visit family and friends in Kano in northern Nigeria, before moving to the university town of Nsukka to be closer to her lover, Odenigbo. Kainene, the darker skinned 'ugly duckling', is her sharp-witted, sometimes acerbic, yet outwardly confident sister. Both are intelligent women who have recently completed postgraduate courses in Europe. Olanna has accepted a position to teach in the Sociology department at Nsukka, while the tomboyish Kainene is moving to Port Harcourt, in the east, to run the family business. Her father's proud description of Kainene is that she is as good as having two sons.

They navigate their privileged lifestyles on the cusp of an unexpected civil war until it is declared over, and then the Ozobia family tries to reinstate their tattered lives to some kind of normality. But so many lives are lost in between and when loved ones like Kainene go missing it can feel worse than death.

Adichie drip-feeds the horrors of the war as tragic scenes are piled onto each other, as the massacre quickly takes root. Olanna is the first of her family to witness first-hand the descent from unrest that scared the Igbo people into sheltering in their home region in the east and then calling for secession. She sees the massacred bodies of family members, recognized only by their clothing, as her ex-boyfriend Mohammed helps her to escape by dressing her as a Muslim and pushing her onto a packed train with other Igbos fleeing back to Lagos. At the end of the three-hour journey, she finds that the comforting familiarity of a calabash, which would usually carry food or small belongings instead holds the severed head of a little girl, with beautifully braided hair, which her mother refused to let go.

Olanna goes from living a comfortable lifestyle on campus with Odenigbo and his cadre of intellectual friends, including the poet Okeoma (likely to be a cameo of Christopher Okigbo who died on the frontline), to living in one room with their daughter, Baby, and their houseboy, Ugwu, among starving neighbours dying of an extreme form of malnutrition

– *kwashiorkor*. Olanna's marriage disintegrates as her revolu-tionary-minded partner descends into alcoholism. Adichie's fully dimensional characters enable us to see aspects of both human nature and of war that create ethical issues. She leaves the storyline wide open for readers to search their conscience to make up their own minds. For example, Olanna seems near-perfect until she sleeps with Richard, Kainene's blonde-haired English lover. She creates this dilemma again when Ugwu is conscripted into the army and he changes from a gentle homebody and teacher to a gang rapist who regrets his actions, and is determined to make amends. But, how can amends be made after such crimes and betrayal? Ugwu faced the same fear as experienced by the character Okonkwo in Chinua Achebe's *Things Fall Apart* (see entry 6), highlighting the challenge and effects of peer pressure on masculinity.

Adichie also provides fully dimensional aspects of lives in Nigeria, as the country slips into civil war in the face of ethnic, religious and regional tensions. Igbo people are starving in one region while, in the north, Mohammed sends Olanna choc-olate, soap and a letter, expressing the hope that she is ok, yet informing her that his polo game is suffering. Expats in Lagos continue to play tennis. Nigerians from smaller ethnic groups feel forced to choose sides. An important dimension of women's lives is subtly touched upon and always apparent; that of the status of women being determined on their ability or choice to have children.

Adichie presents alternative portrayals of the war by using different narrators to avoid portraying 'a single story'. Richard Churchill, who speaks fluent Igbo, appears as a foil to what was happening. Although he considered himself a Biafran, he was more of an outsider on the inside, one who the outside world would regard as having an honest, objective viewpoint since he was a white man. He finds it difficult to stomach the attitude of two international journalists, one of whom is eager to photograph 'the real Biafra'. The other one continually munches on chocolate in front of children in a refugee camp. Richard also writes articles explaining how Nigeria had reached such a point of devastation in its history.

After Kainene sees her houseboy's head cut off by shrapnel and his body running around headless, we see another side to her. She takes a step towards forgiveness by hand-delivering a letter from her parents to her sister, instead of sending a messenger. Her home then becomes a refuge for her sister and family. She uses her business skill to become an effective and caring refugee camp director. The need for forgiveness is found in every aspect of this story: siblings, lovers and countrymen. This story asks how do we forgive? When does the healing begin?

In a country where the bruises of war remain in living memory and the people of Nigeria have had to find a way to live together again, this novel helps make people aware of an important part of the history of Nigeria, Africa's largest populated country. It highlights the impact of colonial rule, when colonizers drew borders around groups of people for the convenience of governance. On a larger scale, it is a wake-up call to governments and authorities whose citizens feel ignored and whose demands to be listened to are not heeded.

THE NOVEL

Originally published by Fourth Estate in the UK, *Half of a Yellow Sun* won the Orange Prize for Women's Fiction in 2007 and the Winner of the 'Best of the Best' in the 25-year history of the Baileys Women's Prize for Fiction (previously the Orange Prize) in 2015. It won the Anisfield-Wolf Book Award (2007), PEN 'Beyond Margins' Award (2007) and was named a *New York Times* Notable Book (2006).

THE AUTHOR

Chimamanda Ngozi Adichie (1977–) was born in Nigeria. She attained international attention when she won the *Zoetrope*: All-Story competition with her short story 'You in America' (2001). Her debut novel *Purple Hibiscus* (2003) won the Commonwealth Writers' Prize in 2005 and the Hurston/ Wright Legacy Award (2004). She received a MacArthur Fellowship in 2008. Her short story collection *The Thing Around Your Neck* was published in 2009. *Americanah* (2013) won *The Chicago Tribune* Heartland Prize for Fiction, the National Book Critics Circle Award for Fiction and *The New York Times* Top Ten Best Books of 2013. *Dear Ijeawele, or a Feminist Manifesto in Fifteen Suggestions* was published in 2017. She was named one of the 20 most important fiction writers under 40 years old by *The New Yorker*. 'The Danger of a Single Story' (2009) is one of the most-viewed TED Talks of all time.

IF YOU LIKE THIS, TRY...

A new generation of African women writers on the continent and in the diaspora are receiving accolades. These include Chika Unigwe's *Black Sisters' Street* (2011) and Aminatta Forna's *The Memory of Love* (2010). Other novels by women writers across the continent include: *From Pasta to Pigfoot* (2016) by Frances Mensah Williams, *Lyrics Alley* (2010) by Leila Aboulela, *When We Speak of Nothing* (2017) by Olumide Popoola and *Noon* (2007) by Sahar El-Mougy. Other novels about Biafra include: *Destination Biafra* (1982) by Buchi Emecheta, *Divided We Stand* (1980) by Cyprian Ekwensi, *Sunset in Biafra* (1973) by Elechi Amadi and *The Man Died* (1971) by Wole Soyinka.

THE WHITE TIGER

ARAVIND ADIGA

2008

Adiga's debut novel, *The White Tiger*, combines compelling storytelling, irreverence, up-to-the minute concerns and a fast pace. Local and global concerns surface, foremost of which are oppression, corruption, greed and global capitalism. A novel about 21st-century India, it remains clear-sighted throughout about India's present and its wasteful abuse of humans – a practice linked to feudalism and exploited by colonialism.

White Tiger's story is told by Balram Halwai, the proud owner of a flourishing taxi service for call centre workers in the city of Bangalore. Balram has made an exceptional rise from being a lowly teaboy in the remote and impoverished village of Laxmangarh, to become a wealthy entrepreneur in Bangalore, a booming IT and outsourcing city. In the course of seven nights and in a series of seven letters to Wen Jiabao, the Premier of China (2003–13), Balram tells the story of his own meteoric rise as a successful businessman. The pretext for his writing to Premier Wen is that he has heard news on the radio that the premier will be visiting Bangalore to learn

about India's world-class entrepreneurship. Balram considers
it a waste of time for the premier to undertake an official visit
which he warns will only prove to be a charade on the part
of the politicians. If Premier Wen truly wants to understand
about new India's rising entrepreneurial position globally,
Balram will provide the relevant information. In telling the
story of his own life, Balram intends to illustrate 'the truth
about Bangalore' and India's real position. This is that the
country is held in a stranglehold of feudal practices inhibit-
ing modernization and the country's duplicity in perpetuat-
ing two Indias: one rich, while the other is mired in poverty.
As the 'white tiger' who has learned how to succeed, Balram
promises to be the premier's 'Midnight Educator' especially
since he imagines China becoming a crucial ally of India in
the future, in which the 'brown man' is due for ascendancy.

The characters involved are primarily from the Stork's
family from Balram's region of India. The 'Stork' who controls
the rivers and exacts payments from everyone using the
rivers, also holds claims to their lives. Typical of the syndi-
cate of wealthy landlords traditionally linked to his village –
nicknamed locally as animals – they extort payments from
the villagers who must also seek employment from them, as
Balram does. His family members play minor roles in the
narrative. Members of the servant class, with whom Balram
mixes in Delhi, also play minor roles in the novel. They open
his eyes to the wider pattern of corruption in the city.

He was initially called Munna, meaning boy, and is given
the name Balram by his elementary schoolteacher on his first
day at school. As Balram, he holds the possibility of realizing

his father's dreams that he become educated. His father hopes that he will break the cycle of oppression that is traditionally experienced. A school inspector names him 'White Tiger' when he outshines everyone else during a surprise inspection. He is promised a scholarship which never materializes. When his father – a rickshaw puller – dies a gruesome death, Balram is abruptly removed from his school, which, in any case is like everything in his village, a sham of corrupt practices. He is made to find work as a child labourer to help support his family. By successfully bribing a taxi driver to teach him to drive, he circumvents the caste system. It is as a driver that he enters the Stork's family, and becomes acquainted with his sons, 'Mongoose' and Ashok. It is Ashok who, having newly returned from the US with a restless, Indian-American wife, Pinky Madam, moves to Delhi and becomes Balram's employer. Pinky Madam's foreign behaviours temporarily upset the family, but help Balram to see alternatives to the feudal–servant pattern of his life. Balram kills and robs Ashok, then escapes to Bangalore and assumes a new identity. He knows that the Stork's revenge will be to have members of his family killed or driven mercilessly out of the village. But he chooses his own freedom above his family's life. Privately, he becomes the White Tiger and publicly he names himself Ashok Sharma, in part assuming the identity of the man to whom he was a servant.

The context of the story is a divided India, one part of which – mainly in the south – is referred to as 'the Light' and the other part, within which Balram grows up and must first learn to accept his lowly status, he names, 'the Darkness', or poor India. Growing up in the Darkness, which is controlled by feudal-style landlords, Balram's fate was destined to be similar to his father's. His luck turns when he gains the job as an assistant driver and, with it, the hope of being given a smart uniform. Thereafter, when he manoeuvres his way into the main driver's job, his desire is to drive the better of the two available cars. Throughout his life with the Stork's family, true to feudal style, Balram dutifully demonstrates his loyalty and trustworthiness, whether he is required to wash his master's feet or be a chauffeur. In New Delhi, as Ashok's driver, however, Balram gradually sees the stark divisions between rich and poor, and observes the urban slum dwellers. The turning point comes when he is strongarmed into covering for his employers by agreeing to go to prison for a possible hit-and-run accident. Balram determines that he is not prepared to live in a cage that he recognizes as the destiny of the acutely poor.

The White Tiger portrays the life of one individual who succeeds against all odds in breaking 'out of the coop' in increments. He has learned that in the new India there are only two ways to survive: 'eat – or get eaten up.' In whichever guise – Balram or White Tiger or as Ashok – he has chosen to eat. The manner in which he achieves this leaves the reader with several questions: to what extent is the novel to be considered as satire, given the route to neoliberal success involves murder and theft? Also, is Balram to be considered a hero or an anti-hero? Is *The White Tiger* solely about India and its achievement in the global economy, or has Adiga handed his readers a contemporary fable about neoliberal capitalism and its interlinked pressures that destroy family and community, tying in with the single-minded determination to gain wealth and upward mobility? The debate is ongoing.

THE NOVEL

First published in 2008 by Atlantic Books, *The White Tiger* won the Man Booker Prize in 2008, to much critical acclaim and some controversy. The source of the controversy lies mainly in questions concerning Adiga's representation of a 'Dark India', how inauthentic this might be, and the possible motive for producing a novel that might be read as negatively portraying India. *The White Tiger* has been adapted for film, directed by Ramin Bahrani, to whom the book is dedicated. The film premiered in January 2021 and was nominated for a best-adapted screenplay award, BAFTA, 2021.

THE AUTHOR

Aravind Adiga (1974–) is an Indian novelist, short story writer and journalist. His articles and short stories have been widely published including in the *Guardian*, *The Sunday Times*, *The New Yorker*, *Financial Times* and the *Times of India*. Following this debut award-winning novel, in 2008, Adiga has published the following novels: *Last Man in Tower* (2011), *Selection Day* (2016) and *Amnesty* (2020). His *Between the Assassinations* (2008) is a collection of short stories. *Selection Day* has been made into a series for Netflix.

IF YOU LIKE THIS, TRY...

Amitav Ghosh's *The Hungry Tide* (2005) is also critical of India's contemporary role and similarly reveals the clash between local and diasporic values. Richard Wright's *Native Son* (1940, Harper Perennial, 1998) is acknowledged by Adiga as an influence. There are many differences to be found between the two novels, which are written at dissimilar historical moments, and are set in considerably divergent continents and cultures. Yet, *Native Son* similarly turns on murder by the novel's oppressed anti-hero, Bigger Thomas. Both Balram and Bigger experience family troubles that become significant within the story. Both live in a sharply divided world of haves and have-nots, and both are chauffeurs to employers whose wealth they could hardly imagine.

44

IN OTHER ROOMS, OTHER WONDERS

DANIYAL MUEENUDDIN

2009

In this collection of eight stories set in the Punjab, Daniyal Mueenuddin shares an aspect of Pakistani lifestyle that is uncommon elsewhere, that of the privileged land-owner class – a reflection of the leftover lifestyle of British colonialism. The stories reveal the lives and actions of Harouni family members, revolving around their patriarch K K Harouni, and their employees.

The collection's title story opens with landowner K K Harouni poised to listen to a distant family member who wants help in finding a job. Twenty-year-old Rusna arrives with a letter of introduction from his ex-wife, whom she assists as a maid and companion.

Rusna, instead of looking for a job, decides to slowly work her way into K K Harouni's life. She starts by going to the house, at his insistence, a few times a week to have typing lessons from his assistant so that she can become more employable. Her companionship alleviates K K Harouni's loneliness and she abandons the typing practice to get closer to him. It is not long before she has an interlocking room next to his so that she can share his bed. After he dies, his three daughters order her to leave immediately. She arrived in a rickshaw, with her belongings, denoting her low status and now she must depart for her family home in a rickshaw. The gains she had purchased on her expense account, now packed into steel-strapped trunks, cannot make up for the loss of her virginity.

The story 'Nawabdin Electrician' centres on an employee of K K Harouni's, who maintains all things electrical on the estate. He makes sure that he is in his employer's line of sight daily, so his indispensability is clear. Nawabdin has a wife, 12 daughters and a son to provide for so he engineers a way to supplement his income. He approaches Harouni for a motorbike and petrol allowance, which he says is to get around the vast estate quicker. He uses the bike for his own business as well. On his way home from work one day, a robber tries to steal his motorbike. People nearby hear his cries for help and they attack the robber. Both Nawabdin and the robber end up lying next to each other in the makeshift clinic at the pharmacy. The robber, near death, asks for forgiveness, but Nawabdin ruminating that his own death would have made his family homeless, refuses to give it.

One of the saddest stories in the collection is 'A Spoiled Man', offering a clearly observed tale of the feudalistic lifestyle of Pakistan's landed gentry. An elderly man, Razak, who owns nothing but his self-made mobile home, is given the position of gardener for a special orchard for the Harouni family. The family and estate is now run by Sohail, a family member who appears in an earlier story. The old man marries a girl with a speech impediment and felt he had everything he could want to end his old age peacefully: female company, a television and two goats. He becomes the favoured gardener of Sohail's American wife, Sonya, who treats him as a curiosity. But in a tragic twist, he loses everything and is punished for having even these small comforts. He philosophises that he expected too much when all he wanted was to end his life securely. He returns to being content with his basic provisions and wants only to be buried on the Harouni estate, which he now regards as his home.

In these stories, the lives of Rusna, Nawabdin and Razak are all dependant on the favours of the Harouni family; it is from this that they all attain a sense of belonging. Other stories, such as 'Saleema' and 'Provide, Provide', also draw on this employee–employer relationship. 'Our Lady of Paris' is a version of *Guess Who's Coming to Dinner*. Sohail is a member of K K Harouni's family. The story focuses on a life-changing incident with his then-girlfriend Helen, while they were both students. They intend to spend Christmas in Paris, and his mother Rafit decides that she and his father will join them. It is clear that she plans to interfere in her son's relationship. While in Paris, she suggests afternoon coffee with Helen to talk about their shared interest, Sohail. Rafit tells Helen that Sohail is expected to return home to Pakistan to take care of the family business and states that she does not feel that Sohail and Helen's relationship will last, because she does not believe that Helen will fit into their high-end lifestyle in Pakistan. Although Sohail and Helen had planned to celebrate New Year outside Paris, Helen changes her mind, suggesting she believes this to be their last chance to be in Paris together and to walk along the Seine.

In linking stories to the family patriarch, K K Harouni, the lives of those who work on the lands of the Pakistani landed gentry are shown to be those of independently minded people and not just an extension of their employer and their estate. It also presents a situation in which stealing from their employer to make their own lives better is to be expected. In all of the stories there is some form of corruption. Some of the women are shown as corrupting themselves as the only way to get what they can in a patriarchal society.

Mueenuddin shows how this cross-section of society who live in close proximity to each other on a family estate, functions as an accepted way of life. By focusing on a central character to link the stories, it is also a subtle way of showing how small the world is, when worlds can be linked through one family.

Exploring the facets of class, culture and power within this feudalistic lifestyle, and a form of ownership which ties the people to the land, shows the family to be influential – politically, economically and socially. It also subtly questions the disposability of people, particularly in societies that ensure that there is a clear demarcation in the employer–employee relationship and, in this, the author's intention is to recognize that change can be for the better, placing himself in the role of an active agent of change for a way of life that is dying out.

THE COLLECTION

First published by Bloomsbury in 2009, *In Other Rooms, Other Wonders* was a finalist for the Pulitzer Prize (2010), the winner of The Story Prize (2010), the Commonwealth Writers' Prize

(2010), a finalist for the National Book Awards and the *LA Times* Book Prize (2009). It was named a top ten book of 2009 by *Publishers Weekly* and *Time* magazine.

THE AUTHOR

Daniyal Mueenuddin (1963–) has had stories published in *The New Yorker, Granta, Zoetrope, The Best American Short Stories* (2008) and the PEN/O. Henry Prize Stories 2010. He also won the 2010 Rosenthal Family Foundation Award from the American Academy of Arts and Letters.

IF YOU LIKE THIS, TRY...

Books by other Pakistani writers such as *Maps for Lost Lovers* (2005) by Nadeem Aslam and *A Case of Exploding Mangoes* (2008) by Mohamed Hanif, a humorous novel based on the conspiracy theories of the 1988 plane crash that killed General Muhammad Zia ul-Haq. Tariq Mehmood's *While There is Light* (2003) follows Saleem, on bail for suspected terrorism in Britain, back to Pakistan to visit his mother before she dies. *Kahani* (2005) is a collection of short stories by Pakistani women edited by Aamer Hussein.

Other interconnected short story collections are *Drown* (1996) by Junot Díaz, *The Lone Ranger and Tonto Fistfight in Heaven* (1993) by Sherman Alexie, *Gorilla, My Love* by Toni Cade Bambara (1972) and *Erotext* by Sudeep Sen (2016). *All Aunt Hagar's Children* by Edward P Jones (2006) is a collection of 14 stories on African-Americans in Washington DC in the

20th century. *The Women of Brewster Place* (1982) by Gloria Naylor contains tales of seven African-American women living in a shared home called Brewster Place, which chronicles the challenges that many Black women face.

HOW TO READ THE AIR

DINAW MENGESTU

2010

This story of two marriages is recounted by Jonas, of his own marriage to Angela, which lasted for three years and that of his parents, Mariam and Yosef, who were together until he left home to start college at the age of 19. Mariam, his mother, is a beautiful Ethiopian woman who married her husband, Yosef Woldemariam, after a brief relationship during a politically active time of young people demanding change in Ethiopia. Yosef narrowly escaped execution for his involvement in political activities and flees first to Sudan, where he remains until he can stow away on a ship bound for Italy to claim political asylum.

Yosef finally arrives in the US, where Mariam joins him three years later. On being reunited, they soon realize that they do not actually like each other. Mariam becomes pregnant soon after she arrives, but that does not stop the physical abuse that Yosef rains on her, the extent of which is evidenced by her multiple bruises. Mariam attempts to leave with Jonas several times, but is held back by the restrictions of doing this with a small child and always returns to her husband. Mariam eventually leaves her husband two weeks after Jonas goes to college in New York, staying with friends in Washington DC. The strained existence that she and Jonas suffered together seems to have forced them further apart, and they see and speak to each other infrequently over the next ten years. Whenever they do speak, they never talk about the past. In the meantime, Jonas marries Angela, a lawyer he meets at the asylum seekers centre where he works. But when his marriage breaks up and he loses the teaching job that Angela secured through her connections, he decides to go on a road trip, tracing the honeymoon route of his parents. Yosef's love of country music had been the deciding factor for the road trip between Peoria, Illinois and Nashville, Tennessee. This is how and when both marriage stories unfold.

After Jonas's father dies he receives his belongings from the boarding house where he lived out his last years with dementia. Jonas discovers drawings of ships and boxes, revealing that Yosef never got over his fear and nightmares of enclosed spaces. He had travelled from Sudan to Italy in a box, his body folded up with only his urine for sustenance in the last three days of his ten-day ordeal. In a similar way, Jonas has blocked out from his own memory, the violence he saw his father inflict on his mother. This was violence he had sometimes experienced himself when his father had threatened him with a knife for being in the way; so Jonas had simply folded himself away in a corner, attempting to be invisible. This traumatic experience rendered Jonas unable to properly express his own emotions.

As an adult he 'forgets' most of his past, not even able to remember if he had friends at school. He often responds to questions about his childhood with, 'I can't remember' or 'maybe that is how it happened' or simply filled in gaps with his imagination, with what could have happened or what he would have liked to have happened – retreating into a world that he would frequently make up on the spot.

Angela can never tell what is true, from the small snippets of his life that he does share. She is infuriated by his non-engagement with her, particularly as she suffers from parental abandonment issues, and carries her own deep insecurities. Both Angela and Jonas tell lies about themselves – to each other and to other people – as a type of game when they are out together socially. Eventually, these seemingly harmless lies catch up with Jonas and he loses his lucrative teaching post.

Jonas' marriage to Angela is the opposite of his parents'. The younger couple share little physical contact and when they do, it lacks intimacy. At breakfast one morning Angela reaches over to fix her husband's tie after she arrives home late again, without a plausible explanation. Jonas grabs her wrist tightly, which Angela sees as a sign that he is not emotionless, that he does have feelings for her; this is the day that she decides to end the affair she has been having as a result of feeling neglected.

Mengestu skilfully weaves minute detail into the bigger picture to chart the deterioration of relationships: one is physically oppressive, the other is mentally oppressive through being non-physical and spiritually absent. Both marriages are doomed not to last – a feeling that is pervasive from the outset. It is due to their own fragilities as human beings that Jonas cannot go on as he is, although his constant trying shows that trauma experienced in childhood remains in the psyche for years. Mengestu seems to offer a template of how to fail in a marriage without being a failure. He paints the picture of Jonas and Angela so explicitly, that neither one of them is to blame, that people can fall out of love easily, simply and sadly as part of life.

Mengestu is not so presumptuous as to preach philosophies, wisdoms or meditations on marriage; instead he liberally sprinkles his narrative with anecdotes, hints of last conversations or last meals, a scene or conversation that marks a change. It allows us to see how our different actions and words can affect those closest to us. The themes of love, redemption, diaspora, abuse and living as a refugee run through the parallel spaces in between the narratives on marriage.

How to Read the Air reminds us of the fragility of human emotions, the complexity of human relationships, the strength of the human spirit and our determination for individual survival. It shows that marriage break-ups are not due to people failing but often due to people hurting deeply, before they have even met. In the pursuit of happiness – or at least peace and contentment – people sometimes search for this in their partners, rather than themselves. We know that the answer is to make a significant life change to free ourselves – as Jonas does by going on the road trip – which at the same time, frees the other person. It also reminds us that the craft of writing literary novels is to make readers conscious of themes without overstating them.

THE NOVEL

The novel was first published by Riverhead Books in the US in 2010 and by Jonathan Cape in the UK. This is Mengestu's second novel and it was a *New York Times* Notable Book of the Year.

THE AUTHOR

Dinaw Mengestu (1978–) was born in Ethiopia, migrating to the US as a refugee with his family in 1980. He is the recipient of a fellowship in fiction from the New York Foundation for the Arts (2006). His first novel *Children of the Revolution* (2007, US: 2009) won the *Guardian* First Book Award (2007) followed by *The Beautiful Things That Heaven Bears* (2007) which won the *Los Angeles Times* Art Seidenbaum Award for First Fiction (2007). *All Our Names* was published in 2014. Mengestu has been awarded *The New Yorker*'s 20 under 40 and The National Book Foundation 5 Under 35; he is a recipient of a MacArthur Fellowship (2012).

IF YOU LIKE THIS, TRY...

My Name is Why by Lemn Sissay (2019), the true story of an Ethiopian baby boy raised in the care system in England after he is unintentionally separated from his mother. This is a story deeply about family, one that was taken away from the boy when he was a baby. *The Shadow King* (2020) is by Ethiopian-American writer Maaza Mengiste, set during the

Italian invasion of Abyssinia in 1935 and told through the experience of a maid. Other writers from 'The Horn of Africa' include Nadifa Mohamed, whose debut novel *Black Mamba Boy* (2010) is a fictionalized biography of her father's life in Yemen. Protagonists in pursuit of happiness in other cultures include *Professor Chandra Follows His Bliss* (2018) by Rajeev Balasubramanyam set in the US and *The Book of Echoes* (2020) by Rosanna Amaka, a story of love and redemption in 1980s South London, when a young couple discover how their lives are linked through ancestors.

NW

ZADIE SMITH

2012

Zadie Smith, talking about her fourth novel *NW*, says, 'If I'm honest with you, I feel that this book is the first book that I've really written as an adult.' Readers, take note, although this richly mature novel has been overshadowed by the dazzling reception of the novels she wrote in her twenties, this is *the* Zadie Smith book to read.

NW explores long-term friendship between girls, specifically that of Keisha (who later changes her name to Natalie), of Caribbean heritage, and Leah, of Irish heritage. The relationship that unfolds between them is carefully built on Smith's realism and reflects familiar rather than idealized friendship. The source of their friendship is highlighted as a definitive 'event' in the pair's history: one saves the other from drowning in a local pool when they are four years old. This event allows them further access to each other beyond the local north-west London schools that they attend. Of only passing significance to the children, this serves as a bridge between the two families, previously separated by difference in their racial and cultural backgrounds.

Keisha's Jamaican mother, Marcia, notes that prior to the lifesaving, Leah's mother Pauline had been 'a bit snooty' with her. Marcia is unaware of how Pauline's snootiness might translate in terms of racialized attitudes. Both mothers are migrant characters who become largely peripheral to the novel; meanwhile, Smith focuses on the increasingly strained relationship of their daughters. It is through the two friends that *NW* transposes – with measured irony – the historically specific Black and Irish outsider position of the Windrush era to this 21st-century fiction. This study of ordinary friendship based on a complexity of difference is rare and lies at the heart of how Smith transforms the canon.

The friends experience modernity as they grow into womanhood. *NW* addresses questions concerning gender and the lives of London's disadvantaged in the 21st century. The characters' life chances are tested in the face of stereotypical ideas about race, gender and attainment, as well as the realities of urban poverty. Moreover, the question emerges: by which values should one live in a globalized modernity? While the term multicultural is readily associated with Smith's writing, we see in *NW* that her carefully crafted characters are often deeply *inter*cultural. They are presented as being both shaped by and rooted within several cultures. Here, the writing is experimental, with Smith's impressionistic brush strokes accompanied by realism in the depiction of her range of characters, serving to alter literature's understanding of humanity.

The fictional housing estate, Caldwell, in which Leah and Keisha grow up, appears to be at the heart of the north-west London postcode to which *NW* applies. From its first pages, the novel reveals a world that might be considered *open*. As such, the area provides varying types of refuge for characters, like Leah, who returns to live in the locality by choice, as well as for those who appear to lack choice and who, in their desperation, connect with others through a habit of screams, real or metaphorical. There is, for example, 'the grim girl' on the estate, only 'four gardens along' from Leah, and who habitually 'screams Anglo-Saxon at nobody.' There is the woman who is 'screaming PLEASE and crying' at Leah's door and who will be discovered living in a squat just a few streets away. Yet, NW is also the space that Leah has chosen to make her home with her husband, Michel. While the couple's familial migration histories might vary from those whose desperation is signalled through screams, their relationship, like that of others in the novel, is based on an integration of intimacy that has long been at the core of intercultural relationships, despite being largely shunned by literary writing.

To fully appreciate *NW*'s intercultural world requires some attention to the ways in which characters cross boundaries of histories, cultures and racial belonging. To this effect, Smith not only sets her characters in motion, but also attends to how they are perceived. Michel, Leah's French-speaking husband from Algeria, is declared Nigerian by his mother-in-law, Pauline, who pronounces all Africans 'Nigerians'. An established resident of NW, and herself a migrant from Ireland, Pauline similarly declares Shar a gypsy and dismisses her daughter's 'sub-continental' correction. By such alerts to complexity, Smith represents London in her fiction as the globalized city that many recognize it to be. Smith's characters reflect this. Furthermore, the globalized context that NW appears to mirror is primarily one of interactions, exchanges and overlaps between characters who are British. This includes Irish, but also Black British and Black European. At the same time, the novel points to a larger understanding of 'NW', not just as a London postal code, but also the geographical area sometimes referred to as the global north west or, more simply, the west. Overshadowing the lives of these characters is the afterlife of coloniality with which much of Western Europe was once thoroughly enmeshed and chooses to forget.

Yet, despite its reminders of the past, NW, concerned with the multiracial, intercultural present, consistently opens up questions about the choices that the characters make. The novel includes a contemplation of a place that might be thought an undesirable residence and insists that we think about the globalized, neoliberal present. Assuming that each character has freedom of choice – as Western democracies insist – how, for example, should Leah's secret ending of her pregnancies, regardless of her husband's desire for children be understood? How free is Natalie – now living with a wealthy husband and their children – to make her choices? Considering her sexual and career decisions should Natalie's freedom be more constrained than her friend's, and what part does race play in our reading of the different lifestyles and choices that each friend makes?

The figurative screams of the desperate have been the subject of memorable literature and that of Dickens, for example, is sometimes invoked in comparison to the subjects of Smith's writing. Still more has been characteristically presented through monocultural, monoracial lenses. Smith's *NW* not only counters such a familiar literary dynamic, but pushes its boundaries to effectively alter the literary landscape and illuminate a present that shows many cultures co-existing together in multicultural and multiracial locations, such as the harsh, urban realities of immigrant life in Kilburn. Most importantly, Smith points to that world – our world – as already intercultural. *NW* challenges us to think again about the humans drawn within the many lauded national literatures, to consider what or who might be missing and to reassess the present and its meanings.

THE NOVEL

NW was first published in English by Hamish Hamilton in 2012. It was shortlisted for the Royal Society of Literature Ondaatje Prize and the Women's Prize for Fiction, and was named one of the *New York Times Book Review*'s 10 Best Books of 2012.

THE AUTHOR

Zadie Smith's tremendous talent saw her first novels attract multiple awards. Her debut novel, *White Teeth* (2000), was the winner of The Whitbread First Novel Award, the *Guardian* First Book Award, the James Tait Black Memorial Prize for Fiction and the Commonwealth Writers' First Book Award. *The Autograph Man* (2002), her second novel, won The Jewish Quarterly Wingate-Literary Prize. *On Beauty* (2005),

Smith's third novel, won the Orange Prize for Fiction, the Commonwealth Writers' Best Book Award (Eurasia Section) and was shortlisted for the Man Booker Prize. Her most recent novel, *Swing Time* (2016) was shortlisted for the National Book Critics Circle Award for Fiction and longlisted for the Man Booker 2017. Her first essay collection, *Changing My Mind*, was published in 2009 and her second essay collection, *Feel Free,* in 2018. Her first short story collection, *Grand Union*, was published in 2019. She is professor of Creative Writing at New York University (NYU).

IF YOU LIKE THIS, TRY...

Helen Oyeyemi's *The Icarus Girl* (Bloomsbury, 2005) in which the Nigerian-English couple is less the focus. It is their daughter whose difficulties spin out of control. Martinician-British writer Ruel White's novella *Heroes Through the Day* is set during a single day featuring London characters, Butch, Derrick and Joanne. Published by New Beacon Books (1990), it experiments with the form of dialogue and monologue that anticipates *NW*. See also Jackie Kay's *Trumpet* (entry 32).

47

THE SWAN BOOK

ALEXIS WRIGHT

2013

What happens when a virus resides in your brain and thinks you want what it does? What happens when you are deemed to be an alien in your own ancestral lands, discounted, forcibly relocated from place to place, suffering violent attacks and denied justice?

The Swan Book chillingly and presciently offers a timely tale of great relevance to today's climate catastrophe, global virus pandemic and erosion of human rights. Oblivia, 'a little Aboriginal kid', has been asleep for a decade in a sacred eucalyptus tree. The ancestral tree is the only witness to Oblivia's rape by a petrol-sniffing gang of young men. In a nod to Shakespeare's Ariel in *The Tempest*, Oblivia is rescued, not by a white patriarch but by Bella Donna of the Champions, a white woman, a refugee from Europe's climate disaster. She is a stranger, a migrant to the 'swamp', the latest manifestation of internment camps for Australia's Indigenous population. Bella Donna anchors her hulk as a habitat for herself and Oblivia, for whom she becomes an 'old *wanymarri* white woman Aunty'.

There are few books that can match the imaginative scope, scale and the stylistic sweep of Alexis Wright's dystopic and allegorical novel. Its poetic and parodic use of language intersperses Waanyi, English, French and Latin to create a brew of exquisite imagery, acerbic observations and ecological encounters. Wright has crafted a perturbing and disturbing tale. It was written in the wake of John Howard's government and its 2007 'Emergency Intervention' into 73 remote Indigenous communities in the Northern Territory (an area of 40 Indigenous language groups). This followed the 'Ampe Akelyernemane Meke Mekarle 'Little Children are Sacred' Report'. When police and armed forces were sent in, they were followed by the media, creating a spectacle that Indigenous intellectual Marcia Langton describes as the 'perpetual Aboriginal reality show'. It evoked the traumatic policies that had produced the Stolen Generations. The novel is framed by the ongoing failure of white settler Australia to unilaterally acknowledge that the continent is unceded and that Indigenous sovereignty is indisputable.

This futuristic novel is set in a world wracked not only by climate change, but also technological damage under the auspices of development. The cataclysmic events of *The Swan Book* take readers into heinous crimes, brutality and degradation, alongside struggles to retain sovereignty over self and surroundings. But there is much buoyancy in what might appear to be unremitting bleakness. This is in no small part due to the narrative that Wright crafts, one that both excites recognition and repulsion, but also enjoyment of the satire by which she represents policy-makers, politics, greed, collusion and the lengths people will go to achieve power.

After years of sailing and reaching Australia with the 'nightmarish' story of her people, Bella Donna's arrival parodically mirrors the first settlers who rewrote history in their nation story that supplanted pre-existing Indigenous Peoples. However, the crucial difference is that Bella Donna is narrated from an Indigenous perspective – one that does not allow colonialist nationalism.

The motifs of imprisonment and refuge underpins Oblivia's and Bella Donna's experiences. Oblivia is mute throughout the book, not having spoken since the rape. She is also trapped within her own mind, inhabited by the virus, unable to articulate aloud all that she is witnessing, hearing and thinking. Her thoughts, recorded in italics, give the reader a dual perspective. As well as the third-person narration, Oblivia's inner responses provide a sharp counter-observation of other characters and remind us she will never recover from her brutal ordeal.

Character and country are inextricable in this novel. Climate devastation co-exists with the suffering caused by dispossession and violence towards humans and non-humans. Wright represents riveting cross-cultural and cross-species complexities through such relationships and interactions as that between Oblivia and the swans she first encounters as a premonition.

The Swan Book weaves a narrative of linguistic exquisiteness with trenchant, expository critique. Wright examines how stories from time immemorial retain traction in the hearts and minds of generations who were removed from direct connection to the land, the elements, flora and fauna. Dreams, memories, time in reverse, before- and after-thought, and future visitations all exist on the same plane of consciousness to produce an exuberant release from Western rationalism and rigidities of linear time.

Wright also represents Indigenous characters who absorb the traits and manipulations of power that support the apparatus of policy-making, government interventions, and community and environmental destruction. While driving Oblivia away in his car after abducting her as his trophy wife, Warren Finch the first Indigenous prime minister tells her she will never return to her home because '*It no longer exists*' and orders the evacuation of the swamp. Oblivia cannot reconcile the man in the suit with the orders he has given via his mobile phone and the explosions she hears of her world being destroyed. Finch locks her up in an apartment tower, The People's Palace in the City of Refugees. While she is guarded by Machine in Finch's home, swans remain powerful presences and she does not give up hope of returning to the swamp. Finch's backstory, his fate and the entwined destinies of Bella Donna, Oblivia and the swans present a deeply affecting plotline for readers to unpack.

This story reminds readers how settler interpretations of what 'reconciliation' entails are problematic in relation to what Indigenous people experience as more pressing – the reparative, re-establishing of connections with family and land. A double provocation is posed. To what degree can people be abused, incarcerated or left bereft of sovereignty before they stop surviving against the odds but, more importantly, what happens if they do keep surviving, no matter what?

Colonial trauma is present and ongoing, a lived hydra-headed reality for Indigenous communities. Wright notes that, 'I use literature to try and create a truer replica of reality.'

This apocalyptic writing unflinchingly reasserts accountability for the impact upon Indigenous Peoples' lives from the moment the British flag was planted to declare *terra nullius* which, in the light of this novel equals the ultimate *'ignis fatuus'* – the title of the book's opening chapter, defined as a misleading goal, influence or delusion, in the face of what will always be Aboriginal Land.

THE NOVEL

This was first published in English by Giramondo Publishing, Australia in 2013 and shortlisted for the Stella Prize in 2014. It was published by Constable in the UK (2015) and Simon & Schuster in the US (2016).

THE AUTHOR

Alexis Wright (1950–) is a member of the Waanyi Nation in the area of northern Australia named the Gulf of Carpentaria. Her novels include *Carpentaria* (2006), which won the Miles Franklin Literary Award and the Australian Literature Society Gold Medal and has been translated into six languages. Her other books include: *Plains of Promise* (1997), shortlisted for the Commonwealth Writers' Prize and *Tracker* (2018), a collective biography of activist Tracker Tilmouth which won the Stella Prize. She holds the Boisbouvier Chair in Australian Literature, University of Melbourne and is Fellow of the Australian Academy of the Humanities.

IF YOU LIKE THIS, TRY...

Anita Heiss's 2021 *Bila Yarrudhanggalangdhuray* (*River of Dreams*). The author is a member of the Wiradjuri Nation, and the novel is set in 1852 in Wiradjuri country in the wake of the Murrumbidgee River's deadly flooding. Of Rembarranga and Tiwi descent, Marie Munkara's *Every Secret Thing* (2009) is described as a collision between faith and culture in the Christian Mission era of northern Australia, when nothing is left sacred and much carnivalesque humour results.

Cristina Calderón is the only remaining native speaker of Yagan, the southern-most Indigenous group in the world. *Hai kur mamashu chis* or *I want to tell you a story* (2005) are stories told by Cristina and her grandmother from the Yagan community in Ukika, Isla Navarino (Chile). The English-language edition was translated by Jaqueline Windh and published in 2013. Fijian Paulini Turagabeci's *The River* (2019) is set on one of the two major islands that comprise Fiji. Grandfather Ilai Levukanailoma, a retired widower with a troubled past, becomes the only caregiver to his six-month-old grandson Tomi in a poignant tale of redemptive love across generations.

48

A BRIEF HISTORY OF SEVEN KILLINGS

MARLON JAMES

2014

The first edition front cover of *A Brief History of Seven Killings* rightly proclaims its 'epic' status and the novel's huge cinematic cast of characters definitely takes the crime thriller to a higher level. James' book is epic in its treatment of history, its many language styles in play and its bold rewriting of the crime genre.

Set in a former colony, Jamaica, the clues discovered in the opening pages of the novel invariably indicate what the narrative holds in store. What the reader first encounters here is death, intriguingly personified against a background in which time is collapsed to bring the dead of the region's history – monarchs, pirates, slave merchants, ghetto rude boys – fleetingly together into 'the flatness of the deadlands'. Notably, the voice with which the novel begins – and which temporarily disorientates the reader – is that of someone who has met a violent death. He is the white politician Sir Arthur George Jennings, whose name alone evokes a postcolonial history linked to Britain's former slave colonies and empire.

Jennings, whose head was 'pumpkin-smashed' in death, pronounces that 'dead people never stop talking', foreshadowing the brutality that will come to light as the action of the novel develops. One of several ghostly narrators, Jennings also figures in the haunting reach of the region's colonial history into the novel's 20th-century setting and into a widespread diaspora, specifically linking the US to the Caribbean. Troubling characters such as Barry Diflorio and Louis Johnson enter the narrative from the US. So does the Cuban who becomes known as Doctor Love. The interest of each lies in the ghetto areas of Jamaica's capital, Kingston, and in engineering political instability; cocaine and guns become central to this Jamaican story. For the same reasons, the gangsters, Weeper and Josey Wales, must travel to the US to build upon the cocaine gains they make through this connection. The killings – more than seven – in Kingston in the 1970s and the Bronx of the 1980s – speak to a long history of colonial and racialized violence resurfacing as slum-dwelling realities of the newly independent post-colony at the heart of James' novel.

How the action of outsiders, primarily CIA agents, escalates the violence and corrosive brutality that runs throughout is narrated by key eyewitnesses. The novel centres on the attempted killing of reggae superstar, Bob Marley, personified by James as the Singer. The young Bam-Bam narrates the second killing, that of his father, and tells of his terror as a ten-year-old witnessing the event. Orphaned as a result of the traumatic execution of both his parents, he reveals that he was given a gun while still too shocked to speak after escaping the murder scene. Although an American would later teach him how to shoot, it is the aspiring gang boss Josey Wales who, three years later, would brutally order Bam-Bam's first gang murder. Wales' effective grooming of younger gang members would also eventually steer the course of the novel.

As Bam-Bam's narration reflects, in the everyday ghetto existence madness flourishes in poverty so searing that people 'can't even afford shame.' Meanwhile, foreign men 'bring guns' and so killings further escalate with the increased availability of lethal weapons, including machine guns. Speaking to the one he believes to have sung himself 'straight out of the ghetto', he confesses to having 'learnt to hate' him. The novel turns on the action of the architect of that hatred, the ruthlessly ambitious Wales, who systematically usurps the place of Papa-Lo or 'Don of Dons', a friend and confidante of the Singer. While Marley is not directly characterized, his figure as the Singer overshadows the novel whether loved, hated, desired or simply remaining an enigma to powerful others.

The narrative's opening instruction – 'Listen!' – echoed by gang narrators such as Demus signals to the reader an important orality, flagging the prospect of being offered distinctive, perhaps unfamiliar voices, markedly for those readers new to Caribbean writing. Additionally, the talking dead allow James to distort time but also to enable astute readers to see situations, perhaps familiar through the media, anew. This strategy draws on African-Caribbean storytelling traditions in which the dead not only speak to, but assume the power to illuminate much that puzzles the living. In this way, James disarms his readers and leads them into a narrative that is often brutal and shocking, in order to question real-life events and their long-term meanings.

James' writing soon comes alive with the Jamaican Creole narration of characters like Bam-Bam and Papa-Lo, whose voices carry the island's lyrical musicality. There are also the Americans with their varieties of English and Hispanics associated with Cuba and Colombia. Wales, though he is strategic about when and how he uses it, even speaks Spanish. The sheer virtuosity of James' first-person narrators jumps from every page. These include gangsters, CIA agents, a *Rolling Stone* journalist and an up-town but desperate one-time lover of the Singer.

There are startlingly few female characters in James' third novel, which though perhaps a point of contention, nonetheless allows a clear focus on the male world the author wishes to interrogate. In that male world, the ghostly narrators, part of James' deep concern with history or what he calls being 'obsessed with the past' and 'obsessed with stories that weren't told or that weren't told in a good way', are all male. So are the gang members and the overwhelming majority of eye-witness narrators, with the result that James' story-world readily exposes the many ways in which women within this specific history have been made and continue to be made sexual objects by men. At the same time, James' male narrators, themselves under fierce scrutiny through the writing, reveal the rigidity of their worldview, including sexual understanding and particularly the ways in which colonialism shaped more than just the social violence that maintains poverty. That is to say, that the same dominant histories of social violence also systematically reinforced ideas of gender. In the case of Jamaica, same-gender sexual relations were specifically prohibited by the

1864 Offences Against the Person Act by the British colonial government. Unsurprisingly, James' homosexual characters, drawn from an overwhelmingly dehumanized, ghettoized, social group, are not in a position to understand their gendered, sexualized position and instead must distort and deny their desire. Questions about internalized homophobia is one of many issues that James' novel raises.

The novel has been described as 'polyphonic' because of the many voices James uses to tell his tale. Its 'masculinist violence' has been highlighted and it has been assessed as a crime novel concerned with suppressed stories. Readers expecting a crime novel must be prepared to do much of the detective work themselves. There are certainly many clues to be found, much of which can be fact-checked. Yet, moving beyond crime fiction, James refuses to tie up the ends for us. He seems to point to detective work as only one level through which this book might be read. A great many layers remain to be excavated along with the questions that arise in this big, nuanced but also darkly humorous narrative.

THE NOVEL

First published by Oneworld Publications in 2014 and by Riverhead Books in the US, *A Brief History of Seven Killings* was received with widespread excitement and positive literary reviews. The novel won the OCM Bocas Prize for Caribbean Literature, the 2015 Man Booker Prize, the American Book Award and the Anisfield-Wolf Book Award for Fiction in 2015. It was a finalist for the National Book Critics Circle Award.

THE AUTHOR

Marlon James (1970–) was born in Jamaica. His debut novel was *John Crow's Devil* (2005). His second novel, *The Book of Night Women* (2009), won the 2010 Dayton Literary Peace Prize and was a finalist for the 2010 National Book Critics Circle Award. He is now a Creative Writing professor in the US.

IF YOU LIKE THIS, TRY...

Marlon James, *The Book of Night Women* (2009) which centralizes women as figures of rebellion, set in the period of Atlantic slavery. If same-sex desire is a theme that is of particular interest, try Patricia Powell's *The Pagoda* (1998), which is set in the late 19th century and focuses on an immigrant Chinese shopkeeper in Jamaica.

THE SELLOUT

PAUL BEATTY

2015

The reader is catapulted quickly into Beatty's bitingly satirical novel. *The Sellout* opens with, 'This may be hard to believe, coming from a black man, but I've never stolen anything.' The narrator's immediate trickster appeal to the reader to consider stereotypes of the Black male is extended in the sentences that immediately follow, listing deviant behaviours that he assures the reader he has never indulged in. However, he soon reveals that he is sitting handcuffed in the Supreme Court of the United States of America, in a 'padded chair that, much like this country, isn't quite as comfortable as it looks.' His case is listed as number 09-2606, 'Me vs America'. Me is his surname, and the charges against him are grave, ignoring the Fourteenth Amendment, reinstituting segregation and enslaving a fellow human.

The Sellout is centrally concerned with racism and Blackness. The novel dares to re-present the situation through a series of absurdities. Neither individual characters nor institutions are spared in this roller coaster exposé. Jokes, puns and allusions run throughout the novel, within which Beatty's language is intentionally irreverent. This world ranges from downright absurd to laugh-out-loud funny; its plot is comic, its characters are zany. Its critique of racial politics and culture in the 21st century hits home.

The Sellout's world is one in which absurdities are accentuated within a landscape that is already familiar, even if only through media representation. Beginning with its setting, the fictionalized Californian town of Dickens on the outskirts of Los Angeles, every possible situation is satirized and presented as absurd. In the novel, Dickens is a city with a 19th-century charter stipulating that it should be kept free of 'Spanish of all shades'. Despite this, Dickens is predominantly Latino and Black, a situation that itself grounds the satire so as to immediately raise questions about race and Blackness. The same charter established an agricultural zone known as the 'farms' within the larger urban area. Though the farms are in the process of disappearing due to gentrification, they ensure the homely smell in Dickens, of cow manure and 'good weed'. In direct contrast is the impact of the Stank, a toxic mix of oil refinery waste, sewage, party-goers' body odour and cologne, which hangs over Dickens as a 'celestial flatulence'. In Dickens, noted as the murder capital of the world, the schools are failing. Its only space reflecting a sense of community – in that it is never vandalized – is the Dum Dum Donut shop. When the novel begins, Dickens has been unceremoniously removed from the map and its road signs from the highways. A gentrification conspiracy is afoot and has added to the residents' suffering.

Key to the plot of *The Sellout* is the death of Me's father – shot in the back by the police. His role of dissuading suicidal residents is passed on to Me. As a result, by saving their minor celebrity, Hominy, from suicide, Me comes to understand Hominy's distress as being directly linked to Dickens' disappearance. Hominy's fans can no longer find him. The dilemma for Me is that he finds himself landed with someone who insists on literally being his slave, complete with beatings. Since octogenarian Hominy is deaf to any refusal, Me acquiesces. Vacillating between fury and indulgence, Me beats Hominy as requested, but he also undertakes Hominy's additional request to revive Dickens. Me's mission gathers impetus after he successfully segregates a bus for Hominy's birthday present, and identifies resegregation as the answer to Dickens' many problems.

Central to Beatty's engagement with the past and present is the narrator and protagonist, Me. Unconventionally raised by his father, whose unrestrained ideas centred on matters of Blackness, Me is a character with no social life. He remembers, though, being the guinea pig of several violent experiments generated by his social scientist father who had altered their surname, Mee, by dropping the final letter. Me states after his father's killing, 'Dickens was me. And I was my father.' As both disappeared from his life, around the same time, he found himself with 'no idea who I was and how to become myself.' Home-schooled and solitary, Me's subsequent self-discovery is grounded in the farm he inherits with the compensation money from his father's unlawful death. Having studied agriculture, in time he develops varieties of those plants that were culturally relevant to him, such as the watermelon. He travels around the city on horseback, surfs for leisure, and generously shares novelty varieties of his weed and fruit such as his square watermelon. Me merits two other names in the novel. He is called Bonbon by his former neighbour and sometimes lover, Marpessa. He is also dismissively referred to as 'The Sellout' by his nemesis, Foy Cheshire.

Beatty treats the past in a variety of ways through the character of Me's father, whose life is permeated with frustration. A devotee to his own science, 'blackology', he was the Black professional typically waiting for 20 years to be promoted. Unacknowledged in his field of psychology, a failure at farming, the blackology home-schooling of his son served as a case study. Within Dickens, psychology gained him the distinction of acknowledging his success with the suicidal. The success he valued greatly was the founding of the Dum Dum Donut Intellectuals club at the local doughnut shop. It is there that Me becomes acquainted with the fraudulent Cheshire, who uses Me's father's ideas to his own financial advantage. It is when Me refuses to take on his father's role in the club that Foy first calls him 'The Sellout'. Through the tension between Me and Foy, Beatty draws attention to the Black intellectual who works against those for whom he appears to speak. Rather like Cheshire, such a character undertakes self-serving roles from which he profits.

The character of Hominy Jenkins brings into view questions concerning media representation, blackface minstrelsy, and figures dismissed as Uncle Tom. In the novel, he is the last survivor of the Little Rascals gang in which he played the stereotypical Black figure at the butt end of visualized and racial jokes. Hominy enjoyed the recognition and the money derived from it. Like Cheshire, whose name alludes to the Cheshire cat in *Alice in Wonderland*, Hominy is waiting for recognition from society; for progress to manifest itself. However, he has been doubly written off, by a system that no longer has use for him and by other Black people who dismiss him as Uncle Tom. Additionally, as a Dickens resident, and as his attempted suicide confirms, Hominy's life is over-determined by race and ghettoization. Unlike Cheshire, his choices and opportunities are severely limited.

The Sellout exposes complexities, ideas and realities that abound concerning race, specifically Blackness. Above all, through its parodying and comic approach, the novel attempts to debunk the idea that the 21st century represents a post-racial era characterized by progress in its response to race. Dickens is segregated in all but name before Me begins his campaign. Me's words, 'I've just whispered race in a post-racial world' resonate throughout the novel. At the same time, the focus is not upon merely the effect of racism but on an opening up of the debate to include those like Cheshire, who claim to speak and write for Black people. The novel is also about identity, particularly Black masculinity. *The Sellout* underscores the ridiculous in how matters of race continue to be played out through frustrations, cynicism, ghettoization, despair and violence in a post-millennial era.

THE NOVEL

The Sellout was published in 2015 by Farrar, Straus and Giroux in the US and in the UK by Oneworld Publications (2016). The novel won the Man Booker Prize and the National Book Critics Circle's fiction award, both in 2016.

THE AUTHOR

Paul Beatty (1962–) is a novelist and poet. His novels include *Slumberland* (2008), *Tuff* (2000) and *The White Boy Shuffle* (1996). His poetry collections are *Big Bank Take Little Bank* (1991) and *Joker, Joker, Deuce* (1994). He is editor of *Hokum: An Anthology of African-American Humor* (2006).

IF YOU LIKE THIS, TRY...

Ralph Ellison's *Invisible Man* (1952 and Vintage, 1995) is the classic African-American novel that studies the urban and treats invisibility as an outcome of racism.

THE WHITE GIRL

TONY BIRCH

2019

What can an Indigenous grandmother do in 1960s rural Australia to stop her blonde-haired granddaughter from being taken away by the authorities because she appears to be white? In *The White Girl*, Odette Brown must save 12-year-old Sissy from two threats: removal by the State and Aaron, the predatory son of the white pastoralist Joe Kane, who had raped Sissy's mother Lila. With Lila's whereabouts unknown, the law does not recognize Odette as Sissy's official guardian, despite being a direct relative. Odette needs to take action and that means breaking the law.

It is generally overlooked that Indigenous People on the Australian continent have the oldest continuous culture in human history. The British invasion in 1788 was justified by declaring *terra nullius* or empty land, and Australia became a version of Britain. White settlers consolidated land acquisition by displacing and slaughtering Indigenous Peoples. Governments implemented punitive colonial policies that ranged from 'Protection' to 'Assimilation' and 'Integration', and murdering the continent's Indigenous population. Indigenous Peoples lived in fear of their children being forcibly removed through designations based upon 'Name. Age. Colour. Blood.'. Removal policies decimated kinship ties and belonging on an unimaginable scale, now recognized as the Stolen Generations. This novel is a loving tribute to them all.

The strength and courage of Indigenous women is celebrated as they protect their families and heritage against malevolent white male violence and repressive laws. The weightiness of the issues is elegantly pivoted by the warmth and vitality of ties sustained against the odds. Odette and Sissy share a meagre hut in Quarrytown, an abandoned mining camp outside the fictional town of Deane – a place that 'carried the blood of so many Aboriginal people on its hands it could never be scrubbed away.' The now-abandoned church mission where Odette was born, and immediately separated from her parents, is also the site of her ancestors' graveyard, replete with memories that she passes on to Sissy. Although a work of fiction, its poignancy compels readers into understanding and recognizing the abusive treatment Indigenous Peoples faced in this era – and the repercussions that continue to shape these citizens' lives today. Under the Aborigines Protection Act and its Aborigines Welfare Board, white authorities had complete power over where Indigenous Peoples could live, work, travel to, and with whom they could mix. When Odette is refused a travel permit for Sissy, local policeman Bill O'Shea reminds her, 'You take her out of the district and get caught, you're likely to lose her for good.' The only means to escape the restrictions was through an

Exemption Certificate that required severing all ties with Aboriginal culture, including one's family.

Birch brings both aspects into orbit in *The White Girl* when the lax and drunken O'Shea who grew up with the Indigenous community he polices, is replaced by the coldly bureaucratic Sergeant Lowe who begins a forensic audit of the town's Indigenous children. Odette's journey in defiance of the Act is prompted by the need to stop her granddaughter from being taken by the authorities. Sissy becomes the eponymous White Girl, escaping with Odette as her Aboriginal servant to the unnamed City. They are pursued by Lowe, whose determination to enact welfare policy borders on pathological calculation and the outcome of this pursuit leads to many surprising encounters and revelations.

Odette increasingly becomes custodian of the stories and photographs of other Indigenous characters, an everywoman holding together the tragedy of her dispossessed people and the replaying of the dreadful story across generations. Unbearably at one point, Wanda, the receptionist at the City Hotel where they are staying asks Odette for a hug, 'It was the first time Wanda had felt the touch of an Aboriginal woman since the day she had been taken away from her own mother'.

The exquisite precision of Birch's knife-sharp, unadorned realist prose twists and turns the narrative with unsparing candour. He crafts a path of painful memories alongside small victories. Characters' weaknesses or vulnerabilities are interwoven with moments where they shine. The narrative unflinchingly shows the effects of gross injustices that cross-generationally contour the lives of the Indigenous

Peoples. He also offers a touching panoply of non-Indigenous characters – those who are victimized or defiantly individualistic who form bonds of friendship and compassion with the Quarrytown community, irrespective of race.

Apart from the local junkyard owner Henry (scapegoated and bullied), Dr Singer (a survivor of the Nazi concentration camps) and the clerk at the Aborigines Welfare Board, many of the white characters are cruel and unsympathetic. Yet, Birch's straightforward prose style has the power to evoke 'sympathy for the devil'. There are glimpses into their back-stories. Aaron Kane, who terrorizes Henry and then Sissy, has been sadistically beaten by his father Joe all his life and the cowardly O'Shea is a hopeless alcoholic who ends his own life. While *The White Girl* creates grandeur in the overlooked and ordinary lives of legions of people like Odette who have stoked resilience against brutality, it also recognizes those who cannot. Lila is not condemned for abandoning Sissy. Bearing a child after rape by a white man is a horror she cannot recover from, and the novel elicits compassion for a woman destroyed and unable to care for her daughter.

There are humorous aspects to the writing, none more so than in the figure of formidable Millie Khan, married to the Afghani cameleer Yusuf. Indigenous Millie is not however, under the jurisdiction of State Welfare. She and her non-Indigenous husband run their own business and have bought back land stolen from her people. She enjoys freedom from persecution by the welfare rules that restrict Odette and other Indigenous Peoples in the town. Her acerbic encounters with

Lowe offer cathartic opportunities to speak back to power. As Millie tells him the idea of 'welfare' is a cruel misnomer, as most of the girls 'are dead, disappeared, or were sent mad by what you did to them in the institutions.'

Indigenous Australian literature is not easily obtainable for British and North American readers. The rewards gained from reading this novel offer an affecting and powerful reminder of resilience and dignity sustained in the wake of the malignant legacy of colonization. It is also a profound story of mothers, daughters, sisters, aunts and granddaughters, testimony to the sincerity of Birch's hope that in writing *The White Girl* he can encourage an 'understanding of the tenacity and love within the hearts of those who suffered the theft of their own blood.' It is a shared history that must be remembered in perpetuity.

THE NOVEL

First published in English by University of Queensland Press in 2019, *The White Girl* was named winner of the New South Wales Premier's Prize for Indigenous Writing 2020, and was shortlisted for both the Christina Stead Prize for Fiction (2020) and the Miles Franklin Award (2020).

THE AUTHOR

Of Indigenous, Barbadian (convict), Irish and Afghani heritage, Koori writer Tony Birch (1957–) was raised in inner-city Melbourne, Australia. He is author of nine books, and also writes poetry and polemical essays. Until his retirement in

2020, he was a Professor at Victoria University and the inaugural Dr Bruce McGuinness Indigenous Research Fellow. Birch's fiction includes *Shadowboxing* (2006), *Father's Day* (2009), *Blood* (2011), *The Promise* (2014) and *Common People* (2017). In 2016, *Ghost River* (2015) won the Victorian Premier's Award for Indigenous Writing, while *Broken Teeth* was shortlisted for the Scanlon Prize for Indigenous Poetry. He is a recipient of the prestigious Patrick White Literary Award (2017).

IF YOU LIKE THIS, TRY...

Sally Morgan's *My Place* (1987), a modern classic, spanning three generations of Indigenous women and set in suburban Perth, Western Australia during a similar period to *The White Girl*. Even though her mother and grandmother were Indigenous, Sally and her siblings had a white father and their mother told them they were Indian. *My Place* articulates Sally's discovery of her true heritage. Other must-read award-winning novels include: Kim Scott's *Benang: From the Heart* (1999), Claire G Coleman's speculative fiction *Terra Nullius* (2017) or intertexts such as Leah Purcell's play *The Drover's Wife* (2016): which centres an Indigenous woman who has had to pass for white to survive the murderous settler environment, and her subsequent novel and film, *The Drover's Wife: The Legend of Molly Johnson* (2019).

AFTERWORD

DECOLONIZING THE LITERARY WORLD

We hope you will continue expanding your literary journey around the world and discover new authors. As colonization involves a group or individual imposing their culture and beliefs over another, our aim has been democratization, to assist you in becoming proactive in curating your own reading choices.

Literary activism incorporates the full range of work involved in the creation, production and promotion of literature and books. Additionally, reader activism can help influence the shape of the contemporary fiction landscape. You can support writers and their books by talking about them, recommending them and by voting with your wallet.

By taking part in any of the activities suggested here you can contribute to literary activism and/or reader activism. This can make a real difference to opening up the literary world. It is an effective way to make publishers sit up and take notice of what readers want and it supports authors financially. If you are a student and your reading lists are monocultural, ask to study the titles in this book; help get new titles onto the curriculum.

VISIT YOUR LIBRARY

Libraries are the only spaces where you can read your books of choice at little to no charge. Libraries need our support so that ideas, stories and information can be freely accessed by everyone. The Great Library of Alexandria in Egypt ensured that Alexandria was considered as the capital of knowledge and learning in the ancient world: libraries are the bedrock of cultural civilization. Many countries have special National Library weeks to promote library activities and resources. National Libraries often have the scope and size to hold a wide range of events and activities that are ethnically diverse and accessible, such as reading groups. Mobile libraries are essential for rural and poorer communities, as they are anchors in these areas. Helping a nearby community, or one abroad, to access books or create a library, supports the notion that knowledge and information should be freely available to everyone. It is vital for governments to invest more in libraries to encourage a vibrant library culture for the health of their nations and to ensure knowledge is accessible to all throughout their lives. It takes a community to support these services.

JOIN A READING GROUP

Reading groups are a valuable activity and potential starting point for your literary activism. Held in a wide variety of social – and sometimes workplace – spaces, reading groups provide opportunities for you to talk about a title, selected democratically by the group, in a very informal way. Why not introduce this book's selection of authors to your reading group? You might decide to take this a step further and set up a reading group around *This is the Canon* and kickstart a reading revolution at grassroots level. A reading group offers a space where open discussion of ideas and the status quo in publishing, universities and schools can happen. This can then feed into wider conversations taking place in editorial meetings, student forums, PTA groups – all of which can bring about change in the books that are commissioned, read and studied.

SUPPORT INDEPENDENT PUBLISHERS AND BOOKSHOPS

Small independent publishers often publish specialist liter-ature, by genre or ethnicity and frequently discover and nurture new voices. Many of them operate as not-for-profit organisations and buying directly from the publisher ensures that your money goes to them rather than large, interna-tional retailers. Try their websites, or you could support your local bookshop. In a similar way, local, independently managed bookshops can champion authors and issues that are less mainstream than the ones on the tables of the larger chains – they rely on your custom to survive against the online giants, and often host book signings and readings with local authors that offer an opportunity to engage with an author or a book directly.

BUY LITERARY MAGAZINES
AND EXPERIENCE NEW WRITERS

Two of our featured writers, Chimamanda Ngozi Adichie and Daniyal Mueenuddin, gained international recognition through *Zoetrope* magazine. Some independent publishers produce literary magazines in print and online. The majority are run voluntarily by literary magazine enthusiasts and have small print runs.

Literary magazines are becoming increasingly diverse. Some publish special issues to focus on themes, genres or a specific group of writers. These raise awareness of the writers that they feature and are great places for you to discover new authors. However, we advocate for writers to be included in general issues too. You can discover and support new writers and magazines through subscriptions such as the US-based *St Petersburg Review*, whose aim from its inception has been to decolonize the space it offers by including a diverse ethnic range of authors and genres from around the globe. Similarly, UK-based *Wasafiri*'s aim is to 'encourage readers and writers to travel the world via the word.'

Informative blogs and websites are also available and worth a look to find out more through articles and interviews, and to spot new book recommendations. The blogs with widest scope can be found on National Library sites such as the British Library, the New York Public Library (NYPL) and the Library of Congress. These reflect the specialist themes of their collections. The British Library website hosts blogs by in-house curators and external specialists such as the 'Untold

Lives' blog, in which stories of groups and individuals that have become hidden from society throughout history are revealed. Another of their blogs is 'Black Britain, Asian Britain'. The NYPL offers multilingual blog channels and specialist blogs on subjects ranging from the history and culture of literature and writing from Africa and the African diaspora, to a 'LGBTQ at NYPL' blog. The Library of Congress has a special selection of Conversations with African Poets and Writers such as Ngũgĩ wa Thiong'o and Chinua Achebe, as well as younger prize-winning African writers. Publishers such as Peepal Tree Press publish regular blogs on themes and writers in Caribbean literature. Many of these blog articles focus on a specific theme, which will introduce readers to selected books. Novelist Pete Kalu is one of a few writers whose blog offers book reviews.

Podcasts are another platform for writers to share discussions about their work. Examples include Rajeev Balasubramanyam's 'Blissful Thinking' and Ellen van Neerven's 'Between The Leaves'. They host their own podcasts linked to themes in their work, such as love, race and feminism, and invite other writers to discuss these themes with them. There are an increasing number of regular book review and author interview podcasts too. Explore these online to find those with a diverse range of authors and titles. Patricia Cumper's and Pauline Walker's 'The Amplify Project' includes writers from different genres talking about their work. Sherman Alexie shares a podcast with author Jess Walter called 'A Tiny Sense of Accomplishment', in which they discuss their lives as writers and invite other writers to do the same.

DONATE TO WRITING PRIZES

Prizes offer writers an opportunity to boost their profiles and if they come with a financial award, it can be substantial enough to enable invaluable writing time. Small prizes need continual donations and sponsors to administrate and provide the winner's prize. Diverse judging panels are important in encouraging writers to submit work, resulting in a democratic and equal approach for these valuable awards. Positive steps forward have seen more prizes open to unpublished writers and those experimenting with new genres and finding it difficult to gain publication. These awards also support writers who have traditionally had less access to the mainstream publishing industry. Prizes such as the SI Leeds Literary Prize for Black and Asian women writers are focused on unpublished manuscripts. Literary activism is itself a political act in some countries. Ahlam Mosteghanemi set up the Malek Haddad Literary Prize to encourage Arabic literature as a direct way to fight against the colonization of the French language in Algeria. Writers also use their awards as platforms to make statements that criticize policies of the authorities, as Haruki Murakami did when he won The Jerusalem Prize for works that deal with themes of human freedom in society.

ATTEND LITERARY FESTIVALS AND EVENTS

Literary festivals can attract thousands of people to often-glorious locations, providing occasions to discover new books and writers. They offer a platform for authors to attract new readers through public readings and engagement with an audience. The largest free literary festival in the world is the Zee Jaipur Festival in India. Hay Festival, based in the UK partnered with publisher Storymoja in Kenya and have held sister-events and projects in India, Lebanon, Bangladesh, Mali and the Maldives.

Do you have a local writing or arts centre? Or access to a national writing centre? These can be great places to discover literary readings and discussions. You can get involved by helping out at events and you could perhaps suggest a series of readings or inviting a new author for a talk. You might go further and get involved with funding bids to reimagine your city as a UNESCO City of Literature, one which embraces a diversity of literature and sharing of different ways and means to enjoy it.

WRITERS AS ACTIVISTS

All of the writers in this book challenge injustice in their writing and some go beyond this to be active off the page too. Some writers are involved in literary activities, social justice and human rights campaigns, and these might be linked to their creative work. Others have established non-profit organizations.

Activist writers regularly use their public platform to highlight other writers to read. One of the first things that Bernardine Evaristo did after she won The Booker Prize was to suggest books by other Black British women writers. Therefore, we encourage you to follow writers that you admire, starting with their websites and social media.

Many of our 50 writers advocate for various causes and voluntarily give their time to issues they believe in. Others are doing this around the world and the result will be a more diverse, exciting literary culture for everyone:

Chimamanda Ngozi Adichie runs The Purple Hibiscus Creative Writing Workshop annually in Nigeria.

Ama Ata Aidoo established the Organisation of Women Writers of Africa (OWWA) with the late Jayne Cortez. In Ghana she established the Mbaasem Foundation to promote and support the work of African women writers.

Ayi Kwei Armah set up Per Ankh: African Publication Collective where he published books, including reprints of his own books and ran a programme for prospective African publishers.

Tony Birch is a climate justice researcher and campaigner in Australia. He is also a champion for advancing justice for Indigenous communities and other people living on the margins of society.

Sandra Cisneros established the Macondo Foundation and the Alfredo Cisneros del Moral Foundation to support writers. She is the organiser of Los MacArturos, for the Latino MacArthur fellows for community activism.

Tsitsi Dangarembga is a political activist who campaigns against corruption in Zimbabwe. Her 2006 documentary, *Peretera Maneta (Spell My Name)* received the UNESCO Children's and Human Rights Award and the Zanzibar International Film Festival Award.

Edwidge Danticat edits anthologies of emerging Haitian writers and is an advocate for issues that affect Haitians at home and abroad.

Bernardine Evaristo supports Black British writers from mentoring to advocating for more recognition and awareness in the mainstream industry.

Khaled Hosseini set up a charity, The Khaled Hosseini Foundation, to provide humanitarian relief and shelter and support for women and children in Afghanistan.

LeAnne Howe produced a documentary, *Spiral of Fire*, for the Indian Country Diaries and has developed courses in Native American Studies for universities.

Arundhati Roy is a human rights activist supporting and speaking out for the poorest people in India, including working with young writers in the 'untouchable' caste.

Ngũgĩ wa Thiong'o is a 'language warrior' who advocates for writing in mother tongue, raising the visibility of African languages and for people centring their own languages in their daily communications.

Alexis Wright is a land rights activist in Australia.

Following the activities of these writers is a good way to explore the issues which they have expressed in their writing – develop your awareness and support their causes. The list above is merely a sample of the wide range of activity the authors in this book are involved in.

Alongside their writing, individual Indigenous writers and groups are active in creating awareness around their culture and history – and speak out regarding land rights and human rights. You can support them by finding out what action they want their readers to take. There are some places to start, such as exploring publishing companies and bookshops. For instance, Birchbark Books in Minneapolis, US, which focuses on Native American / First Nations literature and holds events, too. In Canada, Tomson Highway created music and arts festivals and has been the artistic director for theatre companies that have laid the foundation for the literary landscape in Canada for Indigenous Peoples. In Australia, writer Claire G Coleman is a member of the cultural advisory committee for Agency, a not-for-profit Indigenous arts consultancy. Tara June Winch created a dictionary for the Wiradjuri language and then wove this into her novel, *The Yield* (2020). *Chapter House Journal* is the quarterly creative writing journal of The IAIA (Institute of American Indian Arts) MFA programme in the US.

In terms of thinking about writing as a political act, when you attend literary events do ask questions of writers about their work, and inform yourself of the writer's activism. Taking that next step may mean reading other works by selected writers and considering the issues that their works raise. This can lead to enriched discussions in your reading groups and other networks, encouraging others to explore new books and authors.

You can support businesses and individuals who are making change happen. Use your own voice to lobby for diversity in all areas of writing and publishing. Be proactive in your selection of new and wide-ranging titles to read. And remember, you do not need to agree with everything that the writer has to say in order to value their perspective. Engagement and discussion is key. The nature of literary activism is to lean into the debate and speak out or take action. Our hope is that this book is a step along the road to change.

ABOUT THE AUTHORS

Professor Joan Anim-Addo is Grenada-born. She is an author, librettist, poet, literary critic and historian. She is the UK's first Black professor of Literature. She co-founded the MA in Black British Writing with Deirdre Osborne in 2014, as well as the MA in Creative and Life Writing, at Goldsmiths, London. She has taught and lectured in universities world-wide including the US, Italy, Spain, Finland and Greece.

She is Associate Editor of *Callaloo*, Journal of African Diaspora Arts and Letters, and co-Editor of *Blacklines*, the journal of Black British writing. She co-founded the independent publisher Mango Press in 1995, to bring a diverse range of new writing to readers internationally. These include bilingual editions from award-winning writers in the UK and the Americas.

Her publications include *Imoinda: Or She Who Will Lose Her Name* (2008), the poetry collections *Haunted by History* (2004) and *Janie, Cricketing Lady* (2006), and the literary history, *Touching the Body: History, Language and African-Caribbean Women's Writing* (2007). Her literary writing has been translated into Spanish and Italian, and her writing for the stage has been performed in the UK and the US. She has written seminal histories of the Black presence in Lewisham (1995) and Greenwich (1996).

In 2016, the literary journal *Callaloo* awarded her a Lifetime Achievement Award for 'invaluable contributions to literature and literary and cultural studies'. As Professor Emerita, she remains Director of the Centre for Caribbean and Diaspora Studies at Goldsmiths, London.

Dr Deirdre Osborne is Australian-born. She is a Reader in English Literature and Drama at Goldsmiths, University of London, where she co-founded the MA Black British Writing with Joan Anim-Addo. A key focus of her career has been working with students who follow non-traditional routes into education. In 2017, she wrote the Edexcel Pearson A-level materials, 'Contemporary Black British Literature'.

Editor of the 2016 *Cambridge Companion to British Black and Asian Literature (1945–2010)* she has written over 50 articles and book chapters, and edited collections dedicated to the work of Black writers, including anthologies of many landmark Black British plays: *Hidden Gems Vols. I* and *II* (Oberon Books) featuring Lemn Sissay, Kwame Kwei-Armah, Courttia Newland, Malika Booker, Lennie James and SuAndi. Her critical writing spans late-Victorian literature to contemporary culture through three conceptual models: 'Mothertext', 'Didactic Poetics' and 'Landmark Poetics' (commissioning Grace Nichols's poem 'Breath' in 2020). She is Associate Editor of *Women's Writing* journal (Taylor & Francis). She has received funding awards from the AHRC and British Academy.

As a curator of cultural events, she has brought together leading figures in the arts and politics, nationally and internationally, for diverse audiences. A joint project with Dr David Dibosa, *Exhibiting Embarrassment: Museums, Public Culture and Consequentialist Aesthetics*, explores the legacies of imperial–colonial acquisition in the context of rethinking Britain's cultural institutions in the 21st century. Her essay 'From "Finders' Keepers" to "Lost and Found": Tales from the Museum' was commissioned for the Black British Museum Project's 2021 *Museums Journal* 'takeover'.

Kadija George Sesay MBE, Hon. FRSL, FRSA is a literary activist of Sierra Leonean descent, who works in literary project management and creative professional development with adults and young people.

From 2001 to 2015 she published *SABLE LitMag* magazine for emerging writers of colour. She has edited anthologies of work by writers of African descent in fiction, drama and poetry, and has published and broadcast her own creative work including a poetry collection, *Irki* (2013). Her second collection is *The Modern Pan-Africanists Journey* (forthcoming). She is the Publications Manager for the Inscribe writer development programme at Peepal Tree Press, supporting Black British writers, where has curated a series of anthologies, including *GLIMPSE: The First Anthology of Speculative Fiction by Black British Writers* (2022). She co-founded the Mboka Festival of Arts, Culture and Sport in The Gambia and is currently developing AfriPoeTree, a Selective Interactive Video of Poetry and Pan-African history. Her doctoral research is in Black British Publishing and Pan-Africanism at Brighton University (AHRC / TECHNE Fellowship).

She has won many awards for her work in the creative arts, including *Cosmopolitan* Woman of Achievement, *Candice* magazine Woman of Achievement, *Voice* Newspaper Award for work in the Creative Arts, a Woman of the Millennium and STARS of Sierra Leone Award (for outstanding women of achievement). She is a Kennedy Center Fellow in Performing Arts Management and a Kluge Fellow (The Library of Congress). She received an MBE for services to literature.

ACKNOWLEDGEMENTS

The authors would like to gratefully acknowledge each other's work as co-authors on this joint enterprise, with thanks also to Kerry Enzor for the opportunity, Katharine Reeve for editorial advice and gratitude to Vimbai Shire for her editorial input. Joan Anim-Addo would like to thank her always-generous support network of friends and family. You know who you are! To the newest member of the team, Zoralys – the hope is that this book will contribute soundly to changing the landscape for your generation.

Deirdre Osborne would like to offer thanks to Dr Valerie Kaneko Lucas, SuAndi OBE, the Most Reverend Walter Khotsu Makhulu CMG for conversations about southern Africa, Andrea Medwin for book club perspectives, and to her daughter Isabella Osborne – always.

Kadija George Sesay MBE would like to thank Dr Rajeev Balasubramanyam, Juliette Bethea, Dr Louisa Egbunike, Stella Oni, Nii Ayikwei Parkes, Sudeep Sen, Lola Shoneyin – Director of Ake Festival, the Rainbow VI reading group and the African Literature Association for advice and suggestions. Thanks also to Saffi, Mark, Dani and Ella Haines, and to her parents for constant love and support.